WHICH? W
BUY, SELL AND
MOVE HOUSE

About the authors

Alison and Richard Barr are both practising solicitors in Norfolk. Alison specialises in commercial and domestic property; Richard is also a freelance writer and broadcaster, author of the *Which?* Action Pack *Do Your Own Conveyancing*, co-author of *The New Penguin Guide to the Law*, and a regular contributor to the *Solicitors Journal*.

WHICH? WAY TO BUY, SELL AND MOVE HOUSE

ALISON AND RICHARD BARR

CONSUMERS' ASSOCIATION

Which? Books are commissioned and researched by
Consumers' Association and published by
Which? Ltd, 2 Marylebone Road, London NW1 4DF

Distributed by The Penguin Group:
Penguin Books Ltd, 27 Wrights Lane, London W8 5TZ

Based on *Which? Way to Buy, Sell and Move House* (Consumers'
Association), first published in August 1987, text completely revised and
new material written by Alison and Richard Barr (1993); Scottish section
revised by David Nichols; amendments for 1996 edition by
Veronica McGrath

Cover illustration by courtesy of ACE/Brian Green

First edition October 1993
Amended reprint August 1994
Amended reprint September 1995
Revised edition April 1997
Copyright © 1993, 1995, 1997 Which? Ltd

British Library Cataloguing-in-Publication Data
Which? Way to Buy, Sell and Move House
(Which? Consumer Guides)
I. Barr, Alison II. Barr, Richard III. Series
ISBN 0 85202 660 9

Typeset by Business ColorPrint Ltd, Welshpool, Powys, Wales

Printed and bound by Firmin-Didot (France)
Groupe Herissey
N° d'impression: 37266.

CONTENTS

INTRODUCTION

HOME ownership is still on the increase. Nearly two-thirds of the population either own or are buying their own homes. The impact of home ownership on the economy of the country is huge. If people stop moving house, as they did in the early 1990s, the economy begins to nosedive: makers of kitchen units and furniture go bankrupt; large building companies go to the wall; estate agents close down.

The knock-on effect is that those who own their homes may no longer keep up with payments – forcing more properties on to a depressed market.

But, if the process is reversed, it often seems to be the house market which leads the way out of recession. People become happy again that their homes, their castles, are, after all, worth something – inheritances to pass on to the children in later years.

Changes in the market

In recent years the house market has been through two dramatic changes:

● First there was the boom. Prices went up faster and further than they had ever done before. It was not unusual for some houses to double in price in less than a year. Nobody thought it would last forever, but most thought that the rate of increase would simply slow down or stop.

● That was until the second dramatic change – the recession. The house market not only fell into the doldrums but also into a downward spiral. The unthinkable happened: house values decreased dramatically. All the increases of the boom times were wiped out and most houses became worth less than they were before the previous price rise.

What the book does and does not cover

This book goes to press amid signs of a modest recovery in house prices. Mortgage rates are remaining low. There is still a very long way to go, however, to get back to the situation that existed before the recession. No crystal ball predictions of the future will be offered, except to underline the advice that home buying is not easy. There are many risks and pitfalls. If you are careful, you should not go wrong; follow the advice given here.

Above all, *Which? Way to Buy, Sell and Move House* is intended as a handbook for home buyers. It gives detailed advice on all aspects of moving house and covers in depth the process first of choosing a new home, then of financing it, the legal side and eventually the mechanics of removals.

Note: it does not deal with renting property. Nor does it cover flats or time sharing.

(Addresses and telephone numbers for those organisations marked with an asterisk (*) can be found in the address section at the back of the book.)

A BIRD'S-EYE VIEW OF HOUSE BUYING

IT SOUNDS simple: you live in one house, you decide to sell it and move to another. Easy. Just sign a few pieces of paper, book a van and away you go. Unfortunately, it is seldom like that.

Mr and Mrs Green decided to move to a larger house. They quickly found the house they wanted to buy and put in an offer, which was accepted. They also found a buyer for their own house. After they had been involved in the transaction for many weeks they were told by the seller that he had received an offer of £5,000 more for the house. He would be happy to sell to the Greens, but only if they matched the offer. Reluctantly, they agreed.

A few days later the Greens' own buyer was on the point of exchange of contracts when she informed the Greens that 'because of an adverse survey report' she would only proceed if they reduced their price by £5,000.

Later still, the Greens were told by their solicitor that their seller had now decided to call for a contract race and he would sell to the first person who signed the contract and deposited it with the seller's solicitors.

Unfortunately, the Greens were pipped at the post by a matter of only two hours, so they had to start house hunting again.

Next time they were luckier, but their own buyer insisted on a further reduction in the price 'because of the delay'. However, contracts were eventually exchanged, with completion due to take place three weeks later.

Two days after exchange of contracts, the seller died. The contract was still valid, but completion was held up for several weeks while the technicalities were sorted out. In the meantime, the Greens' buyer made a claim for compensation for the delay in completing.

Feeling much older, and with numerous grey hairs, Mr and Mrs Green moved into their new house and prepared for their first relaxing moment in several weeks. Their peace was broken almost immediately by the postman, who was delivering a recorded delivery letter informing them that the Department of Transport was shortly to begin road-widening work in their new front garden.

Mr Green picked up the telephone to get in touch with his solicitor... the number was unobtainable.

At the same time, in another part of the country, Mr and Mrs White had just waved goodbye to their removal men. They had moved into their new home just under two months after they had first decided to get a larger house.

Everything had gone smoothly from start to finish and the greatest problem they faced, as they looked out of the window of their new living room, was that the lawn needed cutting.

Moving house, especially when accompanied by a new mortgage, is accepted as a highly stressful 'life event'. There are probably several reasons for this:

- the sheer physical upheaval of packing, throwing out and making ready for the move, followed by the unpacking, rearranging and regrets that so many things had been thrown out
- the emotional involvement which inevitably comes with the process of house selection. People do fall in love with houses – and go through withdrawal symptoms if they are let down
- the legwork needed: dealing with estate agents, lenders, removal men, solicitors, not to mention all the public utilities and remembering to notify everyone on your Christmas-card list of your move

- the built-in stress of the legal system. Many attempts have been made to simplify it. No one has yet succeeded.

And yet, it can be done. In reality, the experience is rarely as pain-free as Mr and Mrs White found it, nor as traumatic as the disasters which were heaped on the Greens. None the less, the experiences of the Whites of this world are far more common than those of Mr and Mrs Green.

You, the house buyer, have much more control over the situation than you may believe. This book should help you to keep that control.

Why move?

People may move because of a change of job or a re-location with the job. Or a change in family circumstances may bring a need for more space – or for less.

A home may have become too big after the family has grown up and left, or after the loss of a husband or wife. It may have become too expensive to run because financial circumstances have changed. When children are on the way or where the financial situation in a family has improved, a couple may decide to move into a better house to obtain more accommodation or to improve their standard of living. When the property market is buoyant, a house may also be regarded as an investment, but the experiences of the end of the eighties and beginning of the nineties have shown that property may decrease in value as well as increase. It is probably safer to regard a house as a home, rather than an investment.

Retirement, or the period just beforehand, is, of course, often the time to decide to move into accommodation suitable for older age – perhaps a flat or a bungalow. A move may be unavoidable for those living in 'tied' accommodation.

Whatever the reason for the move, it may provide the opportunity to make an additional change – by switching from town to country living, or vice versa. Before making the choice, any cost of living differences between one part of the country and another – for example, the higher cost of living in the Home Counties – should be considered, and also any climatic differences, particularly moving from south to north.

For many, the thought of living in the country may seem idyllic, but the seaside village that looked so nice during the summer holiday may be like a bleak graveyard out of season. Some of the very things which provided charm – peace, quiet, lack of bustle – can also be disadvantages: the level of many services is much lower in the country than in the town.

Living in the country

There are reasons for and against living in the country.

For
- Environment: the natural beauty of the countryside; facilities for walking and other outdoor activities; fresher unpolluted air; no overcrowding; usually quieter than town living.
- Housing: often more land with the house; more garden space with safer play areas for children; the chance to grow your own food; often more bungalow housing available; suitable for retired people; insurance rates are lower for burglary cover, and for motor insurance; seldom problems over parking.
- Services: it's possible to use coal or wood as alternative heating fuel (there are seldom smoke-control restrictions), perhaps cheap wood supplies are available.
- Social life: the pace of living is slower than in town; more personal contact with neighbours; easy involvement in local activities.

Against
- Environment: areas may be inhospitable in winter – fog, wind, cold; roads are often not salted or cleared of snow quickly; smells from nearby farms are not always agreeable and can be unpleasant in hot weather; the country is not necessarily always quiet (aircraft flight paths?); in holiday areas, there's an influx of summer visitors.

- Housing: not as wide a choice; free-standing houses in exposed positions are costly to heat; you may have to buy more land than you wanted; if in the 'green belt' area, planning permission may be restricted.

- Services: there may be no mains gas laid on (making it necessary to rely on electricity); there may not be mains drainage but, instead, a septic tank or cesspool (emptying required); in many places, there is no (or poor) street lighting; public transport may be sparse (or non-existent) for getting to work, shops, schools; difficulties in wintry conditions; might need a second car for the family; the doctor, baby clinic, hospital, chemist may all be some distance away, health visitors or district nurses are fewer; schools may be limited in number and type, nursery schools few or non-existent; adult classes and library facilities may be far away; choice for shopping may be poor, village shop(s) within walking distance may be expensive and have a smaller range of goods.
- Social life: lack of choice (you have to get on with neighbours and be prepared to join in local community activities); it may take time to get accepted in a village community; public entertainments and sports facilities are limited; there may be fewer neighbouring children for yours to play with; guests will need transport (yours or theirs) to visit.

Living in a town or city

For
- Housing: there is usually more choice of neighbourhoods and houses; more flats are available; there is possibly some saving on heating costs (terraced or semi-detached houses and flats keep each other warm).
- Services: more public transport, health care and school facilities are available; shopping is more convenient, with more choice; there may be more facilities for older people (sheltered housing, local welfare and social clubs), visiting is easier.
- Social life: closer proximity of neighbours can be useful in times of emergency; children may benefit from nearby

children to play with; there's a wider range of entertainments, sports and recreations.

Against
- Environment: close proximity of neighbours may mean a lack of privacy – your house or garden may be overlooked; the pace of living is likely to be faster; there's hustle and bustle and the pressure of people always around; there are traffic or factory noise and smells; your clothes and home are likely to need more cleaning because of traffic or industrial pollution; parking may be difficult and more expensive.
- Housing: prices are higher, you may have to accept a smaller house and a small or non-existent garden; there may be no garage; play-space for children may be restricted or non-existent; insurance rates for burglary cover are more expensive (or unobtainable), also higher rates for motor insurance.
- Services: health and welfare services may be over-stretched, particularly in holiday or retirement resorts. Inner-city schools may have more discipline problems.
- Social life: it's easy to feel isolated in a large city; friends may not be immediate neighbours but may have to be made through your job or hobby, or school (school friends often bring parents together).

What kind of accommodation?

If you are considering living in a different kind of home, weigh up carefully the new factors involved. You may have been living in a rented flat and are to become the owner of a house, perhaps with a garden, for the first time. Or the change may be from a large house with its responsibilities into a small flat with lesser ones.

From flat to house

Moving to larger accommodation can mean additional expenditure for more furniture, carpets and curtains. Heating costs are likely to be higher. If there is a garden, there will be the expense of tools and plants, and the added cost and time required for its maintenance.

A householder changing from a flat to a house must be prepared to accept a greater degree of personal responsibility for the property and be prepared to devote a considerable amount of time to it: roof and gutters, fences and walls, plumbing and drains have to be kept in good repair. But you can choose when and how to get repairs done, and stagger the outlay.

In a flat, insurance for the building was probably not your personal responsibility but rather the responsibility of the landlord or management company (you would have paid a service or maintenance fee). In your own house, it is up to you to take out the insurance for damage to or destruction of the building (as well as any insurance you may want for the contents). If you have a mortgage, the building society or bank may arrange the insurance or, for a small administrative fee, you may be allowed to arrange your own, subject to their approval.

Having a house may mean having a garage for the first time, which can be a big advantage – not only for housing the car, but space for storage, e.g. for your freezer, tools or workbench.

Although a family may find that, with more space, they have better facilities, these will be on more than one floor and they may find this physically more demanding, particularly at first. Various household activities will have to be re-organised and housework re-planned to avoid unnecessary numbers of journeys up and down stairs. If there are small children, it may be less easy to keep an eye on them. Stairs can be a source of injury.

A house can give more privacy and, within reason, permit more noisy activities without worry of disturbing close neighbours. A piano or a highly amplifying sound system may be possible for the first time – and so may a Great Dane or other large pet.

Changing in size or type

When moving into a bigger house you should budget for more expenses. Perhaps more or new furniture and appliances will be needed, more curtaining and floor coverings, followed by higher running costs in the future. If moving to a smaller place, there may be large items to dispose of and smaller (and perhaps more expensive) replacements to buy.

When considering a larger property, bear in mind that the buildings insurance is likely to be higher. You have to insure for the cost of re-building and this is calculated by taking a figure based on building costs per square foot and multiplying this by the area of the building. For a thatched house, the insurance premium may be as much as four times more (though some companies have special packages for this kind of house).

A bungalow is sensible for older people because there are no stairs to climb and it can be run easily and with less risk of accidents. But a bungalow has to be maintained – it may have a greater roof area, and often has a garden. And a lifetime of 'going up to bed' can inhibit some people from sleeping easily on the ground floor.

If the reason for moving is simply to gain more space, consider extending your present house. Moving is expensive and an extension may be less costly, though the cost of an extension is rarely fully reflected in the increased value of the house. If you are looking for less space, think of converting your house into two flats – or even taking in lodgers.

Changing style

Try to anticipate what changes the move may bring in the pattern of your daily life and outgoings, both immediately and in the long term.

Aspects that might be affected include:

- mortgage – monthly payments may be higher/lower (you may previously have been paying a weekly or monthly rent)
- life-insurance premiums – perhaps payable now on an endowment or mortgage protection life insurance policy
- council tax and water charges – may be higher if you move to a larger house or to a different authority's area
- house contents insurance – premiums will increase if you move to larger premises or to a more burglar-prone area

- fuel consumption and costs – may be different (you may spend more/less on electricity, more/less on gas; or use oil instead of solid fuel or vice versa)
- telephone bill – your bill may be higher/lower if more/fewer calls are within local range (it may be a big one for the period of the move, anyway)
- daily travel – there may be a change in the easiest method of getting to work/schools/social or cultural activities (more by car, less by public transport or vice versa)
- car – a second car (or none) may be needed; a garage may be needed; your insurance premium may be higher/lower
- daily timetable – you may get home earlier/later; or have to get up earlier (dark in winter); there may be more/less housework; opportunities may be expanded/restricted for part-time or voluntary work
- neighbours – adjustment to new neighbours (more or fewer, different ages) will be needed; there may be a difference in access to friends and/or family (resulting in more or fewer visitors)
- clothing – a different category of clothes and footwear may be required if moving from town to country or vice versa
- upkeep of property – there may be more maintenance and redecorating (higher ceilings, more woodwork, windows, doors to paint)
- garden (perhaps for the first time) – you may want to alter the layout and/or contents; there's the cost of restocking, upkeep of a fence or hedge, walls or other boundaries; you may need to resurface paths or driveways; tree care may be an added job.

None of these items needs be a deterrent to moving to the place you want to go to. But you may have to adjust your priorities and purse.

Finding a solicitor or licensed conveyancer

It is sensible to decide at an early stage who is to do the mechanics of the legal side of buying or selling. The choice between a solicitor and licensed conveyancer may be very much a matter of personal preference. Both should be able to provide a full house-buying service and carry out the basic legal work for you. The best ones will also give you guidance and support, and act as a forceful intermediary if things go wrong.

Licensed conveyancers are required to operate the same safeguards to protect the public as solicitors, and there may be little to choose on price, particularly as solicitors' charges have come down considerably over the past few years. Licensed conveyancers are able to offer a highly specialised service but one which is limited to house-buying transactions. There are also far fewer licensed conveyancers than there are solicitors.

Coping with legal jargon

'WHEREAS *the said Albert Jones is seised of the property hereinbefore described AND WHEREAS the parties hereto have hereunto agreed for the sale of the said property to the purchaser for an estate in fee simple subject as hereinafter mentioned but otherwise free from encumbrances NOW THIS DEED WITNESSETH as follows . . .*'

The language of lawyers is seen by many as a quaint and at times irritating archaism. The truth of the matter is that lawyers, like most trained professionals, have their own technical language. The difference is that lawyers (as opposed to, say, mathematicians or scientists) have to communicate their thoughts to ordinary people who do not have legal training. It is widely felt that many lawyers are not very good at this. **Chapter 10** looks at the legal side of buying and selling a house, and at the end of this book there is a glossary which will help to guide you through the maze.

What should you do if you are confronted with legal jargon you do not understand? The answer is that you should ask – and keep asking – till you have it explained properly to you. Solicitors and licensed conveyancers have a duty to make sure that their clients understand fully the obligations they are taking on in house buying or selling. Do not hesitate to demand full explanations in plain English.

Organising your work

House buying is the biggest financial commitment in most people's lives. Even if you are not attempting to sell the house or carry out the legal procedures yourself, there is a lot to remember. You will find that things go much better if you are well organised.

- Put everything in a file: you will generate a large amount of paper. (Solicitors attach correspondence to a green treasury tag, which automatically keeps it in date order.) The file will help you to keep control and will act as a permanent record of your house purchase or sale. File a copy of every letter you send. You should also make a note of the details of every conversation: '28 January – spoke to seller. Decided not to buy the house in Turner Road after all.'
- Record financial details: you will be dealing with (directly or indirectly) large sums of money. At the front of your file keep a note of all the money you spend.
- Make sure there is time: you may need time off work, depending on the pressures and time available. You should *not* rush.
- Have access to typing/photocopying/telephone facilities: you will need to make photocopies and be available by telephone. If you need to be contacted at work, make sure you clear it with your employer. Sometimes a fax saves a lot of time. If you do not have access to a fax machine, make arrangements with a local fax bureau – both to send and receive faxes.
- Typed letters and documents give a more professional appearance.

Buy first or sell first?

Probably the most difficult question to resolve is the timing of the whole operation. The legal position is that you are not committed to going ahead either with a sale or a purchase until contracts are exchanged. None the less, you can waste a great deal of money and time if your efforts to sell or buy prove abortive.

If you are selling and buying at the same time, you will not want to risk being the owner of two houses at the same time – or even none. Although bridging finance is available from a few lenders, if you want to conclude your purchase before your sale, it is not to be recommended if you are bearing the cost yourself. It is hardly ever advisable to take on what is known as an 'open-ended' bridging loan when you commit yourself to your new home without having exchanged contracts on the old. If houses are difficult to sell at the time, very few banks would be prepared to make you a loan in this situation.

The general rule is that, in a buyer's market, you should concentrate your efforts on selling your house first before looking too hard for a house to buy, though it costs nothing to get on estate agents' mailing lists and to find out what is available. Once terms have been agreed to sell your house (or at least there is real interest in it from would-be buyers), you can start house hunting in earnest.

In a seller's market (when prices seem to be going up almost by the day) you will know that your house should be easy to sell, and you must then move heaven and earth to find a house to buy at a price you can afford. Very rarely, the house market is balanced. In that situation, you should put equal effort into selling and finding a house to buy.

CHAPTER 2

COSTS AND EXPENSES OF MOVING

BEFORE you start hunting for a new home, you have to work out how much money you will have available so that you know in what price range to look.

Financing the move

Add together:

- the likely net proceeds from the sale of your present home (i.e. after repaying your present mortgage)
- the maximum mortgage you can comfortably afford
- other available capital or savings.

Then, deduct from the total of these:

- the estimated expenses of moving, including the various fees and stamp duty and allowing for essential repairs, possible redecoration or improvements.

The result of this calculation will give you the approximate maximum price you can afford for your new home.

Net proceeds from the sale of your present home

Estimate what price you think your home will fetch. If you have had an estate agent's valuation, you can use this as a guide but you might get more, or less, depending on the state of the market. If houses in your area change hands frequently, you could ask neighbours and friends how much they bought or sold their house for. You can then deduct from this the balance of any mortgage to be paid off on your present home and the estimated costs of selling it.

For very rough budgeting purposes, allow 3 per cent of the sale price to cover these expenses.

Mortgage

Mortgages are covered in detail in **Chapter 6**. Briefly, a mortgage is a loan secured on a home. It is a means of raising the large sum of money needed to buy a house. If you already have a mortgage it will have to be repaid when you sell your home and a new loan will have to be taken out for the next home. The new mortgage could be the same or a greater or lesser amount, depending on your circumstances.

Your savings

Calculate how much you have available in:

- building societies or bank–deposit accounts
- other investments, such as National Savings accounts, certificates, bonds, shares, unit trusts, government stock (but your move may not coincide with the best time for selling)
- a life insurance policy (but current cash-in value may not yield enough to make it worth using).

Remember that you should always keep some of your savings intact in case of any emergency quite unconnected with house purchase. And you may want to keep some of your savings aside to help pay for such items as new carpets and curtains, or for redecorating your new home.

Money for the deposit

You will be asked for a deposit of up to 10 per cent of the purchase price to put down on the house you are buying when you exchange contracts. In some areas of the country, you may be able to use any similar deposit which your solicitor or agent may be holding in respect of the property you are selling, but in other areas this is not possible.

If you do not have the necessary deposit available in ready money, you may be able to get a **bridging loan** from your bank (and should allow for the extra expense of this), repayable on completion of the sale of your present house (see page 182 for details).

Alternatively, there is a **deposit guarantee scheme**, through solicitors, where the premium is generally less expensive than a bridging loan for the deposit. Instead of paying a deposit, you pay an insurance premium related to the purchase price of the house, which covers a deposit of 10 per cent, up to a set maximum. This includes a commission for the solicitor or conveyancer (who may decide to pass this back to you). The insurance guarantees that the 10 per cent deposit will be paid if you default under the contract (but the solicitor or conveyancer will seek to recover the money from you).

You can arrange and pay for the guarantee scheme at an early stage if you want to be prepared; it will come into effect the moment you exchange contracts. This may be cheaper than raising the deposit by way of a bridging loan, but make sure that your solicitor will not make a charge for the deposit guarantee, which would cancel the difference. Your seller may not be willing to accept the guarantee instead of a deposit: he or she may still insist on cash.

A deposit guarantee does not work in the same way as a normal deposit. It cannot be passed down the line as can happen with an ordinary deposit if all parties agree. And when it comes to completion, you will have to be able to provide the money for the full price. In practice, this scheme is rarely used.

Selling

A major cost incurred is the **solicitor's fee**.

Solicitors and licensed conveyancers are free to charge what they choose. The Law Society★ recommends that solicitors' fees should be 'fair and reasonable' based on the value of the house; how complicated the transaction is; how much time is spent; how much skill is involved; the number and importance of documents involved; the place and circumstances of the conveyancing; whether the land is registered or unregistered; the importance of the matter to the client.

It will be well worth getting estimates from more than one solicitor/conveyancer before choosing. Many charge a fixed fee for all the work involved. A solicitor who has given a written quotation will not be able to exceed the quote unless he or she has reserved the right to do so.

As a rough guide, allow for up to 1 per cent of the price (+ VAT); or a flat fee.

Other fees

Other fees you will have to consider are:

- the estate agent's fee – allow 1½ to 2½ per cent of the price (+ VAT). It may be more in certain areas
- or, your own advertising costs if you decide to do it yourself
- the mortgage redemption charge: if repaying within a short period (say, less than five years) this may be up to three months' interest and/or administration or legal fees (these may be especially likely with fixed–rate mortgages).

Buying

Make provision for the **solicitor's/conveyancer's fee**: not based on a scale fee. Allow for about the same as for the sale. See under 'selling' above for the position generally and about written quotations.

The following are statutory fees applicable to the majority of sales.

Stamp duty This is the tax payable on the purchase price of houses costing above a certain figure (at present, 1 per cent if the price is over £60,000), for example:

- house at £60,000 – stamp duty nil
- house at £60,500 – stamp duty £605.

Price of house		Land Registry fee
£0 –	£30,000	£40
£30,001 –	£40,000	£60
£40,001 –	£50,000	£80
£50,001 –	£60,000	£100
£60,001 –	£70,000	£120
£70,001 –	£80,000	£140
£80,001 –	£90,000	£170
£90,001 –	£100,000	£200
£100,001 –	£150,000	£230
£150,001 –	£200,000	£260
£200,001 –	£300,000	£300
£300,001 –	£500,000	£400
£500,001 –	£700,000	£500
£700,001 –	£1,000,000	£600
£1,000,001 –	£2,000,000	£900
£2,000,001 –	£5,000,000	£1,200
£5,000,001 and over		£1,800

Land Registry fee This has to be paid on all purchases on a scale related to the purchase price (see table above).

Local authority searches Fees payable to local authority for information about planning in the area and suchlike (allow at least £60 – more in London boroughs); this is a nominal fee in Scotland.

Other search fees and disbursements These include index map, commons, the coal authority, land charge, company searches; bank transfer fees. Not all are applicable to every transaction, but allow £70 to cover an average house purchase.

Lender's legal fee Usually, your solicitor will act for the lender as well as for you. His or her fee for the purchase will include all the work on the mortgage. You should check this with your solicitor. A few lenders require their own solicitors to act for them. You will have to pay their fees in addition to your own solicitor's fees for acting on your side of the mortgage (if these are not included in the fee quoted for the purchase). There is no statutory scale of charges for the lender's legal costs, either for work carried out by your conveyancer or, if a separate firm is used, by the lender's own conveyancer. However, the Law Society is currently discussing with several lenders the possibility of introducing an 'indicative fee range' which would tell purchasers the likely cost of work carried out on behalf of the lender.

Valuation fee (for lender's surveyor's valuation) This fee is based on the price of the house (+ VAT); it varies according to the lender's arrangements with the valuers. For instance, allow around £125 for a £50,000 house, £165 for a £100,000 house. Ask your lender. See page 90 on structural surveys.

Top-up loan This may be needed for valuation and legal fees.

Mortgage indemnity policy or high-lending fee (if required). This is charged if you are borrowing above a given percentage – usually 75 or 80 per cent of the value of the property. The one-off payment starts at about 4 per cent of amount of extra loan, payable to the lender who organises the policy – see **Chapter 6**.

Mortgage arrangement fee This is payable on practically all fixed-rate mortgages.

Bridging loan If required, the interest will be charged at 3 to 4 per cent above the current bank base rate; this is the bank's charge for arranging the loan (say, £120 or 1 per cent of loan).

Structural survey (allow for more than one survey during house hunting). If you are getting a mortgage, most building societies offer you the choice of a full survey, a house buyers' report or a valuation. It is advisable to have at least a house buyers' report which should throw up major defects in the property.

For the surveyor's fee for a full survey, allow £250 to £1000 + VAT (get a quotation before instructing the surveyor). There could be a reduction if it is combined with a building society valuation. If you are buying an old property, budget for possible extra charges if tests by specialist firms are needed (e.g. drains, electrical, central heating). For a surveyor's intermediate or house buyers' report which is less detailed than a full survey, the fee is linked to the price of the house: allow, for example, £330 for a £100,000 house.

House hunting expenses

Travel and subsistence: allow for meals out, telephone calls, fares/petrol for several visits and overnight accommodation if some distance is involved. Also, will you need time off work?

Insurance

Buildings insurance: the first premium is payable in advance (the amount payable depends on the sum insured and on the area).

Removal expenses

You should be prepared for the cost of using a professional firm; also for tips. It is best to get at least three quotations.

If doing it yourself – budget for packing materials; the cost of hiring a self-drive van (+ VAT and insurance) plus petrol for several journeys, including for the return of the van; the fare for your own return; food and refreshments for helpers. Also, for insurance, allow a minimum premium of £25.

Services

- Gas: are there any disconnection and reconnection charges?
- Electricity: perhaps there will be costs incurred in having inspections and tests, or for installing additional circuits, e.g. for the cooker at your new house
- Telephone: you may have to pay for the installation of a telephone at your new home (up to £116.33 with BT) or for taking over the existing telephone if the line is disconnected at all, even for a day (£9.99). There is no connection charge if a line is unbroken between owners
- Redirection of letters: £6 (one month), £13 (three months), £30 (one year)
- Plumber: perhaps needed for disconnecting and reconnecting the automatic washing machine and/or dishwasher.

Incidentals

- Notifying change of address: cost of cards and postage
- Rubbish disposal
- New locks and/or security devices in your new house
- Kennelling
- Thank-you presents for helpers. Remember child minders, animal keepers, strong friends who heaved furniture and cases and gentle friends who provided meals and comfort.

As well as the expenses of actually moving, also take into account the cost of any immediate repairs (for example, rewiring), improvements or redecoration which might be required in the old and/or new house.

Contingency fund

You must allow for the costs of purchases (or sales) which fall through, and for once-only expenses that could occur.

The contingency fund should allow for paying for immediate repairs to put right faults in items you have taken over from the previous owners and for buying replacements for fittings you expected to inherit (or believed were included in the price) which the previous owner has taken.

If you buy a 'second-hand' house, the purchase price may include the fixtures. But if the house you are planning to buy is newly built, you will have an initial outlay on many items, which, although inexpensive in themselves, do mount up.

It is not possible to do more than set an arbitrary figure for contingencies – say, 3 per cent of the total of the purchase price plus all other expenses.

If you are moving to a smaller place, you could find yourself with additional money through selling any surplus furniture – in which case, your contingency fund can be marginally reduced.

Help with the expenses of moving

If you are offered a new job which will necessitate a move, you may be able to make it a condition of acceptance that you will get help with removal expenses.

For some employees, such as civil servants, doctors and members of the armed forces, the moving allowances are laid down. Doctors who are members of the British Medical Association can get a guidance note on removal and associated expenses from their local BMA office.

Some private employers undertake to bear the costs of moving when they transfer any of their staff from one branch to another, or if the firm itself moves its premises from one area to another.

Be sure to find out beforehand what the employer means by 'costs of moving' and whether this will include:

● all solicitor's fees
● other fees, such as Land Registry fee, stamp duty, search fees
● any surveyor's fees

Basic checklist of expenses

	Estimated £	Actual £
Maximum possible price to pay for house	_____	_____
Solicitor's/conveyancer's fee	_____	_____
Estate agent's fee (if used for selling house)	_____	_____
Advertisements	_____	_____
Land Registry fee	_____	_____
Stamp duty	_____	_____
Fee for local searches	_____	_____
Other searches and disbursements	_____	_____

Mortgage

• lender's solicitor's fee	_____	_____
• own solicitor's fees	_____	_____
• lender's valuer's fee	_____	_____
• top-up loan: charges	_____	_____
• mortgage indemnity policy	_____	_____

Structural survey

• surveyor's fee	_____	_____
• fees for specialist tests	_____	_____

Insurance

• buildings insurance premiums	_____	_____
• removals insurance premium	_____	_____

Bridging loan

• bank's fee	_____	_____
• interest	_____	_____

House hunting expenses

- transport   _____ _____
- accommodation   _____ _____
- time off   _____ _____
- other   _____ _____

Removal expenses

- firm   _____ _____
- hire   _____ _____
- other   _____ _____

Services

- disconnection   _____ _____
- reconnection   _____ _____
- installation of new equipment   _____ _____
- carpet laying   _____ _____
- mail redirection   _____ _____

Incidentals

- change of address _____ _____
- boarding animals   _____ _____
- meals out   _____ _____
- rewarding helpers _____ _____
- telephone calls   _____ _____
- tips   _____ _____
- other   _____ _____

Contingency fund (percentage of total)   _____ _____

FINAL TOTAL   _____ _____

- estate agent's fee (for selling)
- removal firm's charges
- temporary storage of furniture
- temporary rented accommodation while you house hunt or wait to get in
- fares
- overnight hotel expenses for a two-day move.

If you find you need a bridging loan because of the timing of your buying and selling, it is worth approaching your employers to see if they will advance you this, perhaps interest-free or at a low rate of interest. If the move is at their request, the onus is on them to help you with it.

If it is your employers (or the state) who will be paying, keep receipts for everything.

CHAPTER 3

FINDING A HOME

Buying a newly built house

MANY buyers prefer a new house to an old one. This could be a house designed and built to your specifications on your land. For most people, however, buying a newly built house means one being built (or just completed) by a developer, often on a new estate. A house may be advertised before it has been built. The developer or estate agent can show you the site or the plans of the house, with perhaps a glossy brochure, or there may be a show house for you to look at before you choose a site.

If you need a mortgage for buying a newly built house, you will find that lenders such as building societies normally only lend on new houses built under the supervision of an architect or surveyor employed solely by the buyer, or which are built by an NHBC-registered builder or under the Foundation 15 scheme (see below).

National House Building Council

The National House Building Council (NHBC)* is a non-profit-distributing body with a register of some 20,000 builders and developers who undertake to build houses to a set of standards drawn up by the Council. Each house registered with the NHBC is covered by the NHBC's Buildmark warranty and insurance, introduced in April 1988 to supersede the previous NHBC protection scheme. The scheme is not a guarantee for putting right all faults that may occur in that period. It is an undertaking to repair faulty work within the first two years after completion of the property, followed by a further eight-year insurance cover if major structural faults develop. The Buildmark scheme applies to flats and maisonettes as well as houses and bungalows.

- If the builder goes bankrupt before the house is completed, the NHBC will either reimburse the buyer's lost deposit or pay the cost of completion (up to a maximum of £10,000).
- During the first two years (the initial warranty period) after the house has been completed, any defect resulting from a failure to comply with NHBC technical requirements must be put right by the builder at no cost to the buyer.
- During the following eight years (the structural warranty period), insurance cover is provided for any major damage due to structural defects caused by a failure to comply with NHBC requirements. This includes, for example, major settlement or subsidence, collapse or serious distortion of joists or roof structure, dry (but not wet) rot.

The most that the NHBC will pay for putting right any defects is whichever is the lower of: the cost of the remedial work at the date of payment of the claim, or the amount a reasonable person would spend of his or her own money for the work. Under normal circumstances, there is no charge for the investigation of a claim.

The builder registers the house just before he starts to build. The buyer's solicitor is given an 'offer of cover' form by the builder, together with a Buildmark booklet giving full details of the scheme. He completes the acceptance form on behalf of the buyer and sends it to the NHBC. NHBC inspectors carry out spot checks on registered buildings under construction and when the inspector is satisfied that a house has been built substantially in accordance with NHBC's requirements, a 'Ten Year Notice' is issued to the builder. The NHBC sends a copy of the notice to the buyer's solicitor or licensed conveyancer for the buyer (to be kept with the booklet and handed on to the new owner if the house is sold within the ten-year period), and another copy goes to the buyer's lender.

In addition to the Buildmark policy, home owners receive a

Guide to your new home, giving advice on running in and taking care of the new home, and also explaining further what can and cannot be claimed from the Buildmark scheme, what the payment limits are, and how to appeal to the NHBC's conciliation and arbitration procedures should a dispute arise over rectifying defects.

Foundation 15 Scheme

This provides similar cover to the NHBC scheme and is backed by Zurich Municipal*. It is as yet not as widely used as the NHBC scheme. During the course of construction, if the developer goes bankrupt, the sums paid by the buyer to the developer will be reimbursed (i.e. deposit and instalments, if any) or, at the insurers' discretion, the cost of completing the house will be met.

During the first two years after the house is completed (the Developer's Guarantee Period) the insurers will pay the cost of putting right damage or defects if the developer fails to do so and if the defects arise from a failure to follow the Scheme's building requirements.

During the following 13 years (Structural Guarantee Period) the insurers will pay the cost of rectifying defects arising from a failure to comply with the building requirements if there is either an imminent threat to physical health and safety or major structural damage (such as subsidence).

The insurers provide a *Home Owner's Handbook*, a booklet giving details of the Scheme and a final certificate (which will be sent to the buyer's solicitor). These need to be passed over to the new owner if the house is sold before it is 15 years old.

The builder/developer will choose the scheme. A buyer will have no choice – though you should always insist on some form of cover. Mortgages and later sales of the house within ten years might be difficult or impossible if one of the schemes is not in force.

With 'one-off' houses or very small developments, an alternative to the NHBC or Foundation 15 schemes might be the supervision of the works by an architect or surveyor, who will have made interim inspections, a final inspection and issued certificates for these. This is acceptable to most (but not all) building societies and banks, who normally require full details of the architect's or surveyor's professional negligence insurance. From a buyer's point of view this is less satisfactory than either the NHBC or Foundation 15 schemes. In order to get defects put right it will be necessary to show that the builder or the architect or surveyor has been negligent. There is no protection against the bankruptcy of the builder.

The advantages of a newly built house

- Major repairs and redecoration should be unnecessary for the first few years (although you'll probably need to decorate initially).
- If, as is probable, it is registered with the NHBC, it will come with its ten-year warranty and protection scheme.
- If the house is not yet built or not yet completed, you may be able to get some features changed to suit your requirements – the position of a door, sockets, kitchen work surfaces, cupboards, for instance. But you will have to pay extra for this (and the builder may not agree to undertake any variations until after contracts are exchanged).
- The deposit required may be small.
- It may be easier to get a mortgage on a new house than an old one. Many builders arrange mortgage facilities for a whole estate in advance. There is often a link between the property developer and a particular building society, which makes it possible for a loan of a high percentage of the purchase price (sometimes as much as 100 per cent) to be given.

The disadvantages of a newly built house

- The house may not be finished for some time.
- There may be no more than the site and a plan to show to the solicitor and building society or other mortgagee.
- Most building societies or other lenders will not release the final loan until all the work is completed – down to the last coat of paint.

- You generally have to put in fittings, such as cupboards, which previous owners would already have installed in an inhabited house.
- There are often teething troubles – plaster drying out producing cracks, for example.
- The roads on an estate may not have been finished (this may cause problems with a building society's loan – and muddy floors in the house).
- The garden may have to be laid and planted and there may be restrictions on what you can do to the front garden (front gardens on an estate are often landscaped by the developers).
- Even in a rising property market you may not get your money back if you have to sell within one or two years (particularly if the newly built price was a package including 'free' extras, fixtures and fittings which depreciate; general inflation takes care of longer periods).
- You may be required to pay for the new home by stage payments (instalments) and therefore find yourself borrowing to pay for two houses at once.

A crucial disadvantage is that the date you are first given for the house to be ready is unlikely to be met. This could lead to delay and difficulties over the sale of your present house and extra expenses with your removal arrangements – and wear and tear on you. If possible, you should try to get the builder to agree a 'long stop' completion date, so that if he does not finish the work by that date, he will be in breach of contract and liable to pay you compensation – though not many builders will agree to this. Ask your solicitor to advise.

The builder could go bankrupt and so be unable to complete the building or not be available to carry out any work to remedy defects. This possibility is covered under the NHBC or Foundation 15 schemes, but you could still suffer a lot of inconvenience.

Looking for a newly built house

When touring an area, look out for signs of building works,

either single houses or estates. Advertising boards may have
been put up by:

- a national firm which has its own sales organisation (the
  address to contact will be on the board)
- a large building firm working in the district
- an estate agent working in conjunction with a building firm
- a local builder.

It is worth asking local builders, or a national firm, whether
they have any future plans for putting up houses in the area. Ask
local estate agents not only for details of houses being built or
just completed but also about any plans for future estates. They
may recently have sold land to a builder or developer for this
purpose.

A builder who is not on the NHBC register or registered
under the Foundation 15 scheme may be an excellent builder
with a good local reputation but he may be just a good jobbing
builder with no experience of house building – or he may be one
who has been expelled from the NHBC or Foundation 15
schemes. In either case, you will have difficulty getting a
mortgage; you may have difficulty also when you come to sell if
your prospective buyer cannot get a mortgage.

Advertisements

There are some monthly magazines which contain much useful
information on new estates being built, and have regular articles
on different areas of the country, with plenty of information
about new developments, a round-up of mortgage prospects,
and frequent supplements on specific aspects of new-house
building and buying. From specialist magazines, you can get the
names of large developers and the areas in which they operate,
so that you can apply to them for details in the area of your
choice and in your price range.

The local paper will almost certainly carry notices with details
of property developments, and advertisements of recently
granted planning permissions may appear with the names of
builders and developers. The local authority planning officer
and the building control officer know about ongoing and
projected developments, and may be prepared to give you
information.

Timber frame houses

If you want to buy a timber-and-brick house (constructed with prefabricated timber panels as opposed to a house of conventional masonry construction) the Timber & Brick Homes Information Council★ can be asked for the names of registered timber frame builders and for a copy of its twice-yearly list of newly completed timber-and-brick houses in each county. The *Timber & Brick Homes Handbook*, which may be provided by the builder/developer, contains information about what is involved in buying and owning a house of timber frame construction.

Promoting new homes

The New Homes Marketing Board (NHMB)★ is an offshoot of the House-Builders Federation, established to promote the selling of new homes. The NHMB has produced a free leaflet *Your Best Move is a Brand New Home*, describing all the advantages of a newly built house and explaining how to set about buying one.

Finding out about the house and the estate

Find out as much as you can about the reputation of individual builders or developers. If possible, talk to people who live in their houses; if an estate is still being built, talk to anyone who has already moved in. Ask:

- have there been many problems with the houses?
- has the builder put them right quickly?
- does he keep his promises?

Ask if there is a show house on the estate. Some developers complete one house and furnish it as a demonstration model. (But remember that the show house may have a number of optional extras fitted as if they were standard.) A small building firm may have put up a similar house in the district which you could arrange to look at.

Where you have a drawing rather than a finished house to consider, check at the actual site or compare the drawing with the Ordnance Survey map in the local authority planning office. A site plan may be accurate as to what it does show, but may fail

39

to reveal the proximity of railway lines, sewage works, quarries, factory estates and other unsuspected horrors. For the inside of the house, get confirmation of actual dimensions of rooms and stairways.

Some builders fully equip a house and then sell it on its merits. Others provide a basic shell and offer a long list of options – types of doors, floor finishes, kitchen equipment, bathroom suites – to suit the taste and pocket of prospective buyers. There are all sorts of permutations. The brochure may appear enticing, but it is vital to study the detailed specification if the house is not already finished and available to be seen.

The developer's or agent's particulars are sometimes not as detailed as they might be – perhaps because the builder is wary of naming specific materials or fittings, in case at a later date these become unobtainable. The quality of fittings tends to vary, so try to get what you want written into the specification as part of the contract for your house. Be sure to confirm all variations in writing and obtain a written acknowledgement. Insist that all quotations (for additional work or substitutions) are in writing.

Take special care to check exactly what you are paying for. Is the garage an optional extra, for instance (or obligatory even if you do not want one)? Is there planning permission for a double garage if you need one? Find out what type of heating is to be installed and be sure not only that you like the type but can afford the fuel. Some estates are all-electric with no gas laid on – you may feel strongly about cooking or heating with one fuel rather than another.

Roads
On a new estate, the cost of building the roads and laying the drains should be included in the purchase price of the house. The water authority becomes responsible for the drains, the local authority (county council or equivalent) for the roads, cleansing and lighting.

Most local authorities insist on the base of the road and kerbs being laid before building work starts. Later, when the top surfacing has been completed to their standard, the roads are adopted and maintained by the authority. There can be delays since the final making up of the roads is done at the end of all the construction work.

A building society may withhold some of the mortgage money until the roads are completed, unless there is an agreement between the authority and the builder (a Section 38 agreement). This is backed by a bond so that if the builder fails to complete the road or goes bankrupt before doing so, sufficient money will be paid under the bond to complete the road to the authority's satisfaction.

The roads will not be adopted by the local authority unless they are satisfactorily completed. Even then, it may be some time before the local authority passes the necessary resolution to adopt and there may be no street cleansing until formal adoption is finalised.

Drains

In a similar way, the construction of the sewers may be covered by an agreement between the water authority and the builder, secured by a bond (a Section 18 agreement). The house may be connected directly to the main sewer or may be served by a private drain serving a number of houses. This then connects to the main sewer. You will probably be asked to be responsible for sharing the cost of any maintenance of the private drain.

While the house is being built

A prospective buyer who has chosen a specific house should, if possible, make regular visits to see what is going on and check regularly whether the target date is likely to be met and that the construction is being carried out in accordance with the plans and specification. Builders can, and often do, make changes to methods and materials. These may not affect the value, but they may not be precisely what you contracted for. If mistakes are found (a yellow bathroom suite where blue was ordered, for instance), the earlier the builder is warned, the better.

A survey towards the end of the work might be advisable to check, for example, that the agreed boundaries have not been altered.

The price

A builder may quote for a house that has yet to be built a price which he undertakes to hold for a specified period. Once contracts are exchanged, he will have to keep to that price unless the contract specifically provides for price fluctuations. You may be asked to pay a small deposit for the offer to be kept open.

The price of a newly built house is seldom negotiable, especially if it is part of an estate. National firms fix their asking prices and are not likely to reduce them. A smaller firm which finds one or more houses on a particular site remaining unsold may (particularly if interest rates are high or money is tight at the time) make some reduction in order to complete the scheme and so release funds to finance the next development.

Incentives to buy

Depending on the state of the market, builders may provide financial incentives to persuade you to buy. Amongst them is a reduction in price if you exchange contracts within a specified number of weeks. If you do not meet the date, you may lose the house at that price.

The builder may offer to buy your present house in part-exchange for the new one. This avoids the risk of a chain but you may find that the builder's trade-in price is lower than the open market price for your house. Or the builder may pay the estate agent's and solicitor's fees and even the stamp duty and Land Registry fees.

Some builders have their own 'pet' solicitors whom they will encourage you to use. But you are free to use the solicitor or conveyancer of your choice. Note that the same firm of solicitors is not allowed to act for both you and the developer.

Another incentive is for the builder to arrange a mortgage of 100 per cent and/or to offer a mortgage subsidy for a year in the form of a reduction in mortgage rate or refund. All incentives have to be reported to your building society if it does not already know about them. Remember that if the builder gets into financial difficulties he may not be able to honour the obligation to subsidise interest rates.

Paying

Some builders insist on being paid by instalments and they will put the price up if you do not want to pay for the home in full until it is finished. This is more likely to happen when the house market is buoyant or where you own the plot and employ a builder to build a house for you.

If you are obtaining a mortgage and want to have stage payments as the work progresses, at the various stages the lender's surveyor will have to inspect (and be paid a fee).

It is important to tell your building society when you apply for a mortgage that you will need instalment payments. Building societies are generally quite happy to release a mortgage advance by instalments, as long as the value of the work done at any stage covers the amount they have advanced, and as long as the stages in construction tie in with their own requirements.

The society will issue an offer which spells out the stages at which money will be released. Generally, these are as follows:

1 roof plate level
2 roofed in
3 plastered out
4 final completion.

Make sure that the payment stages in the builder's contract are the same as in the mortgage offer. If there is a discrepancy, you may find it easier to get the builder to change than the building society. Get your solicitor to send a copy of the mortgage offer to the builder with a request that the building society payments are accepted instead.

Even though the lender's surveyor will inspect the house at the end of the construction work before paying out, you yourself should check on doors and window finishes and decorations, whether all the services are connected and working and whether any extras you ordered have all been provided.

Look for details:

● have all the walls been painted with the right number of coats of paint?

- do the doors shut properly?
- are any items missing?
- has the builder included everything that was in the original specification?

Unless everything is in order, you would be wise not to complete, but the contract may specify that you cannot refuse to complete if the outstanding items are of a minor nature. At the very least, you should be given an undertaking that the outstanding work will be carried out – and perhaps hold back part of the money till it is done.

It is unlikely that the builder will let you in before he is paid, so if the building society will not advance the money until the house is completed to the surveyor's satisfaction, there may be a critical and frustrating period when the house is to all intents and purposes finished but cannot be occupied. The contract will probably say that legal completion is to be 14 days after notice being given that the house is physically completed. Ideally, you should try to get the buyer of your own house to agree to a completion date based on the same arrangement.

If you have to agree a fixed date with your buyer in order not to lose the sale, you may need to arrange some temporary accommodation.

If the date of moving in is vital (and earlier than the completion of your sale), you may have to get a bridging loan from the bank.

House hunting

It is sensible to use all methods of looking for a new home: estate agents, advertisements, searching the area and word of mouth. Let it be known to as many people as possible that you are looking – friends, relations, neighbours, colleagues, solicitor, shopkeepers, bank manager, postman, landlord of the pub.

Look out for 'House for Sale' signs. These may have been put up by the owners themselves but more commonly they are notices erected by estate agents on behalf of a seller. Unless the board says that viewing is 'by appointment only' or 'no callers at the house', there is no reason why you should not approach the owner direct. The board may even say 'apply within'.

If the owner is selling direct and you are interested in viewing, you can either call and ask if it is convenient to look around immediately or make an appointment to see it later. But, if it is in the hands of an estate agent, you will usually have to see him or her first. Although the board may be that of one agent, the house may be on the list of other estate agents as well.

At times when there is a seller's market (that is, few houses for sale in relation to the number of buyers), property may be bought up so quickly that agents do not need or have time to get their boards up. There is little point then in searching a district for boards: go straight to the agents' offices and put your name and requirements down with them to be given details of any likely properties.

In London and many other areas, there are 'property shops' where details of houses and flats, including a photograph, are displayed. You can get particulars there of any property you think looks suitable and make arrangements directly with the vendor to view it. Some property shops or centres, in particular those set up by solicitors, offer a package deal, including the conveyancing. Some firms of solicitors have established a specialist estate agency department within the firm and are directly involved in the practical and financial aspects of buying and selling property as well as handling the legal side.

Estate agents

To find the names and addresses of local estate agents, start by looking for the names of firms advertising property in the local paper. Also look in the *Yellow Pages* or other business directory.

Most of the estate agents in England and Wales have principals or senior partners who are members of professional associations (such as the National Association of Estate Agents★, NAEA, the Architects and Surveyors Institute★, the Incorporated Society of Valuers and Auctioneers★ and the Royal Institute of Chartered Surveyors★) and are bound by their codes of professional conduct.

A country-wide list of members is available from the head offices and professional estate agents will normally have a list of their fellow members.

When you have located the offices of estate agents, study any advertisements outside. Most agents have window fronts in which they display particulars of properties they sell, usually accompanied by a photograph. These can give you a rough guide to prices and types of property in the area handled by that agent. Only a small proportion of an agent's properties will be displayed in the window so it's advisable to go into the office to talk to the agents. Agents advertise not only in order to sell a particular property, but also to establish their identity in the market: 'I have this type of property for sale, I operate in this area. Entrust me with the sale of your house and I'll handle it like this' – this is what estate agents are trying to put over.

Call on agents who seem to advertise the kind of property you are looking for. If you are restricted to weekend viewing, check which agents are shut on Saturdays and/or Sundays.

Buying the right house is so important that you should certainly not restrict yourself to what is on offer from just one agent. Enquire of all the agents in a locality. The least flamboyant agent may have just the house you are looking for.

The agents you visit will want to know fairly exactly what kind of accommodation you require. So, decide beforehand what is important to you: how many living rooms, bedrooms and bathrooms are the minimum you need, whether with or without a garage or garden and, most importantly, how much you are prepared to pay. Unless you feel very strongly about alternatives such as detached *versus* semi-detached, house *versus* bungalow, keep an open mind and let the agent know you are doing so.

The agent will ask for your name, address, home and work telephone numbers so that he or she can put you on a register and mailing list.

Be prepared to receive details of properties you may think you don't want. Curiously, estate agents find quite regularly that a lot of people buy types of property which they had initially ruled out.

You, as buyer, are not charged by the estate agent and you are under no obligation to him or her. Estate agents are in business to arrange the sale of a property on behalf of their client – the seller. They act as negotiators between seller and buyer but, since they make their living out of the commission they charge the seller, their duty is to him or her and not to you, the buyer.

To get an indication of the kind of buyer you would make, agents may ask you whether you will be a cash buyer or need a mortgage. They will do all they can to make it easy for you to buy (it is in their interest, too) and will be as helpful and cooperative as they can, offering advice about mortgage, survey, solicitor.

The more contact you have with an agent, the more likely he or she is to think of you and get in touch with you specifically when a suitable house is available. Be prepared to spend time initially calling in or ringing up regularly in order to establish a good relationship with the agent.

In a new area

It is not easy to house hunt at a distance. You are unlikely to know the area well enough to be able to assess advertisements or agents' descriptions: sometimes two streets, although adjacent, can be quite different in style and standard, as can opposite sides of the same street.

Estate agents in the locality may send you details of houses but some of these may no longer be available by the time the information reaches you: someone who lives in the area may beat you to it.

If you are not able to go to the area, you can call on an agent in your home town and ask if he or she has any contact with fellow agents in the other area. He or she may have the professional journal *Estates Gazette*, which publishes a monthly regional directory of agents.

A National Homelink Service is operated by members of the NAEA to provide a referral service for anyone moving from one area to another. The Homelink member in your present locality will contact another Homelink member in the area to which you are moving, giving details of your requirements, and the agents 'on the spot' will send you details of likely properties. The names and addresses of Homelink agents in any area can be obtained from the NAEA.

Some agents are linked to a regional or national multi-list

computer system. For instance, the Team group of estate agents have combined to offer their clients a computerised multi-listing service. You register your requirements with one Team agent, and will receive details of properties that match your specifications currently on the books of all the others.

If the area to which you will be moving is some distance away, the costs of travelling to look at houses can be quite considerable. A good estate agent can be helpful in preventing you making unnecessary journeys. He or she should know each property thoroughly and a telephone call for more details or an opinion may help you decide whether a potentially interesting house is worth a journey. He or she can also arrange appointments to see several houses during one visit.

It can be profitable to take time off to go and stay for a few days in the prospective new area so that you can assess the place for yourself and make a few personal contacts. Arm yourself with a large-scale map or street guide so as to make looking easier and quicker. (Many estate agents provide a free map or guide.) Start touring round the area to get the feel of different streets or districts and mark on your map the ones you like.

Relocation agents
There are a number of agencies offering a 'relocation' service throughout the country. They act solely on behalf of buyers and set out to help them find the type of property they want in the area they want. Originally, such agencies were used mostly by firms for the relocation of staff being moved because of their job. Nowadays, many more agencies deal with individuals moving who do not have the time, opportunity or inclination to undertake the tracking down of potentially acceptable properties, particularly in an unfamiliar area of the country.

Relocation agencies vary from the individual consultant to fairly large organisations offering a full range of relocation-related services in the UK and abroad. They advertise in the national press, and many agencies are members of the Association of Relocation Agents★. The ARA can be asked to send a region-by-region directory of its members which also sets out the rules of conduct that an ARA member will abide by.

An agent's knowledge of the local property market should enable him or her to offer advice on the suitability of property and location according to a client's requirements. The agent should advise on a particular property's general value and condition, on planning considerations and resale possibilities. One advantage of using a relocation agent is that he or she is working for you, the buyer, and will get details of properties, view on your behalf and sift and select property within your specifications, so that you do not waste time and risk disappointment seeing hopeless candidates. An agent will negotiate terms for a client, if required, and can also be asked to oversee the sale of the present home.

Relocation services can include as little or as much as the individual client requests, including introductions to legal and financial advisers and to surveyors, making all the removal arrangements, organising storage of possessions, the cleaning and preparation of both the new and the old home, and providing information about the new area and facilities.

It is usual to pay a 'retainer' or registration fee (anything between £200 and £500) for the initial work of researching and selecting suitable property; when a purchase goes through, a further fee (perhaps 1 to 1½ per cent of the price) is payable on exchange of contracts. Any additional work the relocation agent is asked to do will be charged on a negotiated basis.

Estate agent's particulars

Whether you call in person, telephone or write, the agent will give you what are known as 'particulars' – details of properties available which he or she thinks may be of interest. The information may be in the form of a list or even a glossy brochure or individual sheets for each property. You may be sent particulars at frequent intervals until you tell him or her to stop, or until he or she gets tired of you if you do not follow up any of them.

One of the hazards of the house hunting game is that by the time the list has reached you, you may find that the house which you particularly like the sound of has already been snapped up and is 'under offer'. This is a good reason to make contact with agents and ask that they telephone rather than write to you.

An agent's particulars are part of the service of marketing the house for the seller, who would not thank the agent if a description were so worded as to deter potential buyers. It is intended to act as an inducement for the buyer to inspect: the assumption is that no one buys a house on the strength of particulars only. However, the facts given in the description of a property must be accurate – about, for instance, the number of floors or size of rooms. But you may find that because a room is on an upper floor it is counted and described as a bedroom when it may not really be big enough to hold a bed. So, check the room measurements if they are given, and beware if none are quoted.

Measurements are usually straightforward: reception room 16ft 6in × 20ft. 'Maximum' dimensions may mean that the room is not square: it may be L-shaped or have an alcove.

You have to learn to notice what is *not* said and extract the details from the traditional estate agents' descriptive style, which uses such terms as 'exceptional' or 'beautifully proportioned'. Beware of 'immaculate décor' or 'tastefully decorated' which has to be a matter of opinion – usually only the owner's and possibly only the agent's.

Euphemisms

suitable for conversion: in need of a lot of repair and redecoration
bijou: can't swing even a cat
cottage: anything old and small
town house: front entrance through the garage
easy to manage: pokey
spacious: too big for most people to decorate or heat
exceptionally spacious: cold and draughty
full central heating: four storage heaters
conservatory: porch 18in × 3ft
full double glazing: constant traffic noise
interesting: only if you're selling it (can't think what it's for)
individual décor: paper peeling off walls
convenient motorway/railway: runs at back of garden
convenient buses: bus tickets fall into your front garden
convenient school: children fall into your front garden
quiet cul-de-sac: children's playground early Sunday mornings and school holidays

secluded: the shops are a long way away
rural views: views of allotments, cabbage fields, pig sties, or all three
open views: faces league football ground
reasonably priced: overpriced
reduced for quick sale: still overpriced
potential garage space: if only there were access
potential: anything, if only money/time were available (we would have
    done some work but are moving instead)
full of character: full of woodworm, dry rot, damp
exposed beams: on which to hit exposed heads
light and airy: expensive to curtain
deceptively spacious: too many small rooms
potential for extension: cramped
garage space and driveway: no parking
neat garden: minute yard
garden laid to lawn: grass patch
mature garden: overgrown wilderness
sea view: if standing on seat in WC
merits further improvement: can only get better
suitable for d-i-y enthusiast: present owners did nothing
ideal for modernising: quick, before it falls down

The Property Misdescriptions Act 1991 which came into force at the beginning of 1993 may put an end to some of the more bizarre descriptions by estate agents. A similar set of rules to the Trades Description Act is applied to estate agents' particulars. It is now a criminal offence to make a false or misleading statement about a property in the course of an estate agency business. Time will tell if this will curb their more extravagant purple prose.

The particulars may also give the amounts of Council Tax payable, whether it is freehold, or, if it is leasehold, the length of the lease and the amount of the ground rent and sometimes any maintenance charge and, finally, the asking price. The letters 'o.n.o.' (or near offer) after the price are an indication that the price is set high and the seller might be prepared to come down.

An estate agent must, by law, inform you if he or she has a personal interest in a property (perhaps a house is owned by one of the staff). Such a 'personal interest' statement may appear on the particulars.

Photographs of houses serve as a rough guide to the kind of property involved but can be misleading – for instance, they may have been trimmed of their less attractive surroundings – and should be regarded with caution. Remember that the agent is being paid to sell the house; to do this, he or she has got to present it in the most favourable light, without deliberately misleading or blatantly misrepresenting it or its size or position.

Advertisements

Estate agents often advertise the properties they handle in the local and national press. Although in a buoyant market these may well have been sold by the time the advertisement is published, it is well worth studying advertisements to get an idea of prices and of agents and because they are a useful pointer to the current state of the market.

Owners who wish to sell privately often advertise in the 'Property For Sale' columns of newspapers and magazines. Do not be put off buying a house which is advertised privately rather than through an agent. (An agent gives no guarantee of the quality of the house being sold – and remember, he or she is acting for the seller and not the buyer.)

If you are unfamiliar with the area, ask at the local reference library which papers cover the district. It is important to find out on which day property advertisements appear, and get your copy immediately.

Advertisements in the national dailies, Sunday papers and glossy magazines are likely to be for houses at the upper end of the market: local morning and evening papers and weeklies will give a wider choice. Weekly magazines worth consulting include: *Exchange & Mart, London Weekly Advertiser, Daltons Weekly* and *The Lady*. Top-of-the-market property is advertised in such magazines as *Tatler, The Field* and *Country Life*; often these are houses which are to be sold by auction.

House hunter's advertisement

You can yourself put an advertisement in the 'Wanted' column of a local or national newspaper. Specify what you want: house/bungalow; location/position; size/number of rooms; garden?; garage?; price (approximate); and why you would be a good buyer, such as 'no chain' or 'mortgage arranged', 'cash purchaser' or 'bank employee'.

Local newspapers are likely to be more useful and less expensive. Most newspapers offer reductions for repeated inserts; take their advice on which days to place the advertisement. If you are lucky enough to find a house in this way, you can ask the seller to reduce the price since he or she will not be paying an agent's commission.

Buying an old house to do up

If you want to buy an old house and modernise and improve it, you must be prepared for it all to take a long time. You must also ensure that you have the financial resources to carry out the necessary repairs and improvements. There have been changes to the legislation under which there was a statutory right to a house renovation grant where the property was judged by the local housing authority to be unfit for human habitation. All grants for repair and improvement are now discretionary and, in most cases, the grant applicant must have lived in the house and had an owner's interest for three years prior to making the application. Applying to the local authority for and receiving planning permission could take anything from two to 12 months or longer, plus a further six months or more for the building work to be carried out. In some cases, it may not be practical to live in the house while the work is being done. If you are eligible for a renovation grant towards the cost of the works, the local authority may take up to six months to decide the application and any works commenced before the grant is approved will not be eligible for grant.

Before you buy the house, find out what, if any, planning permission you need for the work you would like to do and the possibility of getting a grant. Go to the planning department and the environmental health department of the appropriate local authority and ask what the position is likely to be in your case. The more accurate and realistic the details you are able to provide, the better.

Conservation officers working for district or county councils can sometimes help with general advice.

House improvement grants

Local authorities administer and give grants (towards which the government contributes the greater part) for improving or renovating property.

There are a number of different grants. All grants are discretionary and a three-year prior residence and ownership qualification will apply in most cases.

- **House Renovation Grant** This is roughly equivalent to what used to be known as an improvement grant. It does not cover second homes, homes built or converted less than 10 years ago (unless the application is for disabled facilities), non-essential works, council tenancies or works under the Housing Defects legislation.

- **Common Parts Grant** This covers the cost of repairs or improvements to the common parts of buildings containing one or more flats. The landlord, or all the tenants, can apply.

- **HMO Grant** This grant is for houses in multiple occupation. Only a landlord may apply for this grant.

- **Disabled Facilities Grant** This is designed to help to make the home of a disabled person more suitable for him or her to live in. Anyone registered (or registrable) as disabled can apply, whether owner or tenant.

- **Home Repair Assistance** This is available to private-sector tenants and owner-occupiers. It may also be available to anyone with a right to live in the property for a period of at least five years and to most mobile-home owners and house-boat dwellers, provided that they have resided there for the three-year period prior to making their application. Assistance is available to people in receipt of income-related benefits or who are over 60 years old, disabled or infirm. It may cover any minor works or repair, improvement or adaptation but is limited to £2,000 per application or £4,000 over a three-year period.

Note that grants are now means-tested. Your finances will be taken into consideration in deciding whether to make a grant or how much grant to give. For further information obtain a copy of one of the three free leaflets – *House Renovation Grants,*

Disabled Facilities Grants and *Home Repair Assistance* – produced by the Department of the Environment★. You should be able to obtain this from your local authority along with application forms and statements of local grant policy. It is important not to start work until the grant is approved and you get the go-ahead from the local authority.

The grant you can get is a percentage of an amount called the eligible expense of the cost of the improvement plus some repair work. A local authority can make it a condition of a grant that you carry out certain repairs – for which you may not get a grant. Thus, you might finish up getting only 25 per cent of your total expenditure, even though a 50 per cent grant was promised.

Planning permission

You do not need to be the owner of the property to apply for planning permission (but you must inform the owner). Planning permission is required for many alterations and extensions to a building, particularly if it affects the external aspects and appearance, and for changing the use of a building. The permission has to be obtained from the local planning authority.

Permission is not required for what is specified as permitted development – for example, extending the house within certain limits. But the rules are very complicated and you would be well advised to contact the planning department of your local authority for informal advice from a planning officer. Sometimes, the permitted development provisions do not apply to certain areas, such as conservation areas.

Whether planning permission is needed or not, building regulations will apply to the materials and method of building. The local authority's building control officer should be consulted about getting building regulations approval (in Scotland, building control consent). A fee is payable when you apply for approval.

Listed buildings and conservation areas

Under the town and country planning legislation, the Department of the Environment compiles lists of buildings of special architectural or historic interest. A listed building must not be altered or extended in any way which would affect its character without authorisation from the local planning authority. This is a separate issue from planning permission, but getting listed buildings consent can be dealt with at the same time. The listing extends to the whole of the building inside and out, and the site, even though only part may be 'of interest'.

Certain areas are designated as conservation areas – perhaps a whole town or village, or a square, a street or even part of a street.

No part of a property in either of these categories may be demolished without consent and all trees within a conservation area are automatically subject to preservation orders. The rules are strict and cover outbuildings and boundary walls. Breach of the regulations is a criminal offence.

You can check whether a house is in a conservation area or is a listed building by going to the local authority offices to inspect the list. Do this before buying a house if you have ideas of making alterations or extensions to it at any time. Not only very old houses are listed – a building may be listed that is only 30 or so years old if it is of outstanding quality or design. The local authority search made by your solicitor will show whether or not the house is a listed building or in a conservation area.

Certain grants may be available from the local authority in respect of essential structural repairs to a listed building, and to repair or retain aspects of architectural interest; ask about this possibility at the local planning authority. Grants may also be made by English Heritage for buildings of outstanding interest. Notes for guidance and an application form are available from English Heritage★.

Ancient or unusual properties

If you are prepared to buy a decayed or historic building, the Society for the Protection of Ancient Buildings★ compiles for its members a quarterly list of historic buildings for sale which are in need of sympathetic owners to repair and maintain them.

Some people prefer the challenge of finding a building not originally designed as a home, and converting it themselves. If you would like to know whether there are any redundant properties available in your chosen area or happen to see a disused or unoccupied one, the organisations to get in touch with are:

- for a redundant church, rectory or other church building: apply to the diocesan office or registry (address in the local telephone directory) or ask the vicar
- for disused railway property: ask the British Rail Property Board* for the names of regional estate surveyors and managers to apply to in Birmingham, Bristol, Glasgow, London, Manchester and York
- for buildings in the forest, the Forestry Commission* sells some of its property by auction or by tender through regional offices; a free mailing list for the area/price requested is available from the head office
- for an unoccupied warehouse or other derelict property: trace the ownership by contacting the local authority for the name and address of whoever is responsible for the rates on the property
- for a redundant schoolhouse: ask the local education authority
- for a redundant pub: ask the estate manager of the brewers.

Other types of purchase

There are other ways to buy properties which depend on special circumstances. They all need very detailed consideration and you should take specialist advice. Chief among these are listed below.

Buying from a local authority

Tenants who have lived in a council house for two years or more or in another 'right to buy' property belonging to certain public bodies have a right to buy it at a substantial discount (up to 70 per cent of its value). The discount is calculated on the number of years as a council tenant (maximum 30 years) and you don't have to live in the same council house over that period.

Similar rights to buy are afforded to tenants of a number of other public bodies. A leaflet *Your Right to Buy Your Home* is available from the Department of the Environment.

The procedure is triggered by sending a form to the local

authority (RTB1), obtainable from the authority. It has to respond by telling you its view of the valuation, and you may appeal to the District Valuer if you think it is too high.

Ownership is exactly the same as for any other house, except that if you sell within three years you have to refund a proportion of the discounted price. There may be certain restrictions on the sale if the property is in a rural area or has been specially adapted for use by the elderly.

Buying from a housing association

Housing associations were established to help people who could not afford to buy outright get access to the housing market. Schemes exist which enable buyers to acquire just a share of the ownership of the property (say 25 per cent) and to rent the rest. It is possible then, over a period of time, to increase the share of ownership up to 100 per cent. This is called 'staircasing'. Even if you do not acquire the full 100 per cent you can still sell your share to another buyer if you want to move. Further information may be obtained from the Housing Corporation★.

Secure tenants of registered non-charitable housing associations have the right to buy as shown above. Also tenants of housing association properties which receive funding from 1 April 1997 onwards will have the right to acquire. Contact the Housing Corporation for further details.

A leaseholder's right to buy

If you own a leasehold interest (see page 76) in a house – not a flat – and the lease is running out, you have a right to acquire the freehold or a lease for a further 50 years. The requirements are complex and are likely to be costly, but nevertheless provide a measure of protection to those whose long leases are running out. The right is available only to tenants who have lived in the property for the preceding three years (or three of the past ten years).

The procedure is triggered by a tenant serving the appropriate notice on the landlord before the lease expires. The landlord can refuse to give a new lease, or to sell the freehold, only on very narrow grounds (such as showing a greater need for the house than the tenant). The procedure then involves a means of valuing the property. If the price is too high the tenant has a month to back out.

Buying a mobile home
From a legal point of view mobile homes do not fall easily into normal categories of home ownership. Even though they are difficult to move, they are none the less considered not to be permanent structures and have the same legal status as caravans.

For many years the owners of mobile homes had very little protection from the law. Since the Mobile Homes Act 1983 the position has improved.

If the site is licensed by the local authority and the home is used by the occupier as a sole or main home, the occupancy may only be terminated by an order of the County Court. Grounds for termination are limited, such as breaches of the agreement or failure to repair the home.

The owner of a licensed site must (within three months) let the occupier have a written statement giving details of the right to occupy the site.

It is possible for ownership to be transferred, but the site owner retains some control over the situation and can demand commission or around 10 per cent of the price as a precondition of agreeing to an ownership change.

Mobile homes cost substantially less than conventional houses. If you are considering buying a mobile home, you should insist on studying (and taking advice on) the agreement between the mobile home owner and the owner of the site. Give attention to the site regulations, the services available on the site and its general condition, and the transfer provisions in the agreement (in case you should want to sell on).

Buying a repossessed house

A house which has been repossessed by a lender could be in practically any of the categories which have been considered in this chapter; money is lent on the security of virtually any kind of property. If the borrowers do not keep up with payments, the home will be repossessed.

If you are buying from a lender, the quality of your

ownership will still be the same: a lender in possession has the right to transfer absolute ownership. This is true even if there is a succession of loans on the same property. Lenders have to comply with strict rules about any surplus money which they hold. But that need not concern a buyer. It is something which you should leave for your solicitor or conveyancer to sort out.

A lender who sells a property will not have the same level of knowledge as a normal owner. There will be little point in asking where the boundaries lie, or whether the house is connected to mains drainage or a septic tank. It is also unlikely that a lender will know if there have been any difficulties or disputes with neighbours.

It is also possible that a house which has been repossessed may not have been maintained as well as one which is being sold by a proud and caring owner. If there has been a forced repossession, damage might have been done to doors or windows. Make sure you insist that it is put right. It is also especially important that you ensure that the locks have been changed.

Should you buy a repossessed house?
There is no reason why you should not buy a house which has been repossessed, but you should exercise extra care in your investigations and enquiries. A survey would be virtually essential. There will be very little comeback against the seller if problems are found.

You may also find it harder with a lender. Lenders are required to obtain the best available price. Sometimes they do this by selling at auction; sometimes by insisting on tender documents. You may also be asked to enter into a contract race (see page 97).

The risk is that you could spend a lot of money on investigations, only to find that you have been pipped to the post by someone else.

On the other hand, there may be advantages: the price can sometimes be low, and the lender might be prepared to offer you a loan on favourable terms if you decide to buy.

How to view

When you have spotted a house or been sent details of one you wish to look at, you should make an appointment 'to view' immediately. If you are the first person to view, you stand a better chance of getting the house should you decide it is the one you want.

If there are estate agents, they will make the appointment on your behalf. Sometimes they will accompany you; this can save time. If the owner is out, or the property is vacant but still furnished, and the agents have the key, they will want to go with you since responsibility for the house is theirs. If it is empty, you may be allowed to borrow the key to look round on your own.

If you cannot keep your appointment, you should let the owner or agent know. If, when you get to the outside of the house, you decide without even going in that it is not what you want, it is common courtesy to cancel your appointment there and then by knocking on the door and saying 'sorry, but no'.

Always take a pen, paper or a notebook and a measuring rule with you, and the agent's particulars, so that you can check dimensions, particularly where measurements are quoted as 'max.' or 'overall' or 'approx.'. Ideally, both partners should view together but if one or the other cannot do so, it will help in later discussions if there are notes or plans to refer to.

It is no bad thing to make up a short check list. Write down on the left-hand side, line by line, all the factors you can think of – rooms, situation, all the merits you want and any demerits you do not want – with a few spare lines for points occurring as you go along. Draw vertical columns to the right of these headings, put the address of the house (and succeeding houses) at the top of the column and then tick off 'yes' or 'no', or '3', say, opposite 'bedrooms', or 'good' or 'bad', and so on, so that you have a ready reminder of the comparative merits of possible houses.

First look

It can be distracting to assess a house when it is decorated or furnished to another's taste or in need of decoration. Try not to

61

be influenced by 'wrong' colours and furniture – or none at all – but concentrate on absorbing a general impression and imagine yourself and your family in it. You are equally likely to be misled by a beautifully furnished and newly decorated home – you can fall for it as it looks, forgetting to think: 'How will it look with my possessions in it?'

A strange house on several floors can be confusing at first sight: it may help to make a floor-by-floor plan as you go. But do not waste too much time on this. It is better to go back and do a second tour. Do not let yourself be rushed or pressurised by the estate agent who accompanies you, or embarrassed by the presence of the owner.

As you go over the house, concentrate on the layout of each floor and each room. Do not forget to look at the windows. An empty house without curtains gives an impression of light rooms, but can appear dark and dismal when curtained and furnished.

The height of the ceilings is something to note from the point of view of heating and redecorating and how your furniture will fit. An open-plan house (where the dining and sitting area and kitchen lead into each other, without dividing walls or doors), will need a powerful heating system and good insulation. There are advantages for a parent working in the kitchen being able to keep an eye on a small child playing in the adjacent living area, but there can be problems about privacy, and difficulties when children reach school age and need a quiet place to study or play on their own or as teenagers to entertain their friends.

If the house seems to provide what you need in the way of basic accommodation – sufficient bedrooms, living rooms and so on – and if your first impression of it as a possible home is a favourable one, you should consider it in more detail.

Looking in more detail

No single house will provide all you want. It is up to you to decide what points are most important and which – because others are so satisfactorily provided – you are prepared to forgo.

Think also how permanent you expect your stay to be in the new home. If you are likely to resell shortly, consider whether any aspect of the property may affect your chances of finding a buyer when it is your turn to sell.

Here are points to consider carefully. If the answers to the majority are not positive, the house is probably not suitable for you. The answer to some of the questions may be 'no, but could be arranged'. But take into account that alterations or improvements will put up the cost – quite apart from the time factor.

Points to be considered include:

- is the accommodation what you want?
- is the layout suitable?
- is the situation of the house right?
- what are the facts about the heating, lighting and other services?
- what is the condition of the structure?
- what is the state of the decorations – inside and out?
- what about the garden?
- what about any garage, drive and roadway?
- when will the house be available?
- what is included in the price?

Accommodation and layout
Entrance (hall)

- is there an outer porch (as protection against weather, for delivery of parcels)?
- is there space for parking a pram, pushchair, bicycle, shopping trolley?
- is there anywhere to hang coats, store Wellington boots, gardening shoes, umbrellas?
- is it well lit?
- which direction does the front door face?

Living room(s)
- are they adequate in size? (in an irregular-shaped room or one with a bay window, take the exact measurements)
- is the dining room or dining area convenient for the kitchen? are there steps up or down from the kitchen? (making a trolley impracticable, carrying trays hazardous)
- is there space for the children to play?

- is there space for the piano? (preferably not against a neighbour's adjoining wall)
- are the windows in convenient places?
- where are the electric sockets and are there enough of them?
- where are the lights and switches?

Kitchen
- is it large enough, particularly if you want to be able to eat in it or work in it?
- does it lead off the hall/living room/dining room? how convenient is it for carrying food and shopping to, rubbish from?
- is there an outside door into the garden, for access to the garage or dustbin?
- is there a back porch?
- what does the window look on to? which way does it face? (if south or west, it may get too hot); could you keep an eye on a child in the garden?
- is the window easy to open? is there an air extractor system?
- does the layout of the worktop and sink area suit your way of working?
- is it well lit?
- what storage is there for food? is there a larder? is there space for your refrigerator? for your freezer?
- will your existing equipment fit?
- is there enough cupboard space, drawers, shelves? a tall cupboard for the vacuum cleaner, brooms?
- is the floor covering in good condition? comfortable to stand on? likely to be easy to clean?
- is gas laid on? (check particularly if the present owner has an electric cooker)
- where and how many electric sockets are there? is there one for a cooker?

Utility room
- is there one? or what facilities are there for washing and drying clothes?

indoors: is there space for a washing machine/tumble dryer? ironing area?

outdoors: is there space for hanging clothes to dry? are there any restrictions on hanging washing outside?

Staircase
- is it easy to climb (for small children or the elderly)? are the treads wide enough? risers not too steep? are there awkward curves or bends? are there handrails? is it well lit (top and bottom)?

Bedrooms
- how many?
- are they large enough? for double bed/twin beds/four poster/bunk beds?
- will other furniture (chest of drawers, wardrobe, for instance) fit in? (measure, do not guess)
- is there built-in furniture?
- is there a washbasin? (if so, fill it up and let it drain, and do the same with any others – they can be noisy and react to the plumbing elsewhere in the house)
- are the rooms convertible to nursery/playroom/study/ bedrooms? (consider future needs as well as current ones)
- do they face a noisy road or a bright street light?
- how soundproof are the walls between rooms?

Bathroom(s)
- how many?
- is it large enough?
- is there a separate WC?
- plumbing: can another bathroom/extra basin/shower/WC be installed easily? (check where the water supply and waste piping run in the building)
- does everything work?
- is there an airing cupboard/linen cupboard or space to make one?

Other
- is there an extra room which you could use as a spare bedroom/study/sewing room/boxroom for storage/play-room/workshop?

- is there a loft? could it be used for storage or converted into a room?
- cupboards: are there any built in? or space to put some in?

Situation and location

You probably already know or, if you do not, you should decide now, how important to you it is to have a sunny living room, kitchen or bedroom. A kitchen or living room which never gets any sun can be very dark and gloomy in winter – so, check which rooms are north-facing (cold and dark), which are east-facing (morning sun, best for waking up/breakfasting), which are south- or west-facing (warm and sunny for most of the day). This is especially important if you are viewing on a dull day or a winter evening. If you cannot work it out for yourself, ask the owner or agent and mark the direction of the rooms on your plan. Similar houses on opposite sides of a road may be quite different inside with regard to the light and warmth – and may be different in price, too, on this account.

Work out whether the garden gets the sun all day or only part of the day, or is always shaded. Consider how important this is to you – as a sun lover or as a gardener. Look to see whether any trees, foliage or adjacent buildings take away light from any room. If you are viewing in winter, be observant and allow for trees in leaf during the summer. Do any houses nearby look into the windows or garden? If you are viewing in summer, study whether the trees obscure some overlooking building. Also, trees in leaf are a good barrier to traffic noise, so it may be much noisier in winter.

Think about any possible winter hazards: if the district is hilly or the approach to the house is steep, icy conditions might make access difficult or impossible. Draughts coming through front or back doors and along passages may be fierce in winter – but absent on the gentle summer's day when you are viewing.

- Is the property near the coast (risk of flooding from the sea, coastal erosion)?
- Is there a river or any streams close by which could cause flooding? (this may affect insurance cover)
- The exterior of a house in an exposed position, on high

ground or by the seaside may need more attention in the way of upkeep and insulation. If there is industry nearby, note whether the prevailing wind would send any dirt, smoke or smell towards the house rather than away from it. Will there be any noise?

- What about the siting of the house – the immediately adjacent vicinity (neighbours), the general location and the effect on your journey to work?

If you are interested in the house, it is essential to go back again to see it at a different time of the day, on a different day of the week, and in different weather conditions, if possible.

Check out the following points.

- distance from the railway station (are there parking facilities there?), bus stop and bus routes (and underground), post office, bank, library, shops, launderette, health centre (will it be uphill carrying home heavy shopping or pushing a pram?), schools (how safe is the route?) or college, church or chapel
- access to the countryside/sea, park or recreation ground, cultural and leisure activities
- neighbours: how secluded is the house? are neighbours likely to be a nuisance (children or pets) or vice versa? in a terraced or semi-detached house, which rooms have the party walls? what is the division between gardens? is the next-door garage near your boundary? (late/early car starting); are nearby buildings (restaurant, pub, club, fish-and-chip shop or take-away) likely to cause parking problems, noise at night, cooking smells, or piles of . rubbish? a factory can produce smoke, noise or smells; a farm may bring in smells or flies or straying animals); on a new estate, could further building work or future buildings obscure a pleasant view?

Problems waiting to happen

Neighbour disputes tend to focus on things which are shared: gateways, drives, drains, hedges. If there are any shared facilities will you be troubled by constant use from the people next door? The kindly old couple who may live there now could sell to a family with a much more intrusive lifestyle. Imagine the worst that could happen. Could you live with it?

Other factors that you could find either a nuisance or an advantage (if next-door or nearby) might be a school, a police station, fire station, hospital, church, garage or repairer, kennels, swimming pool or sports ground.

If the next-door property is uninhabited (particularly if it is derelict) find out who owns it and what is likely to be happening.

If you are viewing on a weekday, try to find out whether things change at weekends. Or if you are there at a weekend, consider the other days of the week. For a market town, make at least one visit on market day.

Watch and listen for traffic noise and inconvenience:

- are there heavy lorries going by on weekdays? (none at weekends)
- are there traffic lights/a junction/hill/bend close by? (constant stopping/starting/gear noises)
- is it a favourite route for L-drivers?
- do commuters or shoppers pass or park on weekdays?
- do tourists pass or park at weekends or in summer?
- do nearby sports grounds cause parking problems and noise at weekends/evenings?
- do trains pass within hearing distance?
- is there a motorway or by-pass near enough to be noisy? or are there plans to build one?
- is there an airport or airfield near and is the house under the flight path?
- are there any nasty but short-lived noises such as a milk depot loading crates at 4 a.m. for two hours every day?

If you can find out about the ownership of the adjacent land or buildings, try to discover if there are plans for further developments. Knowledge of the district if you live there already will obviously be a help. Local papers and local gossip are other sources of information. It is unlikely that the seller will tell you that he or she is putting the house on the market because a new battery chicken 'farm' is to be set up in the field opposite.

Heating and other services

How is the house heated? Is all or only part of it centrally heated? (Look for radiators in all rooms; a note on a plan can help later when working out the arrangement of furniture.) When was the system installed?

Is electricity the only laid-on fuel? Or is there a gas supply, even if not currently in use? (when was it last used?)

Is there an alternative to fall back on if the electricity is cut off or the central heating supply fails, such as an open fire or a stove? Are there working fireplaces and what can you burn (is it a smoke control area)?

If you view during cold weather, you should be able to tell straightaway whether the heating system works effectively. If you view in summer, ask for the system to be switched on, if practicable. You should get it tested as part of the survey.

Ask the owners what the past year's fuel consumption and heating costs (including maintenance) have been – if they are able to tell you. When assessing any figures, remember to allow for differences in your ways of life – whether out all day, with or without children or of different ages, elderly people in the household.

- If oil-fired: where is the storage tank (and its vent pipe)? is it unobtrusively sited and what is its capacity? where is the boiler?
- If solid fuel: do you mind having to stoke a boiler? carry fuel? clean out ashes? what type of fuel has to be used? where is the fuel stored – is it convenient for the house/for delivery?
- If gas-fired: where is the boiler? How old is it?
- If off-peak electricity: electric storage heaters – how many and where, what size capacity?, how old and run on what tariff? underfloor or ceiling heating, in which rooms? warm air ducting? where are the vents/grills?
- Loft insulation: is there any, and of what type and thickness?
- Water supply: is it on direct mains water? If not, what water supply is there? Is the supply under anyone else's control (e.g. the pipe runs across a farmer's land from his

supply)? What are the water charges per year? Is there a meter? How is the water heated? Is the cylinder likely to be large enough for your needs? Where do the pipes run?

- Electricity: ask how old the wiring is and has it ever been re-wired (professionally or d-i-y)? Are there plenty of sockets? Does the consumer unit have old-fashioned fuses or modern circuit breakers? If you want to cook by electricity, is there a separate circuit (30-amp, at least) for the cooker?

- Gas: if there are gas fires, how old are they (older types may not be efficient)?

- Drainage: is the house connected to a main drainage system? or is there a septic tank or cesspool? If so, what are the costs of maintenance and arrangements for emptying? Note where any manholes or access points are: if on your premises, you may be independent in case of trouble; if on someone else's land, there may be delay in getting a stoppage cleared. (On the other hand, if the communal manholes are on your site, you may be inconvenienced by calls to get obstructions cleared.)

- TV aerial: is there one? If you see a lot of fancy aerials on nearby houses, it is likely that reception is poor; if the house is under a cliff or hillside, it may be inaccessible to radio signals. If there is a satellite dish, does it comply with local authority requirements?

The structure

Even if you will be having a professional survey of the house or flat done by a qualified surveyor, try, during a preliminary visit, to get as good an impression as you can of the structural condition of the building. If it looks to you to have a lot of faults, you could save yourself the cost of a survey by deciding there and then that the cost of repairs would not justify the cost of the house – or that the repairs would not be possible on your budget. Ask the owner what structural work has been carried out recently, when and why.

An owner is under no obligation to tell you of any faults: it is up to you or your surveyor to discover them. On the other hand, he or she is under an obligation to give honest answers to direct questions: for example, whether there have ever been any problems with dry rot or an insurance claim for flooding. If he or she does not answer truthfully and you can show that you relied on those answers, you can sue him or her. On the other hand, if you discover the problems at an early stage you will save yourself a lot of distress.

Inside
From a structural point of view, the main things to look at inside are the walls and ceilings.

Ceilings
- are there stained patches? (tell-tale signs of leaks)
- are ceilings sagging or cracked? (cracked plaster ceilings in an older house may just be a matter of papering over the cracks, but if cracks look to you to be alarmingly wide or run into corners or over window lintels, there may be a problem).

Walls
- are there stains on walls around the skirting, and crumbling plaster? (signs of rising damp)
- are there any long, diagonal cracks in walls which look as if they have been repaired but have re-cracked? (this may be a sign of settlement)
- is the existing paper or paint shabby, dirty or damaged? (note to what extent redecorating would be immediately necessary and include this in your budget)
- if the house is newly painted inside, ask yourself why? are they just house-proud – or covering up?

Woodwork and floors
- is woodwork showing cracks or shrinkage (going crinkly), especially skirtings? (a possible sign of woodworm or rot)
- if floors are springy, they or the joists underneath may be rotten (on the ground floor) or wormy (anywhere)
- ask what the floor surface is under a fitted carpet, vinyl or lino covering

- are any floor tiles cracked or wood blocks loose or bulging?
- are any floor coverings worn in places that take a lot of traffic? would any need replacing?

Outside

Go outside and study the building from top to bottom. A pair of binoculars can be useful for scanning roofs and chimney stacks. If things look bad from below, they are probably worse up there, and inside too.

If any major re-roofing or repairs have been carried out, find out what, when, and whether any guarantees were attached. For a flat roof, find out how long ago it was laid (felt roofs last about ten years, asphalt up to 30).

Points to look for or ask about include the following.

Roof

- look for any loose or broken slates or tiles, particularly near chimneys and roof valleys. Walk down the garden or to the other side of the road and have a look at any roof valleys that may be visible (if they are cluttered with slipped slates or tiles, the whole roof may be likely to need rehanging)
- do chimney stacks look in good condition or is the brickwork in need of repointing?

Main walls

- are there any bulges or cracks? (may be caused by settlement of the foundations or by tree roots – own or neighbour's). A way of checking for bulges is to stand very close to a wall and look along it. If any part is out of true, perhaps you should look at another house.
- what is the state of the pointing between the bricks? (it should look smooth and full: gaps or cracks allow damp to penetrate). Are the bricks themselves in good condition?
- is there a damp proof course? (not all old houses have one) Are there signs of damp at ground level? If a damp course has been injected, ask for the inspection report and guarantees. Confirm that the work has been carried out to specification
- guttering and down pipes: are there signs of rust or leaking,

stained or green walls? (damp could penetrate the brick-work, or cause wet rot)

- when were the walls last painted? with what material? will they need doing immediately? and how often thereafter?
- is the paint peeling very badly? (there may be a damp problem)
- are walls covered with a cement rendering? what condition is it in? (it will be an expensive maintenance item).

Doors and windows
- do they fit well? do all the windows open and close easily?
- does the woodwork look in good condition? is there any rust on metal frames?
- what is the condition of the paintwork?
- when were they last painted (or varnished)? (every three years is the recommended interval, more frequently in south-facing walls or if the house is at the seaside).

If you go ahead to the stage of having a professional survey done, tell the surveyor of anything you have noticed that you think may be sinister. If he or she confirms your suspicions, you can ask for an idea of how much it would cost to be put right.

There is more likelihood of there being heavier maintenance and repair costs with an older house, so it is even more important to have an old house surveyed and to get an idea of how well it has been looked after over the years.

Some prefabricated reinforced concrete (PRC) house-types have been designated as defective. Before buying a PRC home, a prospective buyer should check with the local authority whether the dwelling is one of these. If so, find out whether it has been repaired in compliance with the Housing Defects Act 1984 and carries a warranty issued by the National House Building Council. If not, you will have difficulty in obtaining a mortgage and in re-selling, and it is probably best to look for another house.

The garden
How important is a garden to you for general recreation (sunbathing, barbecues), for the children and as a gardener?

- is it the right size/too big/not big enough?
- how sheltered is it?
- how much sun does it get?
- is it suitable for a child to play in? are there any hazards? (trees, pond, stream, unsafe access to road)
- is it easily accessible for a pram?
- can you keep an eye on it from the house?
- is it on a steep slope? easy to maintain?
- what state is it in? (if not yet laid out, this could be expensive: purchasing topsoil, laying a lawn)
- is there much grass to cut/hedges to be kept trimmed? (would this present a problem?)
- is there somewhere to store garden tools?
- if outhouses or a greenhouse are included in the sale, what condition are they in?
- is there a standpipe or tap for watering? (may involve additional water charge)
- is it possible to reach the garden at the back of the house without having to go through the house? (also relevant for dustbin emptying).

Trees can be a hazard if they have grown too big or been planted too close to a building or walls (including the neighbour's). Roots spread underground, growing outwards generally in proportion to the canopy of the tree and can affect the foundations of a building and damage drains. Poplars, elms and willows are especially greedy (willows can signify a very damp environment or underground stream).

In some areas, trees in private gardens have tree preservation orders placed on them, prohibiting the owner from lopping or cutting them down without first getting permission from the local authority. Ask the owner if this applies to any tree on the property and get your solicitor to check. All trees in conservation areas are automatically subject to a preservation order.

The boundaries of the property may be marked by walls, fences or hedges, for some of which the owner may be responsible. If the piers of a brick wall or the posts of a fence are on your side, it is more likely than not that the wall will be yours and your responsibility. In any case, it is sensible to inspect the state of any brick walls, wooden fencing or gates. Replacing them can be costly. An unstable brick wall is a danger to life.

Garaging the car
- is there a garage?
- how far is it from the house?
- will your car fit in? (the size of garage is not usually stated in estate agent's particulars; be sure to know the measurements of your own car, including its width with the door open and the height if a hatchback)
- are the garage doors easy to open, keep open, shut, lock?
- is there light and a power point inside?
- what is the approach to the garage made of? what sort of upkeep will be necessary?
- what is the access from the driveway/garage to the road like? (if the road is narrow, will a car parked on the opposite side stop you getting yours out?). Is there clear visibility? (so that you can enter or leave the road safely).

If there is no garage:

- is there a legal access to the property? Planning approval is necessary for a new vehicle access
- is there a car port (a roofed-over area at the side of the house)? can your car be parked? in the garden, yard or on the road? (this affects the insurance premium)
- is there plenty of parking and turning space?
- are there parking restrictions outside? or a residents' parking scheme? (involving an annual charge)
- is there space and access to the road for you to put up a garage (needs planning permission)
- where can visitors park?

Agreeing terms

This section covers both using a solicitor and doing-it-yourself.

Before making an offer

If you like what you have seen, check out some practical aspects before you make an offer.

Ascertain approximately when the seller is able and willing to move out. He or she may be waiting to sell before starting to look for a house or may be waiting for a mortgage or be part of a lengthy chain. If timing is important to you, this will affect your decision about the house.

The legal and financial set-up will have to be gone into in great detail later when it comes to the stage of conveyancing (the legal side of house buying). At this preliminary stage there are many relevant points to check. Some are so important that they may stop you buying the house.

Freehold or leasehold?

If it is a leasehold property, ask about any annual or other financial commitments such as:

- ground rent payable (how much? fixed or subject to review?). Normally this should be no more than a token few pounds a year
- maintenance charges for repairs or redecoration (is any payment imminent? Has the seller been informed of any

future expenditure, and what payments have been made over the past three years or so?)

If it is freehold, there may nevertheless be annual charges for maintenance – for example, roads on a private estate.

Covenants and rights

Are there any restrictions on the use of the house – for example, on hanging out the washing or keeping a pig? Restrictive covenants are obligations imposed by covenant on the owner of a property, forbidding certain activities on the property, such as running a business or putting buildings on parts of it. (You may in any case need planning permission if you want to carry on a professional business from your home address.)

Covenants last indefinitely. It is never safe to ignore them, even if they were imposed many years ago. There is always the risk that someone may try to enforce them. On a housing estate these rules may be part of a 'building scheme' which means that fellow residents can insist that you obey them.

Do other people have rights such as to walk across part of the property? This should come to light when your solicitor receives the draft contract or details of the lease at a later stage. But if there are any indications of this sort of thing, tell your solicitor so that more enquiries can be made.

Consent for building work

Has planning permission for all alterations to the property been applied for? If granted, what work was carried out and by how much did this increase the size of the house? (This could affect your need for planning permission for any future alterations.) If permission was refused, why? Has an enforcement notice been issued?

If you think you would like to make alterations – for example, add a large extension or put in new windows – visit the local planning department to try to discover, before you get too involved, what the local planning authority's attitude is to such alterations.

Also, you can find out by going to the local authority planning department whether there are any plans (or projects) for local buildings, new roads, motorways or industrial development. Every local authority keeps a register of planning applications and the register is open to inspection (as is the register of enforcement proceedings).

Similarly, all building work must comply with the Building Regulations (see page 103). If they do not, your own safety may be affected and the building control department can take enforcement action.

Many of these investigations are covered as a matter of course by solicitors' searches.

Other environmental matters

Environmental policies are gradually moving towards greater protection for members of the public. One proposal (not yet in force) is to operate a register of contaminated land, so that it is possible to find out (for instance) if the house has been built on the site of a municipal rubbish tip or there is other contamination of the land. Even though the register is not yet in force it may be possible by making local enquiries to find out whether the immediate area has a history of land use which could cause you problems.

You or your solicitor can make numerous other enquiries over matters as varied as flight paths, road improvement proposals, planning zones, commons, oil pipe lines, limestone workings, coal, tin or clay mines, radon (especially in Cornwall), rivers and canals or Ministry of Defence activities.

Council Tax band

The Council Tax band, or perhaps the Council Tax payable, may have been quoted in any particulars you have been provided with by the agent or seller. If not, ask for this information. If only the Council Tax band has been given, you can find out from the finance department of the local authority what the Council Tax for that band is likely to be. Water and sewerage charges are levied separately by the local water authority in England and Wales, based on the old rateable value or the Council Tax band of a property.

Vacant possession and sitting tenants

Normally, a house is sold with vacant possession: when it becomes yours, the seller leaves and it will be empty, ready for you to occupy. But if there are already 'sitting' tenants in the house – that is, the owner has let part of it to other people – you should assume that you cannot get immediate possession of those parts of the property. (Some sitting tenants even have the right to transmit the tenancy to the widow[er] or another generation.) You would also probably have considerable difficulty in raising their rent above its present level, should you want to. The subject of sitting tenants is complex and you should get legal advice before you take any steps towards acquiring such a house.

What does the price include?

The estate agent's particulars may mention specific items which the owner would like to sell with the house. When the agent or owner is showing the house, he or she may point out in each room any items being included in the sale, or being offered separately. These would be additional to what are usually termed 'fixtures and fittings', which are accepted as being part of the house. Make sure that all extra items are included in your contract.

Fixtures and fittings

To avoid problems later it is vital to establish clearly which items are, and which are not, included in the sale.

The basic concept is that anything that is part of the fabric of the house is included. Over the years, various removable items, known in law as 'chattels' ('moveables' in Scotland), get fixed to the house and lose their original nature of chattels by becoming part of the structure. One test is the extent to which the items are actually attached and cannot be removed without causing irremediable damage; the other is to consider what might have

79

been the intention of the owner in installing them. But the distinction between a removable and a not-removable item remains difficult to establish.

For example, a case was brought to court over some garden seats and sculptured statues which were free-standing on their own weight and not fixed to the ground. These were judged to be essentially part of the architectural design of the garden and so were not removable (i.e. they were fixtures). In another court case, valuable tapestries had been firmly fixed to the walls of a house in such a way that they could not be removed without causing substantial damage. These were, nevertheless, held to be removable because the aim in attaching them was to enjoy them as tapestries and not that they should form part of the house. So it is not easy for the seller or buyer to know exactly what the law would say in a case of dispute.

Many sellers and buyers are ignorant about what they can take or can expect to have bought, so you should be particularly careful on this point. It may not always be practical or desirable to go through all the items on a first viewing, but at a point before you negotiate a price, you should establish exactly what you are buying and be sure that the seller – as well as yourself – has this clear. Bathroom fittings, light fittings, curtain rails and tracks and TV aerials are commonly disputed items. What has to be done in each case is to clarify what are:

- **items not removable** because they form part of the structure: included in the price
- **uncertain items** which the buyer and seller may regard differently. It should be agreed at the time of making an offer whether they are to be included in the price
- **items removable** since they do not form part of the structure: price to be agreed if sold to the buyer.

Examples of items not removable:

- plumbing and heating installations integrated into the structure
- gas or electric instantaneous water heater
- electric sockets, wall switches and wiring (including lamp-socket holders but not light bulbs)

80

- garden sheds and greenhouses built on foundations and not free-standing
- trees and shrubs in the garden.

Examples of items removable by the seller:

- free-standing gas or electric cooker
- fridge, freezer
- dishwasher, washing machine and any similar detachable equipment
- heaters connected to mains supply only by plugs or detachable means of connection
- electrical fittings beyond the point of contact with mains supply
- lamp shades, light bulbs
- carpets, underlay and felt, curtains (though nowadays fitted carpets are normally included and curtains may be)
- free-standing garden furniture and sheds.

Uncertain items:

- curtain rails and tracks, including brass and wooden rods and pelmets
- fitted bookshelves and other shelves
- built-in kitchen units/appliances
- built-in cupboards and wardrobes/bedroom furniture (the test being the extent to which they are fixed to the structure)
- electric storage heaters, water softener, wall lights
- decorative door furniture and door chimes
- bathroom fittings, lavatory paper holders
- roof TV aerial/satellite dish (nearly always included in the price)
- plants in the garden
- free-standing garden ornaments (depends on their purpose).

When you reach the point where you have decided to go ahead with an offer, ask the owner to go through the house with you, agreeing and listing room by room:

- any fixtures and fittings, whether referred to in any

particulars or separately agreed between you, which are included in the sale price
- any items the seller is willing to leave but for which you would have to make a separate offer.

You should in due course draw up an itemised list together with the seller, with copies for your solicitors, so that there will be no confusion later. (Check when the time comes that the actual item(s) left for you are not inferior substitutes.)

You should assume that anything not on the list of items the seller is to leave behind will be moved by him or her – indeed, he or she must do so in order to give you vacant possession.

If the seller's solicitors are using the Law Society's detailed TransAction protocol (see page 257), the seller will be asked to complete a detailed fixtures, fittings and contents form which will make clear what is being left and what is being taken. This forms part of the contract and is legally binding on the seller.

What you buy

There is no reason why you should not vary any of the 'rules' as to what is or is not removable, provided it is agreed and written into the contract.

Whatever you intend to buy from the seller, inspect it very carefully to make sure that it works or is in good condition (any carpets, for instance, where rugs may have been covering up worn areas, any garden tools or lawn mower which may not have been well maintained) and is not going to cause you additional expense.

The prices for any separate items have to be agreed on the basis of their original cost, the wear and tear the items have had and their condition now, and what a replacement would cost at today's prices. The actual figures are generally wide open to negotiation. But whatever is agreed should be confirmed in writing (tell your solicitor, too).

The owner may try to get you to buy some items which you do not want. If they duplicate what you already have, you are in a better position to refuse them politely. If you do not want them for some other reason – they are not to your taste, perhaps

– you will have to judge whether buying them or not would affect your chances of concluding the whole deal.

The seller will probably be pleased if you agree to buy any residual coal or heating oil; the value of these will have to be worked out later, but the principle can be agreed now. However, quite often these are included in the price.

Making an offer

When you decide that you want to buy a house, make an offer for it without delay. If the seller is offering the property through an estate agent, put the offer to the agent (who can then tell other potential buyers that the property is under offer). Do this even before you have had a survey done – the offer does not commit you provided it is made 'subject to contract and to survey'.

You must make it clear that your offer is subject to contract – whether it is an oral offer or in writing – so that you are covered if:

● you are unable to raise the necessary mortgage or loan
● a survey decides you against continuing with the purchase
● subsequent enquiries disclose some insuperable drawback: for example, road widening or compulsory purchase by the local authority
● you change your mind for some other reason.

If there is any objection to the deal being on a subject-to-contract basis, do not proceed. And do not sign any kind of contract at this stage without taking legal advice.

The price

Most sellers fix a price which they believe to be the maximum they dare ask, and most will be prepared to come down unless several would-be buyers are competing.

To decide whether you are willing to pay the asking price or to make an alternative offer, you must take into consideration:

● how much you can afford to pay

List of items included and excluded

Tick either INCLUDED or EXCLUDED where applicable

	INCLUDED	EXCLUDED
Windows		
double glazing	————	————
curtains	————	————
curtain rails and rings	————	————
curtain tracks and fittings	————	————
pelmets	————	————
blinds	————	————
Electrical		
immersion heater	————	————
switches, points	————	————
wall and ceiling fittings	————	————
night storage heaters	————	————
fitted electric fire	————	————
TV aerial	————	————
Bathroom		
bathroom cabinet	————	————
bathroom heater	————	————
towel rail	————	————
toilet roll holder	————	————
heated towel rail	————	————
mirror	————	————

Kitchen

kitchen cupboards   _____   _____

wall utensils   _____   _____

Garden

greenhouse   _____   _____

garden shed   _____   _____

garden trees, shrubs, plants   _____   _____

flowers and garden produce   _____   _____

garden ornaments   _____   _____

garden furniture   _____   _____

General

fitted carpets   _____   _____

fitted mirrors   _____   _____

door bell   _____   _____

door chimes   _____   _____

heating oil   _____   _____

solid fuel   _____   _____

fitted gas fire   _____   _____

fitted shelves   _____   _____

Any Others (list them below)

. . . .   _____   _____

. . . .   _____   _____

. . . .   _____   _____

. . . .   _____   _____

- the state of the property market (the more potential buyers there may be after the house, the less scope there will be for bargaining; the fewer potential buyers, the more likely the seller will be to accept a reduced price)
- how the price compares with that of similar properties in the area
- how much you want the house and are prepared to pay over the odds to get it.

A TRUE STORY: James and Jane got on well with the people who were selling a plot of land to them. 'You don't want to see a solicitor. They just charge a lot of money and you have nothing to show for it,' said the sellers. The sellers had a friend who prepared the documentation.

James and Jane signed up – then went to a solicitor who found that the plot of land was not the same area as the one on which planning permission had been given.

The sellers bungled the documentation – fortunately, that let James and Jane off the hook, but they had signed documents without proper investigation. They had many sleepless nights before the problems were resolved.

Having made your offer, it may be accepted straightaway or you may have to sit back and wait: the seller may have other prospective buyers about to make offers, or may still want to show the house to other viewers. You can try to persuade him or her that your offer is so good that he or she should not continue with other possibilities but should provisionally accept your offer. It all depends on the personalities involved and the state of the market. A seller who has been waiting for six months for a single offer is unlikely to be difficult.

A strong bargaining factor is whether you can act quickly because:

- you have a mortgage certificate guaranteeing the offer of a loan
- a buyer has been found for your own house
- you have ready money.

If the sale of your own house is likely to be delayed, it may be worth getting the promise of a bridging loan from your bank (or other source) to put you in an advantageous negotiating position. However, in a poor market your bank is unlikely to offer an 'open-ended' bridging loan. Except in very unusual circumstances, you would be ill advised to embark on buying a new home without tying up the sale of your present one.

Saving on stamp duty?

Whether the buyer has to pay stamp duty on the transfer of a property depends on the price of the house. The duty is 1 per cent on the whole price when this is over £60,000; at or below £60,000 no stamp duty is payable (e.g. price £70,000, stamp duty £700).

If the price, including fittings such as carpets and curtains, that you are asked to pay is just above £60,000, ask the seller to separate the price of the house and that of the fittings if deducting their value reduces the house price below the stamp duty threshold. However, the value allotted to these fittings must be a realistic one. It could amount to a fraud on the Inland Revenue if you inflate the value of fixtures to avoid stamp duty.

Preliminary deposit

At the point when you make a firm offer, an estate agent will ask you the name and address of your solicitor or conveyancer (if you are using one) and may ask you to pay a small deposit (say £250) as a token of your intent. This initial deposit has no legal standing and cannot, by itself, bind either party to the transaction. If you decline to pay a preliminary deposit, it is highly unlikely to affect your chances of buying. If you do pay such a deposit, you should get a receipt stating that the deposit was paid 'subject to contract and to survey'. You will not at this stage have had the house surveyed. If a survey reveals any defects requiring attention but not serious enough to deter you or your source of finance, you may want to reduce your offer.

If the sale falls through before contracts are exchanged, a sum paid by way of initial deposit has to be returned in full. Estate agents are required to have a separate 'clients' account' with the bank, into which clients' monies are paid. But be careful. Not all estate agents are members of professional bodies. People have lost deposits if estate agents default.

Valuation for mortgage

A buyer who is applying for a mortgage should notify the building society, or other mortgagee, that he or she has made an offer for a property, and ask that the lender's valuation be carried out as soon as possible. You will have to pay the required fee for the valuation, which is based on the price of the house. (If you lose the house before the valuer has been to it, tell the lender to cancel the visit and to return the fee or keep it ready for your next attempt.)

The valuation is carried out on behalf of the lender to assess whether the condition and value of the house is adequate security for the loan the lender has been asked to make.

A RICS/ISVA (Royal Institute of Chartered Surveyors*/ Incorporated Society of Valuers and Auctioneers*) leaflet on mortgage valuations explains that the valuer takes into account:

- age, type, accommodation, fixtures and features of the property
- construction and general state of repair
- siting and the amenities of the locality
- tenure, tenancies, if there are any, annual payments or other liabilities.

Planning potential will normally be disregarded.

Valuation for mortgage purposes is the amount at which a qualified valuer believes the property would sell in the open market at the date of the inspection. It is not a structural survey, and in no way guarantees that the house is structurally sound and without defects, nor that it is worth the purchase price being asked. If, in the building society's valuer's opinion, the house is worth less than the purchase price, the proportion that will be lent may be calculated on his or her figure – and the amount of loan offered to you may therefore seem a strange percentage of the purchase price.

Low valuation

The offer of a loan may be withdrawn after the valuation survey. You would then have to start again, with a different property – or a different lender. But most mortgage applications ask if you have already applied for a mortgage on the same property, so it is unlikely that you will get an unconditional mortgage from another building society for that house.

The valuer can include a recommendation to the lender not to make a loan unless specified work is carried out, such as putting in a damp-proof course or treating all timbers against rot. He or she may advise the lender to withhold an amount (say, £5,000 retention money or even £10,000) which will be paid out only when the work has been carried out satisfactorily. This can be a problem if you do not have spare cash available – the seller will want all his or her price on the nail. This is where a bridging loan may be needed.

If the lender does lay down such conditions and substantial expenditure is involved, it may be worth getting a second opinion from another surveyor, or there may be an opportunity to re-negotiate the price with the seller. If an agreement cannot be reached, it might be better to pull out of the transaction.

With more minor items of repair, the building society may ask you to give an undertaking to carry these out within, say, six months of completion of the mortgage.

Surveys

Although most building societies let the borrower see a copy of their valuation report, this should not be regarded as a substitute for your own structural survey.

Your own survey

Most building societies allow or even encourage an arrangement whereby the surveyor who does their valuation carries out a survey for the buyer at the same visit. The fee for your survey would be slightly less than it would otherwise be, in view of the fact that the surveyor is already going to visit the property for the building society.

There are standard forms for house buyers' valuation and survey reports used by surveyors who are members of the RICS or of the ISVA. If you want to have your own survey done earlier (so as to avoid delay if there are many other potential buyers), and the RICS/ISVA report is acceptable to the lender, no further valuation report is needed (nor further fee payable).

The standard house buyer's report completed by a building society surveyor when doing the mortgage valuation is not a structural survey. But it provides comments on the condition of parts of the property that are readily accessible or visible and gives an opinion of the market value. There are extensive exclusion clauses in these reports and you are not getting a full investigation and report on possible defects. It may include recommendations for further tests or investigations that seem to be called for. The fee is about halfway between that for a straight mortgage valuation and that for a full survey.

A house buyer's report is unsuitable for many older properties and buildings of unusual construction – pre-1900 buildings, buildings over 200 square metres' floor area and buildings over three storeys in height.

Structural survey

A structural survey should be carried out by a qualified person who specialises in this kind of work, such as a building surveyor or architect. A qualified surveyor may be a member of the RICS (with the letters FRICS or ARICS after the name) or of the Association of Building Engineers★ (formerly the Incorporated Association of Architects and Surveyors) or of the Architects and Surveyors Institute★ (formerly the Faculty of Architects and Surveyors). These professional associations are responsible for maintaining standards within the profession. They can be asked for the names of any of their members in a given area who are qualified building surveyors.

Your solicitor may be able to advise on the choice of an appropriate surveyor if you are buying locally, or a friend may recommend one he or she has used. It is preferable to engage a surveyor local to the property being inspected since he or she may know of any relevant conditions in the area which might affect it. The estate agent/surveyor acting for the seller is not allowed to carry out a survey on the house (because of a conflict of interest) but may recommend a surveyor.

Ask the surveyor how soon he or she can do the survey and discuss how comprehensive a survey to carry out. You should obtain written confirmation from the surveyor setting out the extent of the inspection: this may avoid misunderstandings at a later date. The extent of the survey will depend on the age and condition of the property – and on how much you can afford. It is not only for old property that it is desirable to have a survey done: a recently built house can have serious defects too, through bad design, bad workmanship or neglect.

The extent of a full structural survey is described in *Structural Surveys of Residential Property*, a guidance note prepared by the Building Surveyors Division of RICS. If you want a full structural survey, refer to this booklet.

The cost of the survey

Fees are usually by negotiation and relate to the time taken to inspect the property and write up the report. Generally speaking, the larger the property and the worse the condition of the building, the longer the professional survey will take.

The written report accounts for a large part of the cost, so if you are content to have oral comments, or a less detailed survey taking note only of any major structural defects, you would pay less. However, beware of relying on oral comments only. If defects show up later, you may have difficulty in establishing just what the surveyor actually said.

Be prepared to have to pay for a survey more than once during your house hunting, not only because a survey may show that a property is not worth buying but because a deal may fall through for reasons beyond your control (gazumping, mortgage delay, seller withdrawing), so that you have to start all over again.

The survey report

Give the surveyor as much relevant information about the property as you can, particularly details of any doubtful points you noticed when you viewed it (such as damp patches, odd smells, cracks, obviously recent repairs, state of party walls) and on the siting of the house regarding potential flooding or subsidence.

If you plan to make any alterations or improvements, inform the surveyor before the survey in case there are any snags which he or she might spot. If, for example, you plan to demolish an inside wall to enlarge a room, this may turn out to be a load-bearing wall which it would be inadvisable, or very costly, to remove. And if you are planning complete redecoration, or a rewire or replumb, tell the surveyor. You will save his or her time and your money.

What a survey includes

You are likely to get a general description of the construction and materials used, and comments on the condition of:

- roof – timberwork, cladding, tiles, slates, chimney stacks, flashing, rainwater gutters, insulation
- walls – plasterwork, brickwork, pointing, insulation, decoration, any cracks, damp, bulges
- foundations – soundness, damp-proof course and external soil level, any subsidence, settlement
- windows – state of frames
- floors and joinery – soundness of timber, ventilation, any evidence of wet rot, dry rot, woodworm
- plumbing – bathroom and WC, fittings, waste pipes, tanks and cylinders
- drains – soil and rainwater
- electrical installation – age of wiring
- chimneys and flues
- garden – state of paths, fences, outbuildings.

The report which the surveyor gives you should summarise the condition of these items in as much detail as you have agreed, together with any faults and their importance.

If the house is furnished at the time, it may not be practicable to make a very detailed inspection, which would involve lifting carpets and floorboards, for example. Much depends on how thorough an inspection the vendor permits.

The survey of the electrical installation may be confined to a 'visual examination'. Much of the wiring is hidden behind skirting boards and under floorboards, and it is possible that the surveyor will draw his or her conclusions only from what can be seen. He or she will say so in the report, but you should be aware of the limitation.

Do not hesitate to discuss the report with the surveyor, who will be able to put the defects into perspective. Ask him or her to explain any technical terms that you do not understand.

Ask the surveyor to tell you the approximate cost of putting right any faults which are found and to give you an estimate of how much you would need to spend to put the house into good structural order. Then try offering the seller a price reduced by that amount. Tell him or her why, and be prepared to negotiate. If the seller will not budge, you have to decide how badly you want the house. Your offer being subject to contract and subject to survey, if you decide that you do not want to buy the house, you are not obliged to go ahead: simply tell the estate agent or the seller direct that you are no longer interested.

Specialist tests

There is a distinction between an 'inspection' and a 'test' of such services as the drains, the heating system, the wiring, timber. In particular, discuss with the surveyor whether any central heating system should be inspected or tested.

Where a house is old or appears to be in poor state of repair, the surveyor may recommend specialist tests. He or she will offer to call in specialists (and you have to pay for them). The fact that he or she recommends tests may be sufficient reason for you to incur this extra expense – he or she will usually have diagnosed a potential problem. If the surveyor has found evidence of serious problems, you will have to accept that you are likely to commit yourself to a lot of expenditure. If that worries you, this could be the point when you start looking around for another property.

Guaranteed treatment

If your surveyor's report shows that specialist treatment is recommended (and you are still likely to buy the house), you can get estimates (usually free) of the cost from specialist firms. A list of their members is available from the British Wood Preserving and Damp-proofing Association*. It is worth getting more than one such estimate. You may want to offer less for the house to allow for the cost of treatment and other work needed.

If the firm is a member of the Guarantee Protection Trust* and if the specialist treatment turns out not to have been successful and the firm who carried it out has gone out of business and cannot honour its guarantee, the Trust undertakes to have guaranteed remedial work done again. The one-off fee for treatment costing up to £5,000 is £35 while for treatment costing £5,001-£10,000 it is £60 for woodworm and chemical dampcourse treatment giving 20 years' cover. For remedial wall ties, the cost is £35 or 1 per cent of the contract value. There will also be a small administration fee to pay to the contractor.

National House Building Buildmark Scheme (NHBC)

If the house is less than ten years old, check whether it is covered by a National House Building Council* Buildmark Scheme. (This in itself is no reason for not having a survey.) Find out how many years there are left on the NHBC scheme. The balance is transferred to a new owner, but only for defects which appear after he or she has bought the house. Defects which are (or could have been) apparent before he or she buys will not be remedied by the NHBC unless the previous owner has already claimed. If your surveyor notices anything that may come under the NHBC scheme, it is the seller who must make the claim. Besides, you should be very cautious about buying a house with known defects.

Foundation 15 Scheme

The situation is similar to the NHBC scheme outlined above (see page 35).

Existing guarantees

The previous owner may have employed specialist firms to carry out remedial work for which a guarantee has been given – for instance, treatment for woodworm, for dry or wet rot or rising damp, or the use of special protective coatings for roofs or external walls. Such a guarantee can normally be transferred from one owner to the next, although you may have to notify the company concerned and pay a registration fee. Sometimes a formal assignment of the guarantee is necessary. You should get the original document eventually, usually through your own solicitor, but ask if the surveyor can see it before he or she does the inspection. Make sure you ask your solicitor to obtain not only the guarantee but also the original report and estimate on which the guarantee is based. This will detail what work was (or should have been) done and any qualifications to the guarantee.

Guarantees for damp treatment are often conditional on other works being carried out (such as replastering in a special way or lowering the ground levels outside). These tasks are not usually carried out by the treatment company. If any problem arises, it is often easy for the treatment company to put the blame on someone else.

Some guarantees are for long periods (20 years or more). However, the company which carried out the work might not last as long as the guarantees it gave. If it goes out of business the guarantees will become worthless, unless there is the backing of insurance, such as is afforded by the Guarantee Protection Trust.

The steps on making an offer

- Step 1: see the house you like, go home and think/talk it over.
- Step 2: go to view it again (preferably at a different time of day and day of the week). Find out as much as you can about the neighbourhood, development plans and all environmental matters.
- Step 3: in a buyer's market, put your own house up for sale.

(If everything is still all right (and it looks as though you will get a buyer for your own house):

- Step 4: make an offer at a price you can afford (or a little less) via the estate agent or direct to the seller. Decide who is to do the conveyancing: ask what your solicitor's or conveyancer's fees will be; tell your chosen solicitor/conveyancer of your offer and give him or her the seller's name and address and that of the solicitor.

If your offer is accepted:

- Step 5: put your own house on the market if applicable (and if not already done). Contact the building society (or other lender), complete the application for a mortgage; ask when the valuation can be done (and the name of the surveyor if you want him or her to do a report for you at the same time).
- Step 6: Confirm your offer in writing 'subject to contract and to survey' to the seller direct or to the estate agent; copy to your own solicitor or conveyancer.
- Step 7: Return the mortgage application form with the fee for valuation.
- Step 8: Let your solicitor or conveyancer have relevant details of any potential problems; find out when the seller can move out; warn your bank manager (if a bridging loan is likely to be needed).
- Step 9: If your own survey is required, contact the surveyor, discuss the extent of the survey, draw attention to any aspects of the building you are uneasy about and/or want him or her to check particularly; decide how detailed a report you require (written/oral; specialist tests); confirm your instructions in writing; ask what his or her fee/expenses will be.
- Step 10: Await the outcome.

In the meantime . . .

What happens at this point of the transaction depends on the house, the buyer and seller concerned, and the state of the market. The best would be that your offer gets accepted straightaway. The house is then 'under offer' and the seller should be asked to agree not to entertain any other buyers. Ask the owner (or the agent you are dealing with, if he or she knows) whether the house is on the books of another estate agent as well as the one who has told you about it. If so, you may be pipped at the post from another quarter without you or the other agent being aware of the likelihood.

Newspaper advertisements cannot be cancelled immediately; also, people who have viewed before you may make an offer subsequent to yours. So, expect some bargaining to go on after your first offer.

If you are told, or you sense, that your figure is being matched or surpassed by another, decide fairly swiftly whether to withdraw or to increase your offer, and by how much.

During the period between making an offer and exchanging contracts, neither the buyer nor seller has entered into a legally binding contract. As long as the buyer's offer is still subject to contract, the estate agent handling the sale is under a duty to pass on to his or her client, the seller, all other offers made – right up to the day when contracts are exchanged. So, it is possible for a new buyer, or a previously unsuccessful under-bidder, to enter the field offering an acceptable price which the agent has to notify to the seller.

Contract race

If two or more people want to buy the same property, the seller will sometimes tell his or her solicitor or conveyancer to send out a second (or even a third and fourth) set of contracts to the would-be buyers' solicitors. The buyers then have to race each other, and the first to send a deposit and signed contract gets the house. Solicitors/conveyancers are required to tell the legal representatives of all the known would-be buyers when there is a contract race.

Should you run in a contract race?
Contract races are usually only prevalent at times of shortage of houses or rising prices (or both). However, it is not uncommon

for banks or building societies, when selling houses they have repossessed, to use contract races to get the best price from a buyer who can exchange contracts quickly. This informal 'auction' can cause great distress because many may take part (and incur large expenses) but only one can win.

Contract races are undesirable contests for buyers. The seller is not even legally obliged to sell to the winner. You could run up all the expense of survey fees, search costs, legal bills and have nothing to show for it. The advice is: take part only if you feel you have a really good chance of buying the property.

Gazumping

The unattractive practice of 'gazumping' is where a seller, tempted by a higher offer, goes back on the agreement with the potential buyer and accepts a later, higher bid. This has tended to occur during a rising market with more buyers about than houses. As the law and practice of house purchase now stand, a buyer is not protected against gazumping until he or she has entered into a binding contract. You have to weigh up whether the consequences of binding yourself to a contract prematurely before you have made all the proper enquiries will be more serious than the chances of being gazumped.

A decision by the Court of Appeal in 1993 may give some protection against gazumping in a situation where the seller has agreed not to sell to anyone else provided contracts are exchanged within a specified period. This is known as a 'lockout agreement'.

Gazundering

The equally unattractive practice of 'gazundering' may occur in a falling market. This happens where a buyer, just before exchange of contracts, offers a lower price, in the hope that the seller will accept it, rather than lose the sale of the house.

Pre-contract deposit agreement

The Conveyancing Standing Committee set up by the Law Commission* has recommended a pre-contract deposit agreement which is designed to help deal with the problem of gazumping. The principle is that each side pays a preliminary deposit of 1½ per cent of the purchase price to a stakeholder and signs an agreement that there will be a final exchange of contracts within four weeks. If one side withdraws without good enough reason (the form of agreement specifies the precise grounds), both deposits are released to the other. So a gazumped buyer will at least have some compensation for the expense incurred.

The Conveyancing Standing Committee's recommended form of pre-contract deposit agreement, with an explanatory leaflet and guidance notes which should be read before signing, is available free from the Law Commission*.

The shortcoming of the scheme is that if the seller receives a substantially increased offer, it will still be worthwhile to lose the deposit. Nevertheless, the agreement may be some inducement to both the seller and buyer to keep their word.

With the poor state of the housing market at the beginning of the nineties, this scheme has been little used.

Another option

A workable way of avoiding gazumping has been put into practice by some solicitors. The seller gives the buyer the exclusive right to buy the house in return for a fee and on condition that contracts are exchanged within a specified time.

The example on page 100 shows how it works.

All is not lost

After a series of negotiations, perhaps, which can be nerve-racking for a would-be buyer, who at this stage wants very much to succeed with a purchase, you may be disappointed and have to start all over again elsewhere. But after a seller has accepted a bid and the losers have been informed, it is not

Mary wanted to buy Rose Cottage from Peter. Peter is ready to sell, but Mary cannot exchange contracts yet as she is waiting for her mortgage offer and she has not exchanged contracts on her own sale. She is certain that all these things will be dealt with in the next few weeks. How does she make sure that Peter sells to her and no one else, and that he does not put the price up in the meantime?

The solution is for Peter to agree with Mary that she can buy Rose Cottage at the agreed price as long as she exchanges contracts within × weeks. Peter must be compensated for freezing the price and taking the chance that Mary will at the last minute not go ahead with the deal. He will therefore charge quite a large sum for committing himself to the sale before Mary does – say, £1,000. Mary will lose that money if she does not exchange contracts but not if she goes ahead. Peter should agree to reduce the purchase price by the amount of the option price (the £1,000).

But note: such an agreement should not be attempted without a solicitor (the buyer has to be protected by the agreement being registered in the Land Registry or Land Charges Department).

uncommon that some weeks later the prospective buyer has to withdraw from the transaction for one reason or another. At this point, a disappointed under-bidder may find himself or herself being contacted by the seller or his or her agent to ask if he or she is still interested and willing to re-start negotiations.

If you are bitterly disappointed at being outbid for a particular house (you had already mentally moved in), it is worth telling the owner or the agent so that if anything goes wrong with the first transaction, he or she will remember how keen you were. And do not just leave it to the agent – if the board stays up a while without 'Sold' being stuck over it, a reminder might be to, literally, ring the bell at the right moment. Both agent and seller will now want to settle the matter without further delay and you could be in a good position to succeed at a second attempt.

CHAPTER 5

CARRYING OUT WORK ON YOUR NEW HOUSE

IT IS clearly much easier and quicker to renovate or even decorate a house if it is empty. If financial and other circumstances permit, it may be worthwhile delaying your move for a few weeks to enable work to be carried out. Consider whether you can manage to have completion for purchase (of your new home) earlier than completion for sale (of your old home), even at the cost of a bridging loan. This would allow a period for work to be done while your new house is empty.

If the house is empty (because the owners have already moved, or it is derelict), it might be possible to obtain permission to start work as soon as contracts are exchanged. Whether this will be possible will depend on the goodwill of the sellers.

Even if you 'move in with the builders' you will still need to know before exchange of contracts what will be involved and how much it will cost.

There is often a considerable delay in setting up building works. Planning permissions and building regulation consents take time to apply for and to approve. Sometimes, builders are not available to start straightaway.

If you are buying a house that needs repairs, it is best to get started as soon as terms are agreed (but remember that if the purchase falls through you may have incurred expense to no avail). In any event, you will need to know, before you commit yourself, how much you are likely to have to spend.

Applying for planning permission

For some structural alterations or improvements, you have to obtain planning permission. Apply in good time: it can take some weeks or even months to come through. You can apply even if you do not own the house, but, of course, if you do not buy the house you will lose the money you have spent on applying.

Forms are available from the local planning department. You will also have to submit several copies of site and location plans, along with detailed drawings showing the work you intend to carry out.

Planning permission is usually only concerned with significant changes in external appearance but you should ask at the local planning department whether what you propose needs planning permission.

The Department of the Environment and the Welsh Office publish a free booklet *Planning Permission: a Guide for House-holders*, available at council offices, Citizens Advice Bureaux and housing advice centres. There is also a booklet *Planning Appeals*, a guide to the procedure you can follow after a refusal.

Advice on how to deal with difficulties, refusals or objections can be obtained from chartered town planners, architects and surveyors. Members of the Royal Town Planning Institute (RTPI)* include not only local authority planning officers but also consultants. The RTPI will be able to suggest where to get specialist advice and publishes a series of eight leaflets covering different aspects of planning permission.

If you want to use part of your house for a business or build on part of the plot, you will need to find out about the planning history of the house and the local authority's policies. The RTPI's regional leaflets, *Where to Find Planning Advice*, can help you select a suitable consultant.

Do not let any work start until you have the necessary planning permission, listed building consent and building regulations approval, where these are needed.

Building regulations

The Building Regulations 1991, which have the force of law, operate throughout England and Wales.

The various building regulations are mainly concerned with material work, health and safety, services and fire precautions. They apply to new buildings and extensions, structural alterations to existing buildings and installation of controlled services or fittings.

A copy of the Building Regulations can be consulted in local authority offices or in most public reference libraries. The 1991 regulations are shorter and simpler than previous regulations, and more flexible and easier to use, but a layman would almost certainly need guidance to interpret them. There is a Department of the Environment* explanatory package in 16 parts covering different aspects of the regulations – loading, preparation of site, ventilation, insulation and so on. The total cost is £60 but the booklets can be obtained separately (available also from HMSO*).

For some kinds of building work, you do not need to apply for Building Regulations approval or to give notice. For instance, you do not need to if you are merely repairing a building or replacing drains, sanitary fittings or solid fuel or oil heating appliances, where no structural work is involved. Also, the regulations exempt certain small detached buildings and extensions. Contact the building control officer of your local authority and find out whether the work you are proposing to have done requires approval or a building notice. If so, he or she can let you have the necessary formal notification form and tell you what details and drawings are required.

You have to pay prescribed fees to the local authority, in two parts if you deposit plans for approval (on application and on inspection), or once on inspection if you give a building notice. There are flat-rate fees for small extensions (up to 40 square metres) and for loft conversions; fees for other work are based on estimated cost.

Scotland has its own Building Standards (Scotland) Regulations. You apply for a building warrant – for which you have to pay a lodging fee – and the work is inspected before a certificate of completion is issued.

Timber frame?

If the house is of timber-and-brick construction, it would be advisable to check what can and what should not be done to the walls, and particularly the cavity, before initiating any alterations that would affect the structure. Obtain a copy of the booklet *Living in a Timber & Brick Home* from the Timber & Brick Homes Information Council*. The booklet gives explicit instructions about how to carry out work on a timber-and-brick house. Also, you can ask the local authority building control office to allow you (or your builder) to inspect the drawings and structural calculations submitted by the developer/builder when the house was first built.

Restrictions

If the house is a listed building or is in a conservation area, demolition or structural alteration of any kind would need consent from the local planning office. It is a criminal offence to demolish a listed building without consent. This covers not only the house but also outbuildings and boundary walls. Further information can be found in a leaflet *What is Listed Building Consent?* published by the RTPI.

Some properties are restricted as far as the development or use is concerned by covenants in the title deeds, mostly laid down when the house was first built. A covenant may, for instance, stipulate that certain alterations or additions shall not be made or can be made only with the consent of the person who sold the land on which the property was built. (Some covenants cannot be enforced but, if in doubt, consult your solicitor.) Also, mortgage deeds have a clause stipulating that the building society's (or other lender's) approval must be obtained for any proposed alterations to the house. If a property is leasehold, the landlord's consent will probably be required.

Getting professional advice

For older property, particularly for property constructed before 1850, the Society for the Protection of Ancient Buildings

(SPAB)* can be asked for general advice. SPAB publishes technical pamphlets and information leaflets on treatment and installation in old buildings, and maintains a card index of architects, surveyors, engineers etc. (usually members of the Society) who have experience with work on historic buildings.

It could be useful to have a word with someone at the local authority planning department or engineer's or technical department, or the building control office, who may be able to let you see plans for recent work carried out at the property – layout of drainage, for instance – or of previous structural work or adaptations.

If you want a considerable amount of repairs done, or perhaps some alterations or modifications, it is worth getting preliminary advice from a professional – an architect, building surveyor or similar consultant. For new work – such as extensions, creating new rooms, kitchen layouts – use an architect who has special skill in economic layout and design. If the work is largely remedial and repair, a building surveyor may be a suitable consultant.

Architects and building surveyors offer a range of services – preliminary discussions, preparation of designs, provision of documents or drawings, applications for approval from various authorities. They will obtain quotations and arrange the details of contracts with builders, inspect the work periodically and authorise payments. You can make use of all these services, or seek professional advice at selected stages only. The contracts are signed by the employer (that is you, the person for whom the work is being carried out) and the builder; the architect and however, be able to give you a rough idea of the costs, including their own fees.

The fees charged by an architect or surveyor are determined by the extent of the services provided. Where the work is extensive, fees are a percentage of the total cost (which cannot be known until the work is completed). Some services may be charged on an hourly basis at an agreed hourly rate or, if the client prefers it, all fees may be charged on an hourly basis. Before an architect or surveyor starts working for you, you should, in order to avoid misunderstanding, agree the basics of the charge with him or her in writing.

Architects

An architect has to be registered with the Architects Registration Council of the UK and must have specific academic qualities. He or she has to adhere to a code of professional conduct.

Most architects are members of the Royal Institute of British Architects (RIBA)*. Other professional bodies of architects to which an architect may belong are: the Architectural Association*; the Architects and Surveyors Institute*; the Royal Incorporation of Architects in Scotland*; the Royal Society of Ulster Architects*; and the Society of Architects in Wales*.

No architect has to belong to a professional body and some do not belong to any. Architects who do not belong to a professional body, but who are qualified, are known as 'unattached architects'. The fact that an architect elects to belong to a professional body is a matter for him or her and does not confer any additional qualification or status. The registration qualification is exactly the same for all architects, whether they belong to a professional body or not.

Registered architects in private practice can be found in the *Yellow Pages* and some local planning authorities keep a list of local architects. RIBA has regional offices with lists of local members, and its office in London has a free client's advisory service. RIBA produces a free leaflet *Why use an architect*, and details of architects' fees and services are in the RIBA publication *Guide to the Standard Form of Agreement*.

All the professional bodies of architects also provide an advisory service to help people find the right architect for the right job, and provide booklets relating to terms of appointment and scale of fees. These various booklets are advisory only, in that they are the basis for negotiation, and no professional body of architects compels its members to work to a fixed scale of fees.

Most (but not all) architects carry professional indemnity insurance. They are not required legally to do so. If you are employing an architect, check before you employ him or her that he or she has adequate insurance with a reputable insurance company. If not, it would be better simply to employ another architect who does. If things go wrong, it might be difficult or impossible to bring a successful claim against someone who is uninsured.

Building surveyors

If you had a structural survey done of the house, the surveyor who did that should also be qualified to advise on building work. If not, you can contact the Royal Institution of Chartered Surveyors*; the Royal Institution of Chartered Surveyors in Scotland*; the Association of Building Engineers*; or the Architects and Surveyors Institute*. These bodies provide an advisory service to help people find the right building surveyor for the job; and all suggest a voluntary scale of fees.

Building or design consultants

Firms and individuals who call themselves consultants of various types – architectural, building, design, architectural surveying – are not formally qualified and not registered as architects, but carry out work similar to that of registered architects. They are not bound to adhere to any professional code and may not be insured for negligence. You should ask the consultant during an initial discussion what his or her charges are likely to be based on. Check that the person you want to use has adequate professional indemnity insurance cover.

Builders

Generally, the best way to get a good builder is through recommendation. If you have just moved into a new area, ask neighbours and local estate agents. If you are consulting an architect or building surveyor, he or she should be able to advise you on a suitable builder, as part of the service. Some builders advertise, or put their names on boards outside houses where they are working.

The Federation of Master Builders (FMB)* can be asked for the names of members. Those on the National Register of

Warranted Builders (NRWB, contactable at the FMB) are bound by a code of practice and offer a warranty that defects arising within two years due to faulty workmanship or materials (plus an additional three years for structural defects) will be put right by that builder or another registered builder. The warranty also provides payment (maximum £10,000) towards any reasonable additional costs if the builder ceases trading while your work is in progress.

The Building Employers Confederation* has regional offices throughout England and Wales (the Scottish Building Employers Federation* covers all areas north of the border) which can supply the names of suitable member firms or give a full list from which you can make your own choice. Members of the Building Employers Confederation participate in a guarantee scheme which includes a six-month defects liability period, a further two-year guarantee period covering structural defects and some cover if the builder goes bankrupt or defaults.

If possible, estimates should be obtained from two or three builders, particularly if extensive work is involved. Write out a list of the work you wish to be done, so that each one can estimate for exactly the same job. If you want the new work to match in with the existing building, you must make this clear.

Organising the repairs and alterations

It helps to keep a special notebook (small enough to fit into your pocket or handbag) for notes and decisions, and for recording names and addresses of suppliers, brands and prices of articles, and similar other relevant information. Discipline yourself to use only this notebook and not have recourse to backs of envelopes and other scraps of paper.

It is important to plan the correct sequence in which to do the various jobs, or arrange for them to be done. List all the jobs, then draft a programme, day by day and week by week over the period before you move in, in the sequence in which everything would probably be best carried out. Keep the programme/ timetable by the telephone, so that appointments with servicemen, workmen, delivery men or officials can be put down at the time they are arranged. Note the name of the person you have spoken to when booking appointments by telephone, also the date of the call (written confirmation of instructions is an added safeguard).

Some items have a long delivery time and you may need to place your order as soon as contracts are exchanged – for example, for replacement windows, central heating, fitted carpets, kitchen units – and make the delivery date a part of the sale agreement: get a commitment from the suppliers in writing.

While the house is empty, you will have to make arrangements about getting keys to the workmen and making sure that someone is there when the delivery men are due to come.

Do not make your timetable too utopian but allow for non-delivery, late delivery, workmen's errors, your errors, unexpected snags, sickness, strikes and other malignant acts of man or fate.

The work

Knocking down walls, dismantling wooden fitments, getting at pipes or wiring and so on, are all jobs which create an amazing amount of dust, dirt and debris. Any floor coverings should be protected or removed, and any fittings in the house or flat covered or moved away where possible before any workmen start.

If fitted carpets have to be lifted, see that these are rolled, not folded, so that they do not become badly creased. Watch out that builder's rubble is not 'tidied' under floorboards, in the roof space or even on to a neighbour's flat roof.

Any work that involves making holes in the wall, putting things into or behind walls or ceilings (particularly plumbing or electrical work) is likely to necessitate replastering afterwards and probably repainting. Such work should, therefore, be done before redecorating and final cleaning.

Where a large amount of rubbish and builder's rubble results from demolition work, make it the builder's responsibility to remove it.

Heating and insulation

You may be able to get a grant towards the cost of installing central heating if it is part of a comprehensive improvement plan for your house – but not if you are installing central heating only, or central heating combined with inessential other work. Apply to the local authority for this grant.

Installation may necessitate:

- estimates and preliminary discussion
- up to two weeks' work, depending on the type and size
- having the water supply temporarily turned off
- using a plumber/electrician/plasterer.

The National Association of Plumbing, Heating and Mechanical Services Contractors* and the Heating and Ventilating Contractors Association* can be asked for the names of members in any area.

Grants are available to private householders from local authorities in some circumstances to pay a percentage of the cost of insulating an inadequately insulated loft and for lagging pipes and water tanks. A Department of the Environment leaflet about the homes insulation scheme is available free from the local authority and Citizens Advice Bureaux.

Damp, rot and woodworm

A builder may be able to find and deal with minor localised problems caused by a defective damp-proof course; putting in a new or replacement damp-proof course is a specialist job. An improvement grant from the local authority may be obtainable to help pay for this, but remember that it takes time to get such a grant and you must not start work before it is approved.

The Which? Book of D-I-Y gives advice on the treatment of various household problems.

If you are getting a mortgage, the building society or other lenders may require that damp, rot or woodworm problems be dealt with immediately, as a condition of the loan. They may want a guarantee for the work, in which case it will have to be done by a specialist firm (preferably backed up by the Guarantee Protection Trust* in case the firm goes bankrupt).

Names of specialist firms who are members of their relevant trade association can be obtained from the British Wood Preserving and Damp-proofing Association*.

Roof repairs

It is worth checking the roof again at this stage for any signs of loose tiles or gutters blocked by leaves and dirt. Overflowing gutters are often the cause of damp soaking through walls or under eaves. Fitting mesh guards will prevent leaves from being washed into the tops of any down pipes.

Chimneys may need to be repointed, or the flashing replaced. Check that any television aerial is securely attached, but is not damaging the chimney itself. If any chimney is used to flue-in a gas appliance, it is worth having a 'cage' put over the chimney pot, to save having to call in the RSPCA or fire brigade to release a trapped bird.

Electricity

Plan what lighting you would like in the new home at an early stage, in case any new wiring – for spot lights or wall lights, for instance – will be necessary.

Depending on the age of your new home, it may be a precondition for obtaining a mortgage that its electrical installation is examined in detail to confirm its safety (previous owners may have altered it incorrectly).

In any case, if the house is more than 30 years old, the wiring will almost certainly need replacing if this has never been done. Switches, socket outlets and pendant light cords that are more than about 15 years old are also likely to need replacing.

The electricity company or a private electrical contractor will survey the wiring and provide a report or an inspection certificate. You can get the names of approved electrical contractors from the National Inspection Council for Electrical Installation Contracting (NICEIC)* or from your public library or electricity company shop. The list also indicates those who are members of the Electrical Contractors' Association*. The Electrical Contractors' Association of Scotland* will supply a list of its members in any area and has free leaflets with advice to householders.

The survey will also tell you how the electrical installation is arranged and enable you to plan what lighting, additional socket outlets (for portable appliances) and fused connection units (for stationary appliances) you would like, in case any additional wiring is necessary. Sockets to provide power for electrical power tools or portable devices, such as lawn mowers, must be fitted with a special safety device.

Consider the electricity consumption of lights which stay on for a long time, to illuminate a dark corridor or staircase, for example. Fluorescent lamps use considerably less electricity than tungsten bulbs of similar light output, and have a longer life and in some situations recoup the initial higher cost quickly. Recently, low energy bulbs have become widely available. They fit into normal sockets.

An advantage of rewiring completely, whether this is absolutely necessary or not, is that it gives you the chance to increase the number of socket outlets or to re-position existing ones, according to how you want to use them and where you plan to put your furniture.

The Electrical Installation Industry Liaison Committee has recommended the following minimum number of socket outlets to be provided in homes:

kitchen 4	single bedroom/teenager's room 3
living-room 6	landing/stairs 1
dining-room 3	hall 1
double bedroom 4	store/workroom 2
single bed-sitting room 4	central heating boiler room 1

Rewiring or extending electrical circuits, putting in or moving a socket may mean temporary disconnection of the electrical supply and replastering after running cables under the plaster or through ceilings.

When completed, a new installation (a new circuit for a first-time electric cooker, for instance) or a major alteration should be tested by a qualified electrical engineer (a member of the NICEIC) and a formal test certificate issued. You should notify the electricity company, which may inspect before connecting or re-connecting the supply.

Plumbing

The existing plumbing may need to be modified to install a new sink or basin, an extra WC or shower or to plumb in an automatic washing machine or dishwasher, for example.

A new installation or renewal of plumbing may mean replastering and having the water supply temporarily turned off.

Sanitary plumbing and drainage has to comply with the Building Regulations; if you are in any doubt, consult your local authority's building control department.

Any water fitting to be installed (a shower, for instance) has to comply with the water bylaws, to prevent waste, misuse, undue consumption and contamination of water. The installation of fittings is subject to the approval (and possible inspection) of the local water company, which interprets and enforces its own bylaws, and which should be notified at least seven days before work starts on the installation. (*The Which? Guide to Plumbing and Central Heating* covers both basic and more complicated jobs.)

The Institute of Plumbing* maintains a register of plumbers and can supply a list of registered plumbers in business in a particular area (send an s.a.e.). The register is continually monitored by the British Standards Institution under the PRIMA (Public Register Inspection Maintenance Assessment) scheme. The Institute also publishes an annual business directory of registered plumbers (available in public libraries).

Floors

Wooden floors should be checked for loose joists or supports, loose boards or nails, projecting knots and warping, and big holes or cracks which would have to be filled in.

Flooring has to be laid after any piping for central heating or any rewiring has been completed. Ensure that any nailing is not where pipes or wires run underneath. It is a good idea to mark the floorboards with the position of cables and pipes beneath; this will make them easier to find if anything goes wrong later.

Kitchen flooring – other than carpets or carpet tiles – should be laid before floor-standing kitchen units are fitted and before a dishwasher or washing machine gets plumbed in.

Carpets and underlay should not be laid until floors have been finally cleaned and allowed to dry thoroughly. It is easier to lay new carpets before moving in, but make sure that they will be protected during the move.

Telephones

In most older houses, wiring for the telephone is on the surface along skirting boards or picture rails. The telephone wiring can be concealed in conduits or channels built in while a house is being structurally modified. If the house has an old-style telephone, new plug-in connections can now be installed or extra sockets added to an existing line.

Once you have one plug-in socket and line installed by BT, you can yourself add other sockets if you wish by buying a d-i-y kit from BT or from a telephone shop. Or you can get an electrician to do the connection for you.

There is now a wide range of telephone styles that can be used in a plug-in socket, varying in shape, colour, sophistication and price. BT has a leaflet showing all the models that you can buy or rent from them, and there are many other models for sale through shops and other outlets.

Any telephone or socket kit you buy should be one approved by the British Approvals Board of Telecommunications as suitable for use with BT lines, and which therefore carries the BABT approval label with green circle.

The Telecommunications Industry Association* can give information about items of equipment and the names of independent contractors.

Burglar alarm

It would be sensible to review the security of your new home as soon as possible.

Each house presents different problems. You can ask at the local police station for a crime prevention officer (CPO) to come and give you free advice on the security measures that would be appropriate to your home. Burglar alarms, usually installed by specialist firms, can be fitted to doors and windows, and so can special locks. Some burglar alarms are triggered by pressure mats under carpets or flooring and should be placed in position before carpeting is laid and in places where they will not be set off by any pieces of furniture when these are later put in their permanent places.

The National Approval Council for Security Systems* maintains a register of companies that it has approved as alarm system installers.

Inadvertent damage may be done to an existing burglar alarm system during building work, so check it carefully when all the work is finished.

House cleaning and decorating

Redecoration of any room is considerably easier, quicker and less messy if the room is empty of furniture, carpets and curtains; a professional decorator should therefore charge somewhat less.

Thorough cleaning of the house includes washing paintwork, walls, insides of cupboards, scrubbing floors, cleaning windows. There are firms specialising in general cleaning work who will supply people to do the cleaning with the necessary equipment. Ask for estimates first.

Carpet-cleaning firms will clean fitted carpets *in situ*. Have this done after all other work is finished but allow a few days for them to dry before furniture is moved in. Loose carpets and rugs can be taken away for cleaning on the firm's premises, to be returned before moving-in day. Various types of carpet shampooers can be hired. Some removal firms undertake carpet cleaning.

Doing your own repairs, alterations and decoration

If you are a d-i-y enthusiast, you may look forward to doing a lot of the necessary work in the home. There are some factors you should take into account when deciding whether or not to do any of these jobs yourself.

How difficult is the job?

This may depend on your age, fitness and temperament, as well as your previous d-i-y experience, and what tools and equipment you have.

If it is something you have not done before, you will need to spend some time learning about the job – how systems work, how to design your own, what equipment to use, how to go about it, and so on. The bigger the job, the more diverse the range of small tasks it is likely to involve. *The Which? Book of D-I-Y* is a complete guide to the full range of d-i-y tasks. *Which? Way to Fix It* covers simple household repairs.

Plastering and advanced carpentry are two jobs which require skill and practice.

Does it save you money?

Doing it yourself saves money mainly because you do not have to pay for someone else's time, overheads and profit on materials. The most profitable jobs to do for yourself are those for which the professional rates are high.

Are there any risks?

You could, of course, hurt yourself while doing the job. The results of some d-i-y jobs could be dangerous, particularly electrical work. *The Which? Book of Wiring and Lighting* explains how to do your own electrical work to professional standards.

Only qualified gas fitters are allowed to connect a gas supply to an appliance.

Hiring equipment

You may need equipment for repairs or decorations which you would not normally use and so would not want to have to buy and store. There are d-i-y hire shops in most large towns. If you do not know of one, look in the local paper or under 'Hire contractors' in the *Yellow Pages*.

Your new house empty

It is worth notifying your local authority if a property is to be vacant for any length of time because a Council Tax refund may be payable. If you are carrying out building work which makes the property uninhabitable for a considerable time, you should check with your local authority as no Council Tax may be payable.

You should inform the insurance company with which the building is insured: cover for some risks, such as vandalism or theft, is restricted when a property is unoccupied. Also, arrange for contents insurance for any items (carpets, curtains, kitchen equipment, furniture) that you bought from the previous owner, which are in the empty house. Contents insurance may exclude theft cover if premises are left unoccupied for an extended period.

Curtains give a house a lived-in look and may be a form of safeguard against intruders. Leave some curtains up at your old home if it hasn't yet been sold, and put some up at your new one as soon as possible.

To prevent anyone who is working in the house from running up telephone bills, you can ask the telephone sales manager for an o.c.b. arrangement – that is, outgoing calls barred – until you write to say that you want to revert to normal calling out.

CHAPTER 6

THE MORTGAGE

Getting a mortgage

VERY few people can afford to buy their first home without having to borrow at least part of the cost. Loans to home buyers are usually in the form of a long-term mortgage.

A mortgage is a document which pledges your home as security for the loan. You cannot sell the house without repaying the loan – and if you do not keep up your payments, the lender (known as 'the mortgagee') has the right to go to court for a possession order against you. In the language of mortgages, the borrower is called 'the mortgagor'.

You pay interest at the lender's current rate or at a fixed or discounted rate depending on the type of mortgage. Unless you have an interest-only mortgage, provision is made for the eventual repayment of capital (the sum lent).

Before lending any money, the lender (mortgagee) will want to make sure that you, the borrower (mortgagor), can keep up repayments and that the house you want to buy is worth enough to cover the loan if you default on your repayments.

How much you will be able to borrow will depend on:

- your income – and therefore how much you can afford in mortgage repayments
- the value and type of home you want to buy.

How much can you borrow?

Most lenders work out the maximum they are prepared to lend

by using a multiple of your annual income before tax. For instance, a single person might be allowed to borrow between 2½ and 3 times his or her annual income. So, if you earn £15,000 a year, you would be allowed to borrow up to £37,500 or £45,000 depending on the multiple used. If you apply for a mortgage from the bank with which you have a current/savings account, you may be offered more, especially if you are a long-standing customer.

A couple who are both earning would usually be able to borrow up to 2½ or 3 times the higher income plus 1 to 1½ times the lower income. (Lenders are not allowed to discriminate against women by applying the larger multiple to the husband's income when it is not the higher of the two.) Some lenders use a different formula, adding the two incomes together and multiplying by 2 or 2½. This variation can mean that the same couple could be offered different loans by different lenders (single people could also find variations in the amounts on offer from different lenders).

Unmarried couples are in most cases treated in exactly the same way as a married couple. Other couples or groups of friends can apply for joint mortgages too. But you may need to shop around because lenders are likely to be rather more cautious and the maximum loan could be smaller than the total of your incomes might suggest. If you are thinking of applying for a joint mortgage with friends, remember that each of you is responsible for paying the whole mortgage. If one of you cannot afford to keep up payments or moves out, the other (or others) will have to take over the payments. Sometimes a lender might be reluctant or even refuse to release a borrower from a loan obligation.

The multiples used by lenders vary depending also on the current rates of interest charged to borrowers. In general, the higher the interest rate, the lower the multiple.

The length (or term) of the loan can also affect the multiple used, with larger multiples being available for a 35-year term (though this is uncommon) than for a 20-year term.

What counts as income?

Broadly, 'income' is your basic salary before tax or other deductions. Some lenders will include overtime payments, commission or bonuses but only if guaranteed: they will probably want confirmation from your employer that these payments are likely to continue. In exceptional circumstances, some lenders may take into account future increases in salary or promotion prospects.

Income from investments is not usually counted and neither (normally) is income from social security or other benefits.

Account may be taken of such ongoing financial commitments as hire purchase debts or payments under a court order.

Self-employed

If you are self-employed, the amount you can borrow will usually be based on the average of your earnings over the previous three years or so. Some lenders may base it on your last year's profits but will look at previous years to make sure it was not an exceptionally good year. The lender will not simply take your word as to what your annual income is but will want to see your annual accounts and/or your tax assessments, and may call for information from your accountant.

If you are newly self-employed or have been in business for a relatively short time, you may well find it difficult to get a mortgage. And even if a lender is prepared to grant a mortgage, it may be for a relatively small amount.

But how much can you afford?

Just because a lender is prepared to give you a mortgage of a certain size, do not be led into thinking that you can afford it. Lenders' formulae are based on averages, and your situation could be far from average, e.g. if you have exceptionally high travelling costs to go to work, you will have far less income available than someone who lives only one mile from the office.

Also consider whether your income is likely to drop soon, e.g. if you plan to have children or care for an elderly relative.

If you already have heavy financial commitments, it could mean that you do not really have enough spare income each month to cope with the maximum loan a lender will make. Also, bear in mind the costs of equipping and running a home (particularly if you are a first-time buyer): there are Council Tax and water charges to pay, repairs and maintenance etc. On top of that you are bound to find that there are unexpected expenses – things you need for the house, from doormats to a dining-room table. So check your finances carefully.

What is the value of the home you want to buy?

You are not usually able to borrow the whole of the asking price (or the price eventually agreed). Lenders have to make sure that they would get their money back if you do not keep up your mortgage payments and they have to get a court order to repossess and sell your home.

This means that the lender is unlikely to lend you the full price even if this is within the amount you can afford to repay. Instead, you will be allowed to borrow a percentage. Lenders have a normal maximum percentage that they will offer without qualification. This maximum varies periodically according to market conditions.

At the time of writing, most lenders' normal maximum without an indemnity policy is 75–85 per cent. The maximum percentage may vary with the type of mortgage you take out – lower with a fixed-rate mortgage than with a variable-rate mortgage. As mortgage indemnity policies are now much harder to obtain (see below) many people could find that they have to find as much as 20–25 per cent of the value of the house from their own resources to make up the purchase price.

The percentage you can borrow is not a percentage of the purchase price but of what the lender's valuer reckons that the property is worth. If the valuer reckons the house is worth less than the asking price, even a mortgage of 100 per cent might not be enough to enable you to buy. If the valuation is higher than the purchase price, however, the percentage you can borrow is likely to be based on the purchase price, not on the valuation.

In general, the higher the value of the house, the lower will be the normal percentage that the lender is prepared to lend.

Mortgage indemnity policy

Many lenders are prepared to lend at higher than their normal percentage (a few will provide up to 100 per cent) if the borrower is able to provide extra security for the loan. While a lender may be prepared to accept anything as extra security which could be turned into enough cash if needed, such as a charge on a second property or share certificates, the usual way is through a mortgage indemnity policy. This is an insurance policy which guarantees to pay the lender the outstanding balance of the loan if the home has to be repossessed and sold for less than the amount of the mortgage.

Following poor claims experience, many insurance companies have now withdrawn from issuing these policies. The cost has increased considerably in recent years. Searching enquiries are made about your credit-worthiness before a policy is issued.

Note that even though you pay the premium, the insurance company can make a claim against you personally for reimbursement if it has to pay up under the policy.

What sort of home is it?

The amount of the loan will also depend on the sort of home you are buying. If the house is unconventional or unusual in its construction and therefore likely to be difficult to sell, the loan could be based on a lower than usual percentage of the valuation, or the term allowed to repay the mortgage could be shorter than usual.

In England and Wales a lot of property is leasehold: you are buying the right to live in the property for a certain number of years, after which it reverts to the landlord. You should find no difficulty getting a mortgage on a leasehold property, although the lender will need to check the lease and be satisfied about two things in particular. First, there needs to be a clear and legally binding agreement about who pays for the repair and maintenance of the building. Secondly, most lenders will lend only if there is a reasonable amount of the lease left after the end of the mortgage term. Many lenders want at least 20 years left at the end of the mortgage term; with others, it could be as much as 40 or 50 years. The result of this is that it could be difficult to get a mortgage on a leasehold property with less than 50 or 60 years, or even longer, to run on the lease.

If the property you want to buy has a sitting tenant in part of it, you will have difficulty in getting a mortgage – quite apart from other potential difficulties. This is because it would be harder to sell a home with such a tenant and very difficult to get rid of the tenant, particularly if he or she had been there for some time.

You could also experience difficulty in arranging a loan if the property is used partly for business and partly for living – for example, if it is a case of living over the shop.

How many years to repay?

In theory, a mortgage term (by the end of which the loan has to be repaid) can be as little as five years. But the usual term is 20 or 25 years; longer-term loans – 35 years or more – are available from some lenders. Lenders may insist that a mortgage finishes before you reach retirement age. But many are prepared to offer shorter-term loans to people who are retired.

If you are buying a leasehold property, the length of the lease may affect the length of the term. For example, if the building society requires 40 years of the lease to be left at the end of the mortgage and the lease has 60 years to run, then the maximum length of loan will be 20 years.

Tax relief

When you borrow to buy your own home, you do not have to pay tax on that part of your income which goes towards paying interest on the loan (within certain limits). In other words, you get tax relief on the interest, and the loan, therefore, costs you less. (Tax relief also used to be given on loans taken out for home improvements. Since April 1988, home improvement loans do not qualify for tax relief.)

Tax relief is given at a rate of only 15 per cent, and the government proposes to phase it out completely. You cannot claim tax relief on more than £30,000 of loan and the relief is available only on money borrowed to buy your main home, not for a second home.

Under the scheme known as MIRAS (Mortgage Interest Relief at Source), you make payments to the lender less basic rate tax. For example, with tax relief at 15 per cent, you pay only £8.50 on each £10 of interest owed: £1.50 tax relief is deducted from the gross payment. You would benefit from this even if you did not have enough income to pay tax. If you borrow more than £30,000, you will get tax relief via MIRAS on the £30,000 and pay the interest on the rest in full.

Up to 1 August 1988, where two or more people not married to each other bought a home together with a mortgage, each could claim tax relief on up to £30,000 of loan. This multiple tax relief will continue for the life of a mortgage taken out before 1 August 1988 but is not available for any further or future mortgage – bear this in mind when working out moving costs.

Types of mortgage

You have to pay back the money you have borrowed (the capital) and pay the cost of borrowing the money (the interest). There are two main ways of doing this: by a **repayment mortgage** or an **endowment mortgage with life insurance**, but other types to consider are the pension mortgage, unit-linked endowment mortgage or the Personal Equity Plan (PEP), or interest-only mortgage.

Repayment mortgages

With a repayment mortgage you repay the loan in instalments, along with the interest, so that at the end of the term of the loan you have paid off the capital.

The payments you have to make every month are normally the same throughout the term (except with an increasing repayment mortgage – see below) subject to changes in the interest rate, which will affect the amount of the monthly payment.

How much you pay each month depends on how much you have borrowed, the interest rate charged and the length of the loan. The longer the period of the loan, the longer there is to pay off the capital, so the smaller the monthly repayments. But over the course of the whole loan, your total payments will be much higher because you are paying interest for longer. There would, however, be nothing to stop you increasing your monthly payments as the years go by, thereby paying off the loan more quickly, although this may not be possible during the fixed period if a fixed-rate mortgage.

In the early years of a repayment mortgage, most of each payment you make goes to pay the interest on the money you have borrowed and only a very small part goes towards paying off the capital. But as the years go by, the capital you owe reduces and so the proportion of interest in each payment goes down and the proportion that is paying off the capital goes up – until in the last few years only a very small part of each payment is interest.

How capital is paid off

Since tax relief is given only on the interest part of the loan, which gets less throughout the length of the mortgage (as the capital is reduced), you might expect that the amount you have to pay each month would rise. But most lenders prefer to keep mortgage repayments the same by averaging out the tax relief over the whole length of the loan. This means that the borrower knows exactly how much has to be paid each month. This type of mortgage is known as a **level repayment mortgage** (or **constant net mortgage**) and is the sort of repayment mortgage you are most likely to be offered.

With an **increasing repayment** (or **gross profile**) mortgage, the tax relief is not averaged out, so that repayments start off lower than with a level repayment mortgage. But, as the amount of interest drops, so does the tax relief and the result is gradually increasing payments. The adjustment is made once a year, not every month. The advantage of an increasing repayment mortgage is that in the early years of a loan you get more tax relief because the interest element is higher, so that your payments are less in the early years than they would be with a level repayment mortgage. In later years, the payments are higher, but by that time your mortgage payments are likely to be a much smaller proportion of your income.

Some lenders are prepared to offer formal **low-start** mortgages whereby you make lower-than-normal payments for the first few years and pay interest only (on which you get tax relief). It means that you do not start making repayments of capital for a few years but have to make larger payments in later years. This type of mortgage is not recommended as you are potentially storing up trouble. If interest rates rise, you will have to pay a higher rate of interest on a loan which is larger than you first took out.

Mortgage protection insurance

If there are people who are financially dependent on you, or if you are buying a house as a couple, consider getting insurance which would pay off the loan if you (or your partner if you have a joint mortgage) were to die. In fact, some lenders insist on this. A mortgage protection policy is a relatively cheap form of life insurance because the amount the policy would have to pay out goes down as you pay off your mortgage. If you have a joint mortgage, it may be better to take out two separate policies, one for each borrower, or a joint life policy (which pays out once – on the first death).

What happens if you move?

With a repayment mortgage, you pay off the loan when you sell your house with the money you get from selling it. If you are buying a new home, you then get a new mortgage for that.

Endowment mortgages

With an endowment mortgage, you do not pay back any of the capital until the end of the term. You pay interest on the whole amount of the loan throughout the term and you also have to pay premiums on an investment-type life insurance policy. At the end of the term, (or if you die earlier) the loan is repaid from the proceeds of the insurance policy. With an endowment mortgage there are two separate payments to make.

As the amount you owe does not change, your monthly payments to the lender are constant no matter how long the term of the loan. (The size of your payments will change if the interest rate or the tax relief for mortgages alters. If interest rates rise, you have to increase your monthly payments.)

The mortgage is linked to an endowment life insurance policy for which you have to pay regular (usually monthly) premiums to the insurance company for the whole term of the loan. The policy is taken out for a period to coincide with the term of the mortgage so that, at the end of the term of the loan, the endowment policy 'matures' and the proceeds are used to pay off the capital. Life insurance is automatically included so that, if you die, your mortgage can be repaid by the insurance policy, however short a time the insurance has been in operation. How much an endowment policy costs will depend largely on your age and health: the older you are, and the poorer your health, the higher the premiums. The longer the loan, the lower the endowment insurance premium should be because your 'fund' has longer to build up the amount required to repay the loan.

A simple **non-profit endowment** policy guarantees to pay out just enough to pay off the capital borrowed and no more. A **full with-profits endowment** policy (expensive and rarely offered) also guarantees to pay enough to cover the capital borrowed but, in addition, you will share in the profits made by the company as a result of their investing your premiums. How much you get at the end depends on how well the insurance company's investment fund does over and above the guaranteed amount to repay the mortgage loan.

Much more common is a **low-cost endowment** policy, which is also a with-profits policy but costs much less. If you survive to the end of the mortgage term, you are guaranteed only that it will pay off about half of the mortgage. This is why it is cheaper than a policy which guarantees to cover the whole loan. The insurance company hopes that the rest of the loan will be covered by the profits made by their investment fund during the period of the loan. If their profits were lower than expected, you would have to fund the balance needed to repay the mortgage. In the past, this type of policy was not too risky as, in practice, it does not need a very high rate of return for profits to build up over a 25-year period. In addition, a guaranteed death benefit is built into the policy so that if you die before the end of the mortgage term, the whole loan will be repaid by the insurance policy. In any case, lenders will accept low-cost endowment policies only from insurance companies they are sure are sound. However, the recession in the early nineties gave rise to the very real worry that some of these policies might not produce enough to pay off the whole of the loan. You should think carefully before taking out low-cost policies.

Some lenders may offer **low-start, low-cost** endowment mortgages, allowing you to defer paying all or some of the interest and premiums in the early years. In later years, you will then have to pay more: the amount you owe will have increased by the amount of underpaid interest. These tend to be a very expensive option in the long term and should be avoided.

Unit-linked endowment mortgages

Interest has to be paid to the lender on the full amount of capital throughout the whole mortgage term. The regular monthly payments you make are invested in unit trusts.

At the end of the mortgage term, the units are cashed in and the proceeds are used to pay off the loan. But, the value of the units can go down as well as up and the moment when you need the money may be one when the market is low. Therefore, there may not be enough to cover the sum needed to repay the mortgage. On the other hand, there is the chance of making a much larger profit. This type of mortgage is becoming more popular, but it may be for people who are prepared to take a bit of a risk.

What happens if you move?

You will have to pay off the loan from the proceeds of selling the house and arrange a new loan for your new home. The endowment policy you had for your old home remains in force and can be used to cover the new loan (if the lender agrees), although the length of the mortgage may be limited by the maturity date of the policy and make it shorter than you might wish. If it is not large enough for the new loan, a second endowment policy can be taken out to make up the difference and if the term of it is relatively short (to tie in with the term of the existing policy), the premium will be higher. Alternatively, if the original policy allows, its value and length can be increased to cover the whole of the new loan. But you should be aware that with an endowment policy on which tax relief is being given (i.e. one taken out before 14 March 1984) a change of this sort will mean that you lose the tax relief.

Some brokers and lenders (keen for their commission) encourage buyers to cash in their old policies and take out brand new ones. This is almost never in your interest.

If you do not want another endowment mortgage, you have to choose what to do with the policy:

- cash in the policy (especially in the early years), but this is likely to give a very low return, so is seldom recommended
- make the policy paid-up, but this means that you need pay no more premiums and will get a lump sum at the end of the policy: this will be a much smaller sum than if you had carried on paying the premiums
- go on paying the premiums, treating the policy as an investment (although not one with a very good return)
- sell or auction the policy. This may be possible if the policy has been running for several years. There are companies which specialise in this – your solicitor should be able to advise.

Pension mortgages

A pension mortgage is similar in some ways to an endowment mortgage. You have to pay interest on the whole amount borrowed throughout the term of the loan. In addition, you pay regular premiums to a pension plan. When you start drawing your pension, part of it can be taken as a lump sum and used to pay off the mortgage; the remainder provides a regular pension.

The main advantage of pension mortgages is that as well as getting tax relief on the interest on the mortgage loan, you also get tax relief (at your highest rate of tax) on the contributions you make to the pension plan. This makes a pension mortgage extremely tax-efficient, particularly for higher-rate taxpayers.

WHICH? WAY TO BUY, SELL AND MOVE HOUSE

But there are disadvantages. The most important one is that you are using part of your pension fund to repay your mortgage loan, so that a smaller sum is available to provide your pension (or to be used for other things). And you may be tying yourself to taking your pension at a fixed date in the future, even though this may not be convenient. Very young borrowers who intend to retire and start their pension 35 or 40 years ahead will find it hard to find a lender who will grant a loan over such a long term.

Pension mortgages are available mainly to people who are self-employed or who are employed but have a personal pension plan. Some employers' pension schemes also offer pension mortgage facilities. The percentage of earnings that can be paid in pension contributions to qualify for tax relief is limited.

Not all pension mortgage plans include life insurance, and lenders are likely to insist that borrowers take out enough cover to repay the mortgage loan. Anyone who qualifies for a personal pension plan can include life insurance as part of the plan and will be eligible for some tax relief on the premiums.

What happens if you move?

If you move before your pension plan has paid out, the loan will have to be repaid from the proceeds of selling your old home. You can then link the mortgage for your new home to the pension plan. If the new mortgage is larger than the old one and the lender does not think that the pension plan will pay out enough to repay the loan, you might have to take out another pension plan to cover the extra (subject to the maximum percentage of income allowed for tax relief on the premium) or take out another type of mortgage in addition.

PEP mortgages

Here again you pay interest only on the loan. In addition, you pay contributions to a Personal Equity Plan (PEP). The proceeds are then used to pay off the mortgage but there is no guarantee that there will be enough to repay it all.

The main advantage of a PEP mortgage is that it is a tax-efficient way of building up a fund to pay off the mortgage that suits high-rate taxpayers. The maximum contribution permitted is £6,000 a year (double for a couple) in a general PEP, plus an additional £3,000 a year (again, double for a couple) in a single company PEP. This should be sufficient to build up a fund to repay a sizeable (say £200,000) mortgage over 25 years. These mortgages do however carry an element of risk, and it may be worth considering instead the newer and safer **corporate bond** PEPs now coming in. The flexibility of PEPs, which unlike endowments are not long-term investments, is another point in their favour.

Interest-only mortgages

With this type of mortgage, the borrower pays interest only and the loan is not repaid until the borrower decides to repay it. For example, this might be on the sale of the house, or on the borrower coming into funds which would enable him or her to repay it. In general, only a relatively low percentage of the value of the house is borrowed and this type of mortgage is attractive to older borrowers.

Beware of the type of scheme which provides income for older people: the house is mortgaged to raise a loan. The loan is used to purchase an annuity (an annual income for life) which is then used in part to supplement the borrower's income and in part to pay interest on the loan. It is an expensive way of generating a small extra income; and if interest rates go up, the cost of servicing the loan could actually use up the entire income produced by the annuity.

Interest rates

Most mortgages have a variable interest rate, which means that the lender can increase or decrease the percentage charged (and usually such changes happen with all building societies at more or less the same time). Interest rates do not vary greatly between the major building societies at any given time but there may be a difference of up to 2 per cent with some others. A few charge a higher interest rate for loans over a specified amount (which may be as low as £30,000 or as high as £100,000).

All lenders issue brochures or mortgage packs. It is not easy to compare like with like, but they all have to show the APR (Annual Percentage Rate) in their printed information.

The APR is generally higher than the quoted rate of interest: it includes one-off charges such as arrangement fees, valuation and legal fees and takes into account the way interest is calculated on a repayment mortgage. Most building societies calculate the interest you owe only once a year and divide that into equal monthly amounts: this ignores the fact that each payment reduces the capital you owe – but the APR takes account of this. Where a lender recalculates the interest part of a payment on a monthly basis (as some banks do), the APR is lower.

If you want to compare current interest rates and conditions for mortgages from various sources, look at specialist mortgage magazines.

Fixed-interest mortgages

Many lenders offer fixed-rate loans where it is guaranteed that the interest rate will not change for a stated period of between one and ten years (or even more). Most loans of this kind have fixed interest for between three and five years.

This type of mortgage has become extremely popular, with nearly half of all new mortgages being fixed rate (at the time of writing). This may well be a reaction by borrowers to the high interest rates at the beginning of the decade and the scare caused by the dramatic interest rate rises on Black Wednesday in September 1992.

Should you opt for a fixed-interest loan?

Even the experts have been bad at predicting future interest rates. Quite simply, it is a gamble. If interest rates go down you will lose by taking a fixed-interest option. If they go up you will gain – for the period that rates are fixed. Once you have committed yourself to a fixed-interest loan, it is expensive to change again. Most lenders charge a penalty of three months' interest if you repay during the fixed-rate period.

Flexibility of mortgages

Both PEP and repayment mortgages are more flexible than endowment or pension mortgages in terms of altering the period of the loan, which could be an advantage if your financial situation changes. However, repayment mortgages are not so good if you move regularly because you make very little capital repayment in the early years of each mortgage. This can be got round by sticking to the term of the original mortgage.

Endowment *versus* repayment mortgages

Endowment mortgages are generally considered better value if interest rates are less than 10.5 per cent – *if* you want life cover.

With an endowment mortgage there is a chance that there may be a surplus for you over and above the amount required to redeem the mortgage when the policy matures. However, most endowment mortgages do not guarantee to repay the loan in full, and there is a chance you will be left with a shortfall.

With a repayment mortgage you pay interest only on the reducing capital. If you have made many years of capital repayments, you will be much less vulnerable to a jump in interest rates than you would be with an endowment mortgage.

If you are getting on in years, taking out a new endowment policy becomes increasingly expensive. Here a repayment mortgage – coupled perhaps with a mortgage protection life insurance policy – may be better.

Where to get a mortgage

The first rule is to shop around: there are well over 200 institutions in the mortgage market.

Make sure you know what sort of loan you are being offered; check what costs are involved; find out whether life insurance is included or not or is compulsory; do not take on too big a loan just because the lender offers you that much.

Study the literature of potential lenders: different building societies, banks, insurance companies and other financial institutions.

Most mortgage lenders are very keen to sell all forms of insurance to anyone who takes out a mortgage. This means that:

- most mortgage lenders offer insurance products which are tied to one lender, making it difficult to know if you are getting the best cover and the lowest premium
- with many loans there are 'conditional tie-ins', which means that you have to buy various insurance products in order to qualify for the loan. This makes it difficult to compare different types of mortgage because you have to take into account the tie-in insurance costs, as well as the loan costs when comparing the deals.

To make comparisons even more complicated, lenders do not all insist on the same types of insurance being bought with the mortgage.

Building societies

Until relatively recently, almost all mortgages for home buyers came from building societies who funded the loans from people's investments with them.

Each society has its own guidelines regarding whom it is prepared to lend to, how much to lend and on what type of home. Branch managers may have some discretion to vary the conditions and it is worth discussing your particular case with the manager even if it looks as though the guidelines seem to rule out a loan to you.

When a building society has more potential borrowers than money to lend, it may impose a form of rationing. This could take the form of giving priority to people who invest with that society or who already have a mortgage with the society. So, if you are planning to buy your first home, it may be a good idea to open an account with one or more building societies, just in case. Before doing so, check the society's lending policies to make sure that it will be prepared to lend to you when the time comes.

Banks

Banks have now become prominent in the mortgage market, particularly for large loans. All the high street banks offer mortgages and less well-known foreign banks are also in the market. But a bank (unlike a building society) can decide at any time not to offer any further new mortgages.

There is often little to choose between a bank and a building society as mortgagee. If you are after a big loan, check what the banks, particularly the foreign banks, have to offer.

Some foreign banks offer loans which are geared to other currencies – where interest rates may be lower. These carry an additional risk. Besides the normal changes in interest rates, your loan repayments could also be affected by exchange rate fluctuations.

Other lenders

Insurance companies who offer life insurance may also be in the mortgage market. The chances are that you will be able to get only an endowment mortgage linked to their own policy – few allow a free choice of endowment policy or offer repayment mortgages (this is usually true of banks and building societies too).

Local authorities have to give mortgages to council tenants who want to exercise their 'right to buy' option. A few authorities may offer mortgages to people prepared to buy and renovate derelict houses.

Employers, particularly banks and other financial institutions, often offer mortgages to their staff, usually at low interest rates as a fringe benefit. But before you take one, check what would happen if you were to leave and change jobs: would you be allowed to keep on the loan and, if so, at what interest rate would you have you repay it?

Finance houses and credit companies may be prepared to lend you more than other lenders, but at a higher interest rate. They are unlikely to offer repayment mortgages. There may be a high redemption charge if you want to pay off the mortgage in the first few years (in order to move to a cheaper lender perhaps). They also seem to be faster off the mark than building societies in starting repossession proceedings if you are in arrears.

Builders or the developer of a new site may offer to arrange mortgages for prospective buyers, perhaps offering to get 100 per cent mortgages or lower-than-normal interest rates for the first year as part of a package to induce you to buy. Some schemes depend on the solvency of the builder, and should be treated with caution.

Private mortgages are no longer common, but are a possibility. If a relative or friend offers to lend you money to help you buy a home, at a low interest rate, or none, it would be a cheap source of finance. But make sure a proper business-like arrangement is made between you, with a mortgage deed. You can claim tax relief on any interest you pay on a loan under £30,000, but the lender will have to declare the interest received as income for tax purposes.

You should be careful if the person from whom you are buying a house offers you a loan. It may be just because the seller is desperate for a quick sale but it could be because he or she knows that getting a mortgage will be difficult due to structural or other problems. Get your solicitor to check the terms carefully before agreeing, and make sure the house is properly surveyed.

Using a mortgage broker

Mortgage brokers do not themselves lend money but make arrangements for you to borrow from someone else. If mortgages are not in short supply or you want to buy a fairly ordinary house with an average sort of mortgage, there is little point in paying a broker. You will probably do just as well by going straight to a lender. But if you are hoping to buy an unusual house, or one which most lenders are not too keen on (for instance, one with a sitting tenant or a home combined with a shop), or if you want a very large loan, or mortgages are in short supply, a broker could be useful or even essential.

Brokers vary from those who make all their money by selling endowment policies at one end of the scale to highly respected independent advisers at the other. If you pay the broker a fee you are more likely (but not guaranteed) to get some impartial advice.

If a broker offers you a repayment mortgage, you may have to pay an arrangment fee of 1 or 2 per cent of the loan. If you are offered some sort of endowment mortgage, or a pension mortgage, you should not have to pay a fee as the broker will get commission from the insurance company which provides the endowment policy or personal pension plan. If the broker asks you to pay a deposit, it must be repaid to you (all but £3) if you have not taken up any loan arranged by the broker within six months. This right is given to you by the Consumer Credit Act 1974.

A good broker should give you a choice of mortgages to suit your circumstances. Get written quotations setting out all the payments involved (including any arrangement fee) and study the figures carefully. If you are in any doubt about anything, ask for an explanation and get your solicitor to look over anything you have to sign. And there is nothing to stop you going to a second broker to see what that one has to offer you.

Anyone called an 'insurance broker' has to be registered with the Insurance Brokers Registration Council. But anyone can adopt the title 'mortgage broker' or 'insurance consultant'. Many mortgage and insurance brokers belong to bodies which have codes of conduct for their members to follow and which will investigate customers' complaints. You could write to one or both of the following bodies for lists of members in your area: the British Insurance and Investment Brokers Association (BIIBA)★ or the Corporation of Insurance and Financial Advisors (CIFA)★.

Estate agents

The selling agents may offer to arrange a mortgage for you. Many estate agents are owned by insurance companies, banks or building societies, and may therefore offer you endowment or pension mortgages – from which they will benefit.

Getting information from a lender

As soon as you start looking for a house to buy, it is worth going to visit several potential lenders to discuss a loan.

Information you should find out from booklets or a personal visit includes:

- the interest rate:
  - for different amounts lent (rate may be higher for larger loans)
  - for different types of mortgage (repayment/endowment/ pension-linked)
  - for first-time buyers
- what payment will you have to make per £1,000 borrowed?
- when and how payments have to be made:
  - in the first month?
  - in the rest of the financial year?
  - thereafter?
- what will happen when the interest rate changes?
- what fixed-rate loans are available – will there be an arrangement fee?
- do they offer fixed interest rates for the early years?
- what percentage of valuation is the normal maximum loan?
- how much more you can borrow with extra security (and what security is acceptable)?
- which types of insurance must be bought as a condition of the loan (e.g. house contents, buildings, mortgage protection etc.)
- will there be a redemption charge if you pay off the mortgage within so many (how many?) years?

Under the Financial Services Act, firms that sell endowment or pension mortgages have to be authorised to carry out their business and have to abide by a set of detailed rules. One important feature of these rules is that firms have to make it clear whether they are giving completely independent advice to their customers on what their best choice is, or are tied to selling one company's products.

Applying for a mortgage

You may be asked at an early stage to fill in a form giving some details of your income and commitments. Many lenders offer a **mortgage certificate** to potential borrowers. This states how much they would be prepared to lend you (subject to the value of the property you will want to buy). Such a certificate constitutes an offer to lend but is usually valid for a limited period – six weeks, perhaps, or three months. A mortgage certificate could be useful if you need to persuade a seller that you are a serious buyer who will have the finance to proceed.

The application form asks for full details of your (and any joint borrower's) financial commitments and income. You will have to give details of your employment, your bank, any previous mortgage or your landlord. The lender will probably contact all of these to check that you are a credit-worthy and reliable person to lend to.

A self-employed person may have to submit audited accounts. If you are freelance or working on an irregular basis, you may find it difficult to get a loan unless you can produce a large part of the purchase price yourself. With what is known as a 'non-status' mortgage, the amount borrowed is not related to earnings, but some evidence of financial stability will be required, such as an accountant's or bank's reference, and the interest rate may be higher.

When you have found the house

Once you have made an offer for a house, you will have to apply formally for the loan.

You have to give details of the house you want to buy, including the price. You also have to say how much you want to borrow and may be asked where the rest of the purchase price is coming from.

Once you have filled in the application form, you will have to pay for the lender to value the property. This is a valuation only, not a full structural survey, although most banks and building societies offer you the opportunity of arranging through them a house buyers' report or a full structural survey. The fee is based on the purchase price (or the valuation, if that is higher). If the lender decides not to give you a loan as a result of the valuation, you will not get the fee back. Neither can it be refunded if you decide not to go ahead with the purchase, whatever the reason.

When the valuation has been done, and the status enquiries are complete, the lenders will let you know whether they are prepared to lend, how much and on what terms.

Mortgage conditions

Conditions will be laid down by a lender, which the borrower has to undertake to observe. These will in most cases include:

- keeping the home in good repair
- not letting all or part of the home without the lender's permission (this means you would need to ask before you have tenants in the basement, for example, or take in lodgers or paying guests)
- not altering the property without the lender's permission
- informing the lender of any local authority proposals which would affect the property
- keeping the property insured
- not applying for an improvement grant without proper permission.

They may also include:

- undertaking to carry out certain repairs or improvements within a specified period
- not taking out any further mortgage without permission.

Insurance

Insurance for fire and other risks to the building is always a condition of granting a mortgage. Most building societies and banks arrange the insurance with a selected insurance company or a borrower is entitled to choose from a number of insurance companies named by the lender. If he or she wants to use another company (perhaps current insurers), he or she would have to get the lender's approval (and may be charged for this).

The loan

If the amount you are offered is enough to allow you to go ahead, you should have no problems. But you could either be turned down or not be allowed a large enough loan to enable you to complete the purchase.

Turned down for a loan?

If your application is rejected, you should ask the reason. It could be:

- because of your circumstances (your income, credit record, age or occupation)
- because of problems with the property such as its condition or type
- because the lender does not have the money available to lend, although this is unlikely in the present climate.

If the problem is you or the house, a different lender may well use different lending criteria – though you may be asked to disclose if a previous application has been turned down.

If the problem is a bad report on you from a credit reference agency, you should ask the lender for details of the agency concerned. You are entitled, on payment of £1 to the agency, to a copy of your record. If it is incorrect, you can ask for it to be put right.

If the problem is a shortage of funds, the lenders may be prepared to commit themselves to granting your mortgage in the near future, perhaps within the next month or two. But there would be no harm in seeing whether a different lender does have funds available.

For older properties, particularly if in need of repair, the loan may be a lower percentage of the price than normal. Most lenders stipulate that the loan is conditional on repairs being carried out within a specified period, and may hold back some of the loan until these are completed and the lender's inspector has approved the work.

Need a larger loan?

If the loan you are offered is limited because the lenders will not lend more than a certain percentage of the valuation, they may be prepared to lend you more with a mortgage indemnity policy (although since the early 1990s these are much harder to come by).

If the reason for the offer being low is your income, do think carefully whether you really can commit yourself to the loan you were requesting. Perhaps if you looked at a cheaper home, you would have no problems in getting the (smaller) loan you would need.

Top-up loan

Consider whether you are being realistic in the amount of loan you applied for. If you know you can cope, you may be able to get a second mortgage or top-up loan from an insurance company or bank. The first lender will normally have to give permission (not all lenders allow borrowers to have a top-up loan) and to approve the insurance company or other provider of the second loan.

You are likely to have to pay a higher interest rate on the top-up loan than on the main mortgage and may have to take out an insurance policy to cover it. The conditions of the top-up loan may be stringent: for example, you could be asked to pay three months' interest as a charge for early repayment.

Cost of obtaining a mortgage

The costs which have to be paid by you, the borrower, are:

- the lender's valuation fee
- the lender's solicitor's fee for handling the mortgage application
- your own solicitor's fee (if you use one) for handling the mortgage.

The lender's solicitor's job is to check the legal ownership of the property, carry out necessary searches and enquiries and to draw up the mortgage deed laying down the conditions of the loan.

Your own solicitor may also charge you a fee for providing the lender with the documents about the ownership, and for checking the mortgage deed.

If you are getting a building society or bank mortgage, your solicitor will usually act for both you and the building society. Most solicitors include the necessary mortgage work within their charge for the purchase rather than charging separately for it.

Possible additional costs

If you have:

- a mortgage from a bank, you may have to pay an 'arrangement fee' when you take it out
- a second mortgage or top-up loan, there may be a charge for obtaining this and the bank or insurance company solicitor's fee for handling it; your own solicitor may also make an extra charge, especially if he or she is not acting for the second lender
- an endowment mortgage, the lender's legal fees will usually be higher than for a repayment mortgage
- a mortgage indemnity policy or high-lending fee (required if your loan is for more than a certain percentage of the value of the property), this would entail a single premium, payable as a lump sum or added to the mortgage loan
- a stipulation by a lender for repairs (for example, eradication of dry rot or woodworm), and, if the lender retains a sum out of the mortgage loan until the work has been done to its satisfaction, there may be a fee for inspection
- a bridging loan from the bank to make up the purchase price if you buy before selling, or have to wait until repairs are carried out before taking up your loan, the bank makes a charge for arranging such a loan
- a mortgage other than an endowment, premiums for a mortgage protection policy to provide cover for the sum being borrowed may have to be paid throughout the period
- a newly built house which is still being constructed, and the lender is releasing the mortgage loan in stages, you have to pay a fee for the lender's surveyor's inspection and certificate at the various stages, and will have to pay the interest on the earlier parts of the loan from the time you first receive any money.

Insuring in case of hard times

Some lenders offer insurance policies which pay your mortgage payments if you are unable to earn because of illness or unemployment. These policies are not cheap, perhaps adding £10 to £15 to the monthly payments on a £30,000 loan.

Read the small print carefully before agreeing to have one of these policies.

The wider the circumstances in which you can claim, the better. Some policies pay out only if you are unable to work because you are ill or have had an accident. Others include redundancy – though not always if you volunteer for redundancy. A few policies cover a wider definition of unemployment, e.g. if you are sacked or lose your job but are unable to claim redundancy payment, perhaps because you have not worked for the firm for long enough.

Make sure that your work is covered by the policy. Some do not pay out if you normally work part-time, even if you earn good money in that time and have been doing so for several years. Most policies cover self-employed people only for periods of illness, not for unemployment.

Some policies do not pay out on redundancy or unemployment if you have been with your employer for less than a certain time.

Most policies will only pay out for mortgage payments for one year, some for two years; you are unlikely to find policies paying out for longer than this.

Problems with mortgage payments

The early years of the 1990s saw an unprecedented number of homes being repossessed by building societies and other lenders. If you find that you cannot keep up your mortgage payments, do not assume that you will automatically lose the house. There is much that can be done to help the situation.

There are different general considerations depending on the type of your mortgage.

There are some hints on how to try to ensure that you do not lose your home:

- If you are unemployed and/or are claiming income support, ask for assistance from the Department of Social Security to help with interest payments (not capital repayments).
- If you fall behind with your payments, contact your lender at once (before he or she contacts you) and explain the position. Some lenders now have helplines. Ask for advice on what can be done.
- There is also a Housing Debtline on 0121–359 8501
- *Do not* ignore letters from the lender. Respond promptly to each one.
- Consider going to a debt counsellor. Many Citizens Advice Bureaux offer this service free of charge.
- Be very wary about borrowing more to pay off the arrears, particularly if you are being offered a loan by a finance company. Interest rates are often much higher, and you could find that you simply get deeper into debt.
- If court proceedings are issued, comply with the time limits and go to all court hearings. Writing a letter to the court explaining your circumstances is *never* sufficient. Courts do have wide powers to suspend possession orders if there is a reasonable prospect of the arrears being cleared.

Repayment mortgages

The lender may agree to extending the term of a mortgage – for example, from 20 to 30 years. This will not necessarily reduce the monthly payments by very much (especially in the early years of the mortgage when interest forms the largest part of each payment). Or the lender may agree to your paying interest only for a short period, particularly if your problems are likely to be short-lived.

If interest rates rise, you may be able to extend the term of the mortgage rather than have to increase your monthly payments.

If you get into arrears, and there is sufficient value on the home, the lender may agree to capitalise the arrears (i.e. add them to the loan). Be careful about borrowing your way out of debt.

Endowment mortgages

Extending the term of the mortgage may not make any difference to the payments you have to make because the amount of interest you owe would still be the same. And, again unlike a repayment mortgage, there is not the option of reducing payments by paying interest only because that is what you have been doing all along. Moreover, you have to keep paying the endowment insurance premiums – otherwise, the loan is not covered and the lender may foreclose on the mortgage or force you to sell your home. The only option is to consider changing to a repayment mortgage. If you have paid the premium for many years, the endowment policy could be surrendered and the proceeds used to reduce the amount of capital you owe. A better option might be to sell or auction the policy – there are companies which specialise in this.

Pension mortgages

As with an endowment mortgage, you do not have the option of reducing your payments to the lender by extending the term of the loan or making interest-only payments. And if you stop making the pension plan payments, the lender has no guarantee that the loan will be repaid, so could ask you to pay off the mortgage, forcing you to sell your home. Unlike an endowment policy, a pension plan cannot be cashed in early so there is no chance of being able to get a lump sum to repay part of the capital and then transferring the rest to a different sort of mortgage.

The negative equity trap

Because of the fall in values in the 1990s, many people are living in houses where the value is less than the amount outstanding on the mortgage. Because, traditionally, building societies have insisted on loans being repaid as a condition of agreeing to a sale of a house, this presents problems for those in that situation who want to move – even those who have maintained all their monthly payments and are not in financial difficulties.

Many lenders have introduced schemes to help those with negative equity. If you have to move – for example, because of your job – you may transfer the negative equity from your present to your new home (but you would not be allowed to increase your loan).

There are no easy answers, but if you find yourself in that situation, it probably does no harm to point out to the lender that it shares some responsibility for the situation (by virtue of lending too much) and invite a shared approach to resolving it.

FINDING A BUYER FOR YOUR HOUSE

Groundwork

YOU CAN decide either to handle the sale yourself or to commission one or more estate agents to make the arrangements on your behalf.

An agent will do some of the work for you but you must be prepared for this to cost considerably more than if you do it all yourself. Without an agent, you will be spending your time rather than money – at a time when you are probably occupied with buying as well as selling a house. It may not take longer to find a buyer privately than if you engage an estate agent, but it could do.

If a new industrial or office development is imminent and a firm is likely to be importing new staff, it will probably do its house searching through an agent. Locals contemplating a change, on the other hand, have more opportunity for studying local newspaper and any 'For Sale' boards.

If you advertise your house extensively and do not manage to sell it, you may have difficulty persuading an agent to take over from you. This is not a matter of agent's pique or jealousy but of practical experience that a house known to have been on the market for a long time acquires a reputation of being unsaleable, with the suspicion that there must be something wrong with it somewhere – even if this is unwarranted.

Selling without an agent

If you want to sell your house privately, these are the steps you will have to take:

- prepare your house for sale
- decide on an asking price
- decide which items are to be included in the sale, and prices for them
- draw up the particulars to give to potential buyers
- spread the word
- answer all enquiries
- arrange the appointments to view the house
- show round all viewers
- evaluate the merits of rival bids
- negotiate a final price with the buyer you choose.

Preparing the house for a sale

It is always a difficult decision to make: how much to repair and redecorate the house before selling? The answer depends to some extent on who you think might buy. Young or first-time buyers are more likely to pay a little less and do their own work on the house. Older people might want to move in without sharing their lives with the decorators in the first few months. Nevertheless, a house which looks sad, dirty and neglected will never be easy to sell.

A good test is to look at other houses (whether or not they are for sale) and consider what would attract you or put you off. A well-decorated house (which has all the signs of having been cared for) is likely to create a much more favourable impression than one where the paint is cracked and the floors still have last year's Christmas lunch on them.

On the other hand, your idea of the ideal decorative finish may not be shared by an intending buyer. The orange wallpaper with the purple blobs may have great appeal to you, but the buyer may consider it will clash with his or her lime green and crimson carpet.

The answer probably is a compromise: carry out essential repairs and do some redecoration if needed, but use noncontroversial colours (pale colours – cream or off-white are probably safest). You should certainly scrub the place like it has never been cleaned before.

Pay attention to detail: make sure that everything works. Expired (or missing) light bulbs create a bad impression, as do dripping taps, broken electrical light fittings and blocked gutters.

Smells
You may be fond of a good fry-up or enjoy boiled cabbage. But if your buyers are knocked backwards by the reek of a fish-and-chip shop or a school canteen, they are unlikely to start with a favourable impression.

Children and pets
Bonzo, the Alsatian and St Bernard cross, may not hurt a fly, but strangers will not be aware of his docile nature as he bounds across the lawn to greet them. They may simply decide to move on to the next house on their list. The effect of jam-and-chocolate-coated children could be the same. Both species should be kept well under control during a visit by prospective buyers.

Don't forget the outside
The garden should be tidy and the grass cut. On viewing days, the garden path should not be an obstacle course of children's toys. If your hobby is to break up old cars, remove the evidence to the other side of the county.

Fixing a price

It is not always easy for a do-it-yourself seller to be as knowledgeable as a local estate agent on what would be the right price to ask. An agent's expertise lies in knowing current market trends, what similar local property is selling for, and in judging what would be an attractive but proper price for a particular house and any of its contents.

If your house is one of several similar ones – in a post-war estate, for example – it is easier to judge a price than if it is an older one which may be in a better or worse state of repair and redecoration than neighbouring ones, or a house for which there is no comparable one in the immediate area.

To find out current asking prices in the neighbourhood, study the windows of local estate agents, and advertisements in local papers for similar houses. Remember that the price asked is not necessarily the figure at which the property gets sold.

It is not always reliable to believe what neighbours or friends report were the sale prices of neighbouring properties.

The condition of the house itself ought to be considered before a price is settled. If you have decided not to repair or decorate, and your house needs attention, you should expect a lower price than for an identical house in good order.

Valuation

You can ask a local estate agent to give you a valuation for your house. If you are not selling through him or her, there may be a charge: ask first what this charge would be. If you do decide to have a valuation, make it clear that you are asking for a valuation – not instructing him or her to sell. It is advisable to get the arrangement and fee confirmed in writing.

If you are uncertain about the saleability of your house – whether there are structural problems that could deflate the price or make it difficult to sell – ask a surveyor to look over the house. The survey may reveal one or more faults which would justify a buyer in asking for some reduction on account of them. If so, build into your asking price some allowance for this and keep in mind what figure would finally be acceptable. If, however, you make clear to potential buyers any defects you are aware of, you should not have to reduce the price because of them later – though the price is always a matter for negotiation, and you cannot force a buyer to accept a particular price.

Bargaining

Make the asking price as attractive a figure as possible: £64,500 or even £64,450 is better than £65,000. It is sensible to set the asking price higher than the one you expect to settle for, so that there is some room for manoeuvre. If you want a quick sale and think a little bargaining will attract a buyer, you can quote a figure and add o.n.o. (or near offer) – and wait for one. Any buyer hopes to start negotiating at a somewhat lower figure than he or she is prepared to settle for and each party may finally decide to reach a compromise.

The buyer may ask for a reduction because you are not having to pay an agent's commission on the sale, or may try to get as many extras as possible included in the price.

For inclusion in the sale

You may have included in the asking price any items in the house which you wish to sell with it. Or a separate price can be asked and negotiated for these. In either case, as the seller, you should be quite clear about what will be regarded as fixtures and what you are entitled to take away with you.

You should also consider which items belong to you rather than the house, but which it would be more sensible or convenient to sell with it, such as a washing machine or dishwasher already plumbed in, the fridge or cooker.

If the kitchen contains units constructed to house a particular size or brand of equipment, it may be more sensible to leave these where they are. As a selling item, a well-fitted kitchen comes high on most people's list and to remove specially designed equipment could be short-sighted. A decision on this may also depend on whether you know yet what you need in your new kitchen.

Made-to-measure curtains, perhaps with matching pelmets, are often best sold with a house since they are unlikely to fit satisfactorily into a different one, and adapting them may be uneconomic. Similarly, all fitted carpets are better left in position for the next owner. Curtains and carpets are usually included in the sale price. If you do want a separate price paid for them, the condition they are in should be taken into account when fixing a second-hand price for them. Bear in mind also what the buyer is saving by not having to buy new carpets.

Fixtures
By law, you must sell as part of the house anything that is a fixture (unless it is specifically agreed between the buyer and

seller that particular fixtures are excluded). For full details of the legal position regarding fixtures and fittings see **Chapter 4**.

List of items for sale

When you have reviewed the house and garden, and decided what to sell, make a list, pricing items according to their quality, original cost, age and current condition. When it comes to showing the house to viewers, point out these items specifically.

To avoid misunderstandings or subsequent queries, it may be worth your while to duplicate a list of any items which you are selling separately, together with other information about the house, along the lines of the 'particulars' which estate agents draw up.

When it comes to final negotiations with your buyer, you may find that he or she does not want some of the items you want to sell. He or she is quite entitled to reject these but, if you want to stand firm, you are in a stronger position – it depends on how badly the buyer wants the house: he or she may feel obliged to buy the contents you offer.

How to prepare sale particulars

All estate agents prepare sale particulars describing, usually in glowing terms, the properties they are selling. Although it is by no means essential to have sale particulars, they could well help to sell the house, especially if you are advertising out of the locality.

There is no set format to preparing sale particulars, but it is usually best to start with a general summary giving the address, type of house (bungalow, semi-detached, chalet etc.), number of bedrooms, locality and price. Add a sentence or two on situation ('set back from road', 'quiet cul-de-sac'). Don't be tempted to give the kind of misinformation which some agents go in for (for instances of this see page 50). It is safer and better to describe the house as it is. Exaggerated claims will lead to disappointment. Nevertheless, do not leave out any special features. If the house has recently been renovated or has central heating, say so.

Next, include a description of every room in the house. Plan this so that when you later come to show people round, they can follow the order set out in your sale particulars.

Give measurements (which must be accurate) for main rooms (no need to give the size of the cupboard under the stairs unless it is very spacious). As you go through each room, highlight any special features, as well as facilities such as the number of radiators, electrical sockets and telephone points. Do not include in your sale particulars any item which is not included in the price.

Remember to describe the whole house. Cupboards, attics, cellars should all get a mention, along with plus points (double-glazing, burglar alarm, cavity insulation, roof insulation and so on).

Having dealt with the inside, move on to a description of the garden, garage, fuel store and outbuildings. Again, do not include items which you plan to remove.

Similarly, if you intend to take fixtures which would normally be included in the price, you should say so in the particulars. If you leave it till later, you could cause annoyance and this might upset the progress of the sale.

Next, deal with things which are not included in the sale, but which you are prepared to sell, e.g. 'the carpets may be purchased for a price of £1,000 (or to be negotiated)'.

You can either fix the price or invite offers 'in the region of' or 'not less than' £XXX. If the market is uncertain, you can leave the figures blank in your master copy, and add them later. That will save you having to advertise too loudly that you have made some price reductions.

Make sure you include directions to find the house (including the nearest public transport).

Finally, it is helpful to give additional information, including the mains services which are connected (and those which are available but are not connected), the type of heating and the actual amount of Council Tax and water rates payable. The name and address of the local authority is also useful. If planning permission has been granted for an improvement – a conversion or extension, perhaps, or a garage – which has not yet been carried out, do not forget to mention this.

End with your own name and telephone number, and an indication of the arrangements you offer for viewing.

WARNING: Misrepresentation

You must make very sure that your sale particulars are accurate. If you make incorrect statements, even innocently, you could lay yourself open to being sued for damages for misrepresentation, or cancellation of the contract (or both). This applies equally to any information given orally to a proposed buyer.

By all means put in a disclaimer like this: *These particulars are believed to be accurate, but they are intended as a guide only and do not form part of a contract.* (But it will not necessarily get you off the hook if the particulars are misleading.)

Producing the sale particulars

Plan the layout, allowing for one or more photographs to emphasise the main features.

The particulars should be typed out neatly. An electric typewriter or good word processor will give a smarter finish. This will be your master copy, which should then be photocopied. Don't expect hundreds of enquiries, but you might have two dozen prepared for your first edition. You can always have more copies made later. A buyer who is really keen might need several sets of the particulars to show to his or her solicitor, mortgage broker, surveyor etc.

Photographs

If you have a camera, there is no reason why you should not produce your own photographs. A few simple rules will enhance the effect of your photograph. Avoid elementary errors, such as incorrect focusing, wrong exposure. You should certainly opt for colour.

Frame your picture so that it shows the best features of the house. A close up of the dustbins and septic tank may have practical significance, but will not bring the punters rushing to buy. Cut out unnecessary intrusions: a foreground of parked cars, or the gas works in the distance are bound to be off-putting. On the other hand, if you can successfully frame the photograph so that elegant foliage lends appeal then do so. Do not confine yourself to outside views. If there is a feature which would photograph well (like a well-equipped kitchen or attractive living-room), a photograph of this should also be included.

It is best to experiment. Run off a whole film, then look critically at the results. With luck you will have some good pictures from which to choose two or three for your sale particulars. Get your local film shop to run off the necessary numbers of prints of these and stick them to your particulars. Do not photocopy your photographs. They never really come out well.

Advertising

Before you can have any hope of selling your house, you must tell the world it is on the market. Do it in a way which makes people interested enough to come and take a look.

There are many different ways of letting it be known that you have a house for sale. Some are cheap; others could be very expensive. You need to plan a campaign. Here are the choices.

A 'For Sale' sign outside the house

Some people are reluctant to take this step. They feel it might encourage burglars or nosey neighbours. The decision must be a personal one, but there are many advantages. Many house hunters tour around the neighbourhood and a 'For Sale' sign might be the first indication that the house is, indeed, for sale. It will help people who have already contacted you to find the house. There could well be people in the locality looking for a house, either for themselves or relatives.

If you are concerned about being pestered by people who do not have an appointment (or burglars), you can always put on your sign: 'For Sale – please telephone for appointment on xxx xxxx'. You can easily make your own sign or, if you want a more professional appearance, some stationers' shops stock signs, or you can have them made up specially.

WARNING: Size and number of signs
Prosecutions have been successfully brought where 'For Sale' signs do not comply with the law. You are permitted to have either one board up to 2 square metres in area, or 2 boards 'conjoined', together not exceeding 2.3 metres.

Cards in local shops

Many newsagents' shops and sub-post offices (and even supermarkets) have a window or wall set aside for advertisement cards. This is a very cheap way of advertising. If you want it to be eye-catching, take the same care with your card as with your sale particulars. Use fluorescent card, and add a colour photograph.

To reach as many people as possible, place cards with a number of shops. Inevitably, this is a limited way of advertising – but you could be lucky.

Property shops

You may be able to use a 'property shop' in your area. You have to fill in a fairly detailed form giving information about the property and allow it to be photographed. You pay a fee for the details and photograph of your house to be displayed in the 'shop'; some shops charge per week for displaying property. Most include indefinite display in their initial charge. Some property shops 'computer match' available properties with the buyers who are interested. The seller and any interested purchasers get in touch with each other direct and negotiate individually. There is no commission to pay on a sale, but the fee you pay is not refunded even if you do not sell.

In a few places, property centres have been set up by local solicitors. At such a centre, details of properties are shown and one of the centre's solicitors undertakes the selling transaction for you. The fee you are charged is based on the selling price of your house and includes display of the property and the conveyancing. The Solicitors Property Group* can tell you where to find such centres.

Your notice board at work

If your employer has a notice board for use by employees, consider putting up one of your cards there too.

Newspaper advertisements

Newspaper advertising can take many forms. At its lowest level, you can simply place a classified advertisement in your local paper. The next step up would be an advertisement in the regional paper for your area.

If you want to reach a wider public, you can advertise in one of the specialist magazines, such as *Exchange and Mart* or *Daltons Weekly*. Many national daily and Sunday newspapers have property sections. Top of the scale advertisements go into the glossy magazines like *Country Life* or *The Field*.

The medium you choose depends to some extent on the prevailing conditions and the kind of house you are selling. In boom times, you only have to whisper that your house is on the market before you have dozens of prospective buyers arriving at the door. Most of the time the property market is quieter, which requires active marketing. You should budget to spend quite a large sum of money on advertising. How much depends on the type you will use. Consider the alternatives:

Local paper

People who intend to move into an area frequently buy the local paper to find out what is available. You are therefore likely to reach not just the locals. Because this is the cheapest option, it gives you most scope. You need not confine yourself to three abbreviated lines. You could well include a photograph and an eye-catching description. Look at other private advertisements and improve on them. Try to arrange it so that your advertisement appears on the same page as estate agents' advertisements – perhaps with a bigger photograph than the agents use to advertise their houses. Most local papers will arrange the typesetting for you and can give advice on the wording. It is best to plan to advertise for several weeks, rather than exhaust your budget on one big advertisement.

Regional paper

The regional paper will cover one or more counties. Because of its wider readership, its rates will inevitably be higher than the local paper – so you are unlikely to be able to create the same 'splash' with your advertisement. It is still worth considering as it is cheaper than national advertising.

National advertising
Consider this if you have a house which has something unusual; perhaps you own two acres and offer an opportunity to join the 'Good Life', or you are in an area where prices are still low and you are trying to encourage people to move or retire to your house.

Drafting an advertisement

An advertisement should include the following basic information:

* type of house (e.g. detached, semi, terraced, bungalow)
* location
* number of bedrooms
* number of living-rooms
* number of bathrooms/separate WCs
* heating system
* garage
* garden
* freehold or leasehold
* price
* telephone number for appointments to view
* possibly also the number of floors, Council Tax band and any desirable amenities, such as nearness to station, schools etc. If there are some special features which are out of the ordinary or which would make good selling points, include these so as to give as attractive a picture of the house as possible.

The length of your advertisement will be dictated by price. You can probably afford to be quite expansive in a local paper, but have to cut your wording to the bone if you advertise nationally. Find out the cost before you start preparing the advertisements.

There are certain space-saving abbreviations which are customary in property advertisements, and costs can be cut by using these. Some of the more common ones are:

CH = central heating	clk = cloakroom
p.b. = purpose built	gge = garage
CHW = constant hot water	exc. con. = excellent condition
conv = converted	rm = room
FH = freehold	c & c = carpets and curtains
rec = reception	lge = large
GR = ground rent	f & f = fixtures and fittings
kit/brkrm = kitchen/breakfast room	det = detached
WC = loo	o.n.o. = or near offer

Using too many of these abbreviations will condense the entry to such a degree that it becomes virtually unreadable, and certainly not eye-catching. Compare the following two advertisements (2 ads) both for the same house:

Arch. des. det. hse. 1975. 4 lge bdrms, 2 bath, 2 WC, 30 ft sit rm, sep d/rm, study, mod. kit/brkrm. gas CH. Dble gge. patio. 1/4 acre walled gdn. £00,000 FH. Tel. . . . ,

Architect-designed house, detached. Built 1975 in wooded area 10 mins from town centre, standing in 1/4 acre of own ground. 4 large bedrooms, one with bathroom ensuite; 1 other bathroom, 2 WCs, sitting-room 30' × 14' with picture window on to patio, separate dining-room, study; kitchen recently modernised, pine wall units and breakfast area. Gas CH. Double glazing throughout. Double garage. Well-stocked walled garden. Freehold £00,000. Tel. . . .

Make a video?

More and more people own video cameras. If you are one of them and are trying to attract interest from outside the area, consider making a short video film of your home, using the following guidelines.

Don't spend too much time on the technicalities. Cecil B. De Mille is unlikely to give you a contract. All you need to do is give a general impression – both inside and out, though if you are aiming to send the tape to people not familiar with the area, you might include a few opening shots of your town/village or neighbourhood.

Take views of the outside of the house from different angles, including the road. Home in on the features. Hold your shot for long enough, but not for too long. You do not want your buyers to fall asleep while watching.

Use it to complement your sale particulars inside the house. Show the special characteristics, but don't zoom in on every socket and radiator. If you do a commentary, be sparing unless you are sure you are good at it. It is probably best simply to say where and what you are filming, rather than attempt a travelogue dialogue.

You can make copies of your master with your video recorder, but tapes are expensive. Unless you do not mind risking the loss of a few pounds, you should ask for a deposit (at least the cost of a blank tape).

Other means of selling?

There is no limit to the ways in which you can advertise your house – from a large advertisement painted on the side of your car, to handing out leaflets in a shopping centre (but watch out for breaches of the law or bylaws), local radio or teletext or even hiring a balloon. You can try anything if you have the imagination and resources.

Answering enquiries

All being well, your advertisements and publicity will start to produce results – in the shape of enquiries and telephone calls. You ought to arrange for someone to be on hand to answer any enquiries. (If you are available only during evenings and weekends, say so in the advertisement.) Keep a pad by the telephone to record names and times of appointments – you will probably find it easier to deal with one viewer at a time (although having two viewers looking round at the same time creates a competitive environment and could improve your chances).

161

Do not try to judge your enquirers by the sound of their voices. The surly voice at the end of the line may turn into the most enthusiastic would-be buyer. The objective is to get him or her to come to see the house. Sound helpful, but not too enthusiastic (even if it is the first caller for a month). Viewing should, ideally, always take place in daylight.

It goes without saying that you should be ready for the appointment. The house should be in tip-top condition – and you should be there! Nobody will buy your house if they travel 50 miles to find it locked up.

Prepare an information kit

Have to hand essential information about the running of the house, such as heating and electricity costs. Your bills for the last two or three years are a good indicator. If you are not on mains drainage, your buyers will need to know how often the septic tank has to be emptied and how much it costs to do so. Add to your pack documentation about guarantees, servicing of central heating, and instructions for any equipment which will be included in the sale (central heating, water softener, waste disposal unit etc.).

It is helpful to give local information, such as details about schools, shops, churches, local recreation facilities etc. Your tourist information centre or local authority may be able to let you have local guides and maps at little or no cost. It is a helpful gesture to hand these to prospective buyers, especially those from outside the area.

The viewing

You will probably find that your first few attempts are a little difficult. It is hard to remember to point out important features in a place which you may have come to take for granted. Don't worry about this. If you sound hesitant or nervous that could well create a good impression. Most people do not take kindly to 'hard sell'. On the other hand, don't let your nerves keep you talking non-stop. Follow the general guidelines below.

Invite the visitors into your living-room or lounge. Start your grand tour with the inside, beginning with the downstairs and

---

WARNING: security

There are unscrupulous people who use the invitations in house-sale advertisements to plan burglaries, or to steal whilst posing as prospective buyers. Be vigilant. One elementary precaution you can take is to show people by appointment only. Ring back everyone who contacts you – even casual callers. You can do so on the pretext that you need to check with your wife/husband for convenient times to view. In that way you will at least have the name and telephone number of anyone who arranges a visit.

Do not leave valuables or jewellery in easy reach when showing people around.

---

moving upstairs (if applicable). Generally, try to follow the order of rooms in your sale particulars. It is a good idea to say that you are doing this. If they do not have a copy, offer them one, and.a pen to make notes. Show the main rooms (living, dining, kitchen) first and the bedrooms and bathroom next. After they have seen the inside, take them outside (have an umbrella ready in case it pours with rain) and show them the garden and outdoors.

Point out the features, but do not over-sell. The fireplace you like so much may be the one thing they will want to remove! Indicate what is and what is not included in the price. If there are items you want to sell as extras, tell them about these too.

Once you have shown them round, offer them a coffee and ask them if there is any information they need. Here your information pack will be useful. You should be able to have at your fingertips answers to most questions which are raised. Remember to offer a local guidebook or leaflet if it is available, especially if they don't live locally.

Should you let them look round by themselves? Many people would welcome the opportunity to view a house on their own. They can then feel free to look more closely at the house, and discuss it privately together. You will have to make your own assessment as to whether it is safe to allow them to go round the house unaccompanied. On the whole, it is a good selling ploy to allow this. You will, of course, still be in the house, and will be able to see if their coats are bulging with hidden loot when they leave!

At the end of the viewing

Do not press your visitors for a decision. If they are wavering, you could easily push them the wrong way. Simply ask them if they have any more questions. It is the house, after all, which will sell itself if they like it.

Make it clear that they are welcome to come back to have another look (some prospective buyers inspect a house many times) and offer to supply them with any further information they might need now or later.

Before they go make sure:

- that they have your sale particulars (more than one copy if they want them)
- that they have your telephone number, and know how to contact you at all times (at work, for instance)
- that you have their name, address and telephone number.

Don't build up your hopes

Appearances are deceptive. Enthusiastic enquirers often disappear without another word. Others, who appear to show no interest at all, could buy the house without even bargaining over the price. The chances are that your first visitors will not buy, and you may have a long wait before you even receive an offer. Take advantage of the opportunity to practise your guided tours and your sales pitch.

Selling through an estate agent

The advantages of using estate agents to sell your home are:

- they take some of the work and worry off the shoulders of the seller
- they have more experience in judging the market value of a house and how best it should be sold (and whether by private treaty or auction)

- they have better facilities for publicising the sale, and ready access to more would-be buyers
- they offer better security – for example, an elderly person or someone living alone can ask for the agent's representative to accompany all viewers
- they can ask if an interested buyer has adequate means or mortgage facilities already arranged and will, if required, negotiate a mortgage on behalf of a buyer.

The agent's prime concern is to achieve a speedy and, as far as possible, a trouble-free sale, for all parties concerned. If an applicant's 'buying power' is established at the outset, it is to the benefit of all concerned. Agents have access to mortgage funds from a variety of sources.

The use of computers by groups of estate agents is increasing. Details of your property are fed into the multi-list computer system and are then available to all agents participating in the scheme, who can offer the property immediately to prospective buyers over a wide area.

Finding an estate agent

If you have already found a house to buy through an agent, do you then go on to ask the same agent to sell yours? There is something to be said for doing this: the agent will have more to lose if he or she cannot sell your house. But be careful that the agent does not down-value your house in order to achieve (effectively) two quick sales.

To compare local estate agents, find out:

- what type of property they sell
- whether they belong to one of the professional associations
- the extent of the services offered
- on what basis they charge and what is included.

Studying shop windows, newspaper advertising and the display boards of different estate agents will give an idea of what business they handle, how extensive it is, and whether it covers a special market or deals with all types of housing. The style and flavour of the text may reflect the style of the firm.

The number of 'For Sale' boards in the area reflects agents' activities and the number of 'Sold' stickers their effectiveness. But some local associations of estate agents agree that none of their members shall erect 'For Sale' boards, and the local authority may impose restrictions.

Most estate agents belong to one or other of the professional associations: the Royal Institution of Chartered Surveyors (RICS)*, the Incorporated Society of Valuers and Auctioneers (ISVA)*, the National Association of Estate Agents (NAEA)*, the Architects and Surveyors Institute (ASI)*, the Association of Building Engineers*. They have codes of conduct for their members, who have to participate in indemnity schemes protecting the public from fraud.

Be wary of unqualified estate agents; some of these people are not particularly scrupulous. Estate agents do not have to be registered to carry on business, but if convicted or found in breach of certain obligations under the Estate Agents Act 1979, they can, in the last resort, be prohibited from doing estate agency work by order of the Director General of Fair Trading. Any complaints should initially be made to the local authority trading standards department.

The estate agent's inspection

Ask someone from the estate agents to call to look at the house. It is a good thing to ask specifically who will be dealing with your house and to meet him or her personally at the outset. (Do not necessarily expect the senior partner to deal with you.) The agent should make a thorough inspection in order to be able to assess the value of the house, taking into account its position and condition. You can then discuss, and get advice on, what would be a suitable and attractive asking price – not necessarily the same figure as the valuation. (If you seek advice from more than one agent, do not necessarily give instructions to the one who suggests the highest asking price. It could just be a not-very-ethical ploy to get your instructions.)

He or she should take measurements of rooms, and note other details, such as heating, special features and so on, for the description to be circulated. You should have ready details of

Council Tax and water rates, any ground rent payable and any service or maintenance charges.

If you want, he or she will offer advice on which items to leave in the house, what price to ask for them, and whether to carry out renovations.

Get the agent to tell you what arrangements he or she proposes to make for advertising the property. These could be:

- insertion in the agent's list of houses for sale, fed into a computer, mailed to buyers on the register or handed out at the office
- a special circular dealing only with your property
- an advertisement in a local, regional or national paper or magazine.

The agent may arrange for photographs to be taken for publicity purposes. The cost of a specially printed brochure, with photographs, may not be included in the fee, and you should check what this cost will be.

If there are special circumstances (for example, you are selling because of financial problems or a marriage breakdown), tell the agent; point out that there could be circumstances where, through no fault of your own, you may have to abandon the sale.

An energetic agent will return to the office, draft the particulars, print them out and mail them – often on the same day, Also, he or she may telephone any buyer he or she thinks would be interested, and who might visit even before seeing the particulars.

Agents do not necessarily confirm with the seller (or even show him or her) the house description or an advertisement. You should say if you want to vet the text before it is printed or duplicated. It is worth doing so, even if it causes a day's delay, to make sure that the particulars are accurate.

The estate agent's fee

Under the Estate Agents Act 1979, you must be told in advance in what circumstances an estate agent will charge you and what the fee will be (or at least how it will be worked out) and you must be told if the estate agent or any of his or her associates has a personal interest in the transaction.

Estate agents generally base their fees on the selling price of the house and according to the type of agency contract you have with them. For sole agency, you might pay 1½ or 2 per cent of the final selling price; for multiple or joint-sole agency fees are negotiable between 2 and as much as 3½ per cent. Charges can vary markedly according to area (see *Which?* March 1992 and May 1994). An agent may more rarely operate a sliding scale, charging, say, 2½ per cent on the first £20,000 of the selling price, 1½ per cent on the rest. An agent sometimes charges a flat fee, irrespective of the selling price. It is worth shopping around; it is possible to negotiate a fee.

In some parts of the country, fees are all-inclusive. Elsewhere, you may find that commissions are lower but that you have to pay certain expenses up-front. These may include advertising, printed particulars and occasionally even the cost of a sale board. You must be given an itemised bill for these extras.

Even where an estate agent has approached you direct asking if you are willing to sell because he or she has a client anxious to buy your house, you will be charged commission if you do so.

Sole agency

You may instruct more than one agent to sell your house, but an agent may reduce the fee if you grant him or her sole agency – this means that you put your property exclusively into his or her hands. It is quite common to give one agent a sole agency for a limited period of, say, six weeks. If, after the agreed time, no buyer has been found, you can appoint another agent instead of or in addition to the first. In any period of sole agency, it is important not to instruct another agent or you may find yourself having to pay commission to both.

There should be a clear agreement on what basis the agent will receive commission: namely, that he or she introduced the buyer who actually completes the purchase. Do not undertake to pay commission to an agent for introducing a buyer 'ready, able and willing to buy': this would mean that if anything went wrong and the sale did not go through, you might still have to pay the agent's fee. Nor should you agree to any agent having 'sole selling rights' – this would entitle him or her to a commission, even if the eventual buyer was not introduced by him or her.

There have been unpleasant court cases where two agents have claimed commission for the same sale, or where an agent has tried to claim commission where no sale has happened. The wording of the agent's letter confirming instructions is very important. If you disagree with what is said, get the matter cleared up then. Do not hope for the best later. In some circumstances, it may be sensible to ask your solicitor to advise you on the wording of the agent's terms.

Extras

There is VAT to pay on agent's fees and on any advertising costs. Ask the agent which services are included and what will be extra. If advertising costs are not included, do you have to pay all, or only those above a certain figure? Ask the agent whether advertising is in local or national papers or magazines – costs differ a lot.

If details of the advertising costs which will be incurred, either broken down to the column centimetre rate or per advertisement, are given to you at the outset, you can be aware of the precise charges for which you will be liable. You can set your maximum for extra publicity costs and instruct the agent accordingly.

Some estate agents make a charge for the 'For Sale' board. Do not necessarily accept this, and certainly do not agree to pay for a 'Sold' sign.

Whatever agreement you make with the agent, get it confirmed in writing. The agent may well ask you to confirm acceptance of the charges, in writing.

Showing the house

Estate agents usually leave the job of showing viewers round a house to the owner, saying that he or she is best fitted to do it. So, even when selling through an agent, you have to be prepared to give up time for this. You may be able to make appointments ahead, or you may find the agent sending round viewers from the office who want to be shown round immediately. If you are out at work all day, appointments will have to be made for evenings or weekends. (If you can never be at home at the time potential buyers might want to view, you should leave a key with the estate agent and make it a condition that someone from the estate agent's office will go round with the viewer.)

(See also pages 162 to 164.)

When the buyer's surveyor comes

Expect to have to put yourself to some trouble when the time comes for the valuer or surveyor to inspect. He or she is unlikely to come on a Saturday or Sunday, and will not come in the evening, because he or she will want to inspect in good daylight. A valuation for a lending institution may take only 15 minutes or so, but a full structural survey on a big house will take some hours. When the appointment is made, enquire how long the surveyor is likely to take, so that you can organise your day accordingly.

It will do no harm to prepare for the surveyor. Have steps or a ladder available if possible; make sure all doors and windows are unlocked, including the garage; check that the roof hatch can be moved; check that inspection covers can be opened; have the hot-water system running, and the central heating too, in the winter. Finally, get someone to take the dog for a walk and restrain the children, or vice versa.

Selling an empty house

A house which is furnished and, better still, occupied, is a more attractive proposition to viewers than an empty one. Even if the furniture and decorations are not to others' tastes, the house itself will make a better impression. But the situation can arise when you have to move, taking your furniture with you, before finding a buyer. All that will remain in the house you are selling will be the fixtures and fittings and any items which you are hoping to include in the sale.

When the house is empty, it would be advisable to appoint an estate agent to help with the sale. You should agree with him or her in writing:

- that all viewers be accompanied by the agent or a member of staff
- arrangements for the custody of the keys (squatters in the guise of potential purchasers have been known to have keys copied)
- a list of the items to be included in the sale, and the price of any others which are being offered separately.

Preparing an empty house

If a house is left vacant during the colder months of the year, consider leaving on some kind of heating to prevent the place getting too damp or pipes bursting (not to mention a cold reception for any viewers). A house which has been left empty and shut for any length of time tends to smell either fusty or damp, particularly at a time of year when it would normally be heated.

If a little ventilation can be arranged without risking making it easy for trespassers to enter, this is helpful. In winter, if heating is not possible, the water system must be drained. Remove the telephone or safeguard it against unauthorised use, so that you will not get a bill for calls made to Australia by some unidentified person. See that someone visits regularly to clear the stuff that comes through the letter box – it is a bad sign to have to shove the door open against a mountain of circulars.

Negotiating a sale

Through an estate agent

There is no need to enter into negotiations about price with a buyer if you have appointed an estate agent – this is what you pay him or her for. He or she will act as pig-in-the-middle, passing offer to seller and reconsidered price to buyer. If there are several interested buyers, the agent will try to encourage offers and counter-offers between them. It is in his or her interest to get as high a price as possible because the commission is based on the selling price. But he or she may prefer to get a quick sale and forgo an extra £100 of commission.

Your estate agent may suggest that, as a token of intent, the buyer whose offer you have accepted should put down an initial deposit of perhaps £250. This is of no advantage to you (or your buyer), and it is not as common as it used to be. You (or the estate agent) must get the buyer's full name and address, and that of his or her solicitor/conveyancer, and give him or her yours.

Without an estate agent

If you are not selling through an estate agent, you yourself must act as negotiator. The chances are that the first offer will be less than your asking price. If it is so much less that you could not accept it under any circumstances, you will have no difficulty in rejecting it. Before you do, take stock. Is there a reasonable prospect that you will receive a better offer from this buyer or another? Are you sure you have not pitched your price too high? Could you proceed at that price if you had to (bearing in mind your other commitments and the price of any new property)?

It is sensible to consider all offers calmly. Don't rush to accept or reject any offer.

With or without an estate agent

The following are factors to consider.

Your mortgage and financial requirements
How much is owing on your present mortgage? How much can you afford to borrow on your next property? You should obtain a redemption figure on your existing mortgage and see your lender to obtain an indication of what will be available to you, having regard not only to your means but also the house you want to buy.

The house you want to buy
Have you found a house? If so, have you agreed terms to buy it

and are you under pressure to proceed? If you have already agreed to buy another house, there could be more justification in accepting a lower offer for your own house.

What is the market doing?

If prices are rising, you are much more likely to achieve your asking price than if the market is static or falling. If house sales are sluggish, you could be waiting a long time for another offer.

Checking out your buyer

If you are using an agent, that will be part of his or her job, but you are still involved in the decision making: it is your decision which buyer to go for.

Some buyers are a much better prospect than others. There are even people who obtain a sort of perverse pleasure in making offers for houses which they have no intention of buying. There are others who are so desperate that they will invent anything to secure the house. You have to assess whether your buyer will really buy your house, at the price agreed and within the timescale you have contemplated. You may not have a choice, in which case you have to do the best with any buyer who makes an offer for your house, but if there is more than one, you might rate them in order of preference as follows.

1 The buyer who has actually sold his or her house, moved out and been paid for it. Such people are quite rare, but would be top of the list for reliability, provided, of course, that they do not have difficulties with any mortgage they may need. However, they also know they are in a strong position, and can use it to drive a hard bargain.

2 The first-time buyer. First-time buyers are potentially reliable as they do not have the problem of selling their own property. But – a big but – many houses are beyond the means of first-time buyers. You will need to know that these buyers really do have the wherewithal to go ahead. Ask for some assurance that they can borrow the necessary money – and can pay the balance that they do not borrow. Make sure that they can proceed without delay.

3 The buyer who has sold his or her house 'subject to contract', i.e. has found a buyer, but nobody has yet committed

themselves legally. Many will say at this point that they have actually sold their house. That is not correct, and you should discount such claims. Here you need to know, again, how he or she is going to finance the deal. Can he or she borrow the extra money to make up the price? You should also try to find out whether he or she is selling to a first-time buyer, or to someone who also has a house to sell. In such circumstances, there is likely to be a chain and therefore problems.

4 The buyer who has not sold his or her house. By all means talk to people in that situation. After all, until you find a buyer, it is the same situation as your own. Nevertheless, you would be unwise to negotiate very seriously with someone in that position. It could be months before he or she can proceed. Do not take the house off the market until the situation becomes clearer.

Hard bargaining

Any act of bargaining requires similar skills, whether you are trying to conduct the next wage round with the management or asking the greengrocer to knock six pence off tomatoes. There is often bluff and counter-bluff. Both sides make strenuous efforts to show that they are only marginally interested in the transaction proceeding and that there are plenty more houses/ buyers available.

No advice can really be given on this skill. It is often this quality which makes the difference between a good and a mediocre estate agent. The chances are that the more you do it, the better you may become. If the buyer is genuinely keen and the price is within range of your expectations, most people can reach a compromise. If you do come to an agreement, be sure to cover the relevant points: the price, and what exactly it includes; extras, such as what they are and how much you will sell them for; the expected completion date.

Agreeing terms

Try not to be drawn into some unsatisfactory formula, such as agreeing a right of first refusal to a buyer. That ties your hand without giving you any assurance that you will sell the house.

It is agreed **subject to contract** as follows:

Property: Bide a Wee, The Street, Large Snoring, Norfolk (described in the attached sale particulars)

Price: £50,000 plus £1,000 for the carpets as fitted

Sellers: Albert Raven Sleepy and Denise Dozy Sleepy

Buyers: Larry Edward Snodgrass and Melanie Florence Snodgrass

Completion: Aim for 1st July

Buyer's mortgage: £40,000 to be applied for from the Large Snoring Providential Building Society

Buyer's solicitors: Messrs Snoozing, Dreaming and Nightcap, Bank Chambers, Large Snoring (for the attention of Miss Nightcap)

Seller's solicitors: Messrs Fleecem, Screwem and Cheatem.

Until you have agreed terms, it is best to consider that the house remains firmly on the market.

When you do reach agreement on all the essential details you will need to move on to the legal procedures. You and your buyer might like to draw up a note of what you have agreed. It might look like the above:

It is best not to sign this memorandum, in case you exchange contracts by mistake! However, it records your intentions and you and the buyers should each keep a copy. If you are using an estate agent, he or she will produce a similar memorandum and send it out to all concerned. Remember that the transaction is still not legally binding.

Synchronising the transactions

If you yourself are in the process of buying a house, you will almost certainly wish to exchange contracts on your sale and purchase simultaneously. It would, therefore, be unwise to wait until you are ready to exchange contracts on your purchase before accepting a 'subject to contract' offer on your sale: it will take your buyer several weeks to get to a situation where he or she can also exchange contracts.

To speed things up, you can ask your solicitor to send off the necessary forms to initiate the local authority search. When the replies come, they can be sent directly to the buyer's solicitor. Some local authorities take a long time to deal with these enquiries, so this procedure can save time.

Under the TransAction protocol, your solicitor will send off the search anyway.

The next steps

If you are using a solicitor/conveyancer, your next step is to inform him or her that you have a buyer and to hand over the relevant details – the buyer's name and address, his or her solicitor's/conveyancer's name and the address of the firm, the conditions and price you have agreed, particularly the details of any items included in the sale or being sold additionally, so that these can be incorporated in the contract. The completion date will not be agreed until exchange of contracts but, if you have discussed possible dates with your buyer or if you or he (or she) has special requirements, it is always a good idea to let your solicitor know.

The estate agent does not withdraw the house from the market until contracts have been exchanged unless you, the seller, request this. It is your decision whether the property should be left on the market until contracts are exchanged. The estate agent will be in a position to advise you whether or not to leave it on the market in case the initial interested purchaser should drop out for any reason. If any further offer is received, that person must be advised that there is already an offer on the property, and the initial interested purchaser must be informed of a subsequent offer received.

Many sellers are concerned about choosing who will succeed them in the house, and, having found a buyer they like the look of, they do not want to be bothered with any other offers. The agent may not want to disturb your peace of mind, but he or she does have a clear duty to report all offers to a seller, whether or not the property has already been provisionally sold.

If you tell the agent to withdraw the house, he or she will announce that the property is 'under offer' – often adding this notice to the advertising board outside the house and the shop window if the house is displayed there. Do not forget to get back the keys from the estate agent if you had left them with him or her (to show people round while you are at work, perhaps, or to let in the surveyor). If your house was on the books of more than one agent, inform them all when you no longer need them.

You can stipulate that the exchange of contracts be within a specified period – for example, one month from the date the draft contract is issued to the buyer is a reasonable time for a registered property. This may be worth doing when the market is good and there are several potential buyers around, but not in a poor market where buyers are few and far between.

Your solicitor/conveyancer prepares the contract in draft form to send to the one on the other side.

Contract race

Where there are several equally acceptable offers, it is possible for a seller's solicitor to send out contracts to the solicitors of each of these potential buyers, with a note advising them that the first received back, signed, will get the house. This can be efficacious, but contract races can rebound on the seller: once the buyers know that they risk losing the property, they sometimes all pull out.

Breaking the chain

If you are selling through an agent who participates in a chain-linking scheme and there is a threatened break in a chain of buyer/seller/buyer because your potential buyer has dropped out, ask your agent whether the property is suitable for the chain plan. This means that the agent will arrange to buy your house at a discounted price based on a valuation arranged by the agent, so that the rest of the chain can continue. The house is later sold by the agent, who recoups his or her expenses from the proceeds of that sale. (With the *Chainmaker* service, if the house is eventually sold for more than the agreed valuation, the difference usually goes to the original seller.) It is fairly rare these days due to the decline of the housing market, but you may still be able to find an agent who participates in the scheme. If or when the housing market picks up, chain plans may become more universally available again.

Paying off your mortgage

Your existing mortgage must be repaid when you sell your house. Usually your solicitor will deal with the work involved in redeeming (i.e. paying off) the existing mortgage on the house you are selling, and the fee for this work will generally be included in the fee for the sale. A few building societies or mortgage companies employ their own solicitors to deal with the redemption and you will have to pay the charge made by their solicitors. Some lenders charge a mortgage redemption fee (this may be as much as three months' interest) if the mortgage is paid off within the first years. Most lenders will waive this charge if a new mortgage is being taken out on the next property with them.

The mortgage deed stipulates the length of notice you need to give (or what interest you will have to pay in lieu of notice) when you want to pay off what you still owe. If your completion date is sooner, you may have to pay the stipulated interest but building societies do not always enforce this.

Insurance

You must continue with the insurance of the house until exchange of contracts, when the responsibility passes to the buyer, but it would be wise to keep your own buildings insurance policy going until completion day. If the place burns down between exchange of contracts and completion, and the buyer has not insured, a lot of litigation might be needed to get your money.

Under the terms of the TransAction protocol it remains your responsibility until completion. Keep the contents insurance policy going up to completion day. If you are not going to continue with the same contents policy in your new house, do not cancel it until after the move.

Letting the buyer in

After contracts have been exchanged, the buyer may want to borrow the keys to get into the house (for measuring up, for instance). If you are still living in the property, you can arrange for the buyer to visit while you are at home. If the house is empty and the estate agent contacts you about this, tell him or her to ask the buyer to sign that the keys are issued 'for viewing purposes only: I/we will not take possession'. This is some safeguard against the possibility of an unscrupulous buyer moving in and then causing trouble over completing his or her payment, possibly even claiming protection as a tenant. As a general rule, however, it is unwise for keys to be released to a purchaser after exchange of contracts without a written under-taking prepared by the seller's solicitors and signed by the prospective purchaser. A better alternative may be to ask the estate agent or a member of staff to accompany the buyer.

CHAPTER 8

COUNTDOWN

ONCE you have agreed to buy a new house and to sell your own (if applicable) the procedures for moving house get under way.

Countdown to exchange of contracts

Chapter 7 gives a detailed description of the run up to exchange of contracts.

In practice, as exchange of contracts approaches, you should:

1 be in contact with your solicitor to go through the paperwork and sign the contract
2 check that your finances are in order – everything budgeted for and your loan offer received
3 make sure that your solicitor knows of everything you want included in the contract. If, as part of the deal, the seller has agreed to carry out work or include extra items in the sale *do not* rely on a gentleman's agreement. Get it written into the contract before exchange
4 pay the deposit to your solicitor (if you are a first-time buyer or the deposit on your sale cannot be used or you are topping it up)
5 have discussions with your seller and buyer as to possible completion dates
6 if you have not already done so, check possible completion dates and make provisional arrangements with a removal firm, but do not confirm these until contracts have actually been exchanged.

The date for completion must be agreed at the time contracts are exchanged and is specified in the contract. You may well be involved in two completions – one when your new house becomes yours and, if you are selling as well, when your old one ceases to belong to you. Before fixing the date for completion, both buyer and seller should be certain that they have somewhere to move to on the day.

Ideally, everyone would have two or three days to move from one home to another, but the complex financial arrangements involved in house transfer do not permit this. Unless you are prepared to go to the expense of a bridging loan, you will be stuck with everything happening on the same day. Do not agree to a completion date unless you are sure you can meet it.

If anything should go wrong for the seller's move into his or her new home, he or she cannot expect to remain in the old one: on the date of completion, the seller has to give you vacant possession, and to move out on or before that day with all furniture and belongings (except any that are being sold with the house).

Countdown to completion

The period between exchange of contracts and completion gives you an opportunity to make all your preparations for the move. The moving date is fixed (except, possibly, when you are buying a new home and the contract might specify that the builder will give notification of when the house is ready to move in) and you can confirm the tentative arrangements which you may have made since you first agreed terms for the house.

The legal side of things will be taken care of by your solicitor, but make sure that you stay in contact. There will be plenty of activity on that front.

Practical matters before completion

While the legal matters are being taken care of between exchange of contracts and completion day, there are practical things you can get on with and administrative matters you must not overlook.

Bridging loan

In the rare case where you have to complete your purchase before your sale, your bank might let you have a bridging loan, provided you have exchanged contracts on the sale of your own property and have a firm offer of a mortgage in respect of the purchase. (A few building societies are willing to provide a bridging loan for their borrowers.)

But beware of bridging finance – unless you are not having to bear the cost (for instance, your employer is footing the bill). It is expensive to set up. Most banks charge a setting-up fee of 1 per cent (or a flat fee of £100+) of the loan just for agreeing to lend you the money. On top of that, you will be paying a higher rate of interest.

There is tax relief on the interest on a bridging loan taken out in order to be able to buy a house or flat. If you are still making the mortgage payments on your previous home because you have not yet managed to complete a sale, there is tax relief for a period on both sets of interest payments. The MIRAS (see page 124) scheme does not apply, so you have to claim this relief specifically.

If you have exchanged contracts on your sale, you will at least know that the end is in sight and you can calculate accordingly. But if contracts have not been exchanged, you will need an 'open' bridging loan, because you have no guarantee that the house will sell quickly (some houses take many months to sell). People who take on open-ended bridging loans pay out hundreds, even thousands of pounds in interest. When the market is poor, many banks refuse to give open bridging loans except in very exceptional circumstances. In any event, it is almost never sensible to take on an open-ended bridging loan.

Insurance on the house

From the date when contracts are exchanged to buy a property, the house may no longer be at the seller's risk for insurance purposes. In this case, the buyer must be prepared to take out insurance for any damage to the building itself.

With leasehold properties, the landlord sometimes carries the insurance. Make sure that there is no doubling up of your insurance arrangements.

If you are having a mortgage, the lender will make it a condition that the property is insured, and may offer to arrange cover. If you are getting a building society mortgage, you should be offered at least three companies to choose from, although not all building societies keep to this. Most societies will allow you to arrange your own insurance, but they will want to approve the policy as providing adequate cover for their security, and will charge a fee for the 'administrative costs' of doing so.

The building society often pays the first premium, to make sure that the insurance is effective, and the amount is then deducted from the money you get when your mortgage loan comes through. Some building societies also pay the subsequent insurance premiums and add the amount once a year to the monthly mortgage payments, or allow the borrower to pay part of the premium each month.

A large building society may arrange insurance by means of what is called a block policy, under which a number of buildings are insured. No individual policies are issued, but the building society should give its borrowers full details of the cover provided by the policy.

As soon as contracts are exchanged, ask your solicitor to ensure that insurance cover is in force. However, if the TransAction protocol is being used, the property may remain at the seller's risk for insurance purposes. This is also usual where you are buying a new house from a developer. There is no point in having two insurance policies on the same property – and it can sometimes lead to difficulty in making a claim.

Notify the insurers of your present home that the cover for 'contents' should be transferred to the new address from the day you move in. If you are moving in over several days, get the insurers to hold the contents covered for both addresses.

You have to tell your insurers if you are not moving into the new home straightaway. The cover on a home which is not lived in is generally less extensive.

If you are selling your house, you should keep the insurance cover in force until completion has actually taken place. After that, remember to cancel it, and claim a refund of the unused premium.

Check whether the **sum insured** is adequate. The sum for which you insure should not be the market value (the amount you are about to pay for the house) but the cost of rebuilding it if it should be destroyed, including the cost of clearing away debris and rubble, the architect's and surveyor's fees. This is what is meant by the **reinstatement cost**. Also, there should be an allowance for permanent fittings such as central heating and double-glazing.

The amount for which a house is insured governs how much you will get if a fire or other accident destroys or damages it. If under-insured, you may only be paid a proportion: for example, if you insure for £60,000, but at the time of the incident the reinstatement cost is £90,000, and a fire does £15,000 of damage to the house, then you will receive only two-thirds of the cost of repair (£10,000), even though your claim is well within the amount of your insurance cover.

The Association of British Insurers* issues a free leaflet *Buildings Insurance for Home Owners*, available from the ABI and at some building society and insurance company offices and Citizens Advice Bureaux. This explains how to calculate the amount to insure for on specific sizes and types of houses in various regions of the country, based on rebuilding costs. The figures given in the leaflet are, of necessity, averages. Your house may be more, or less, expensive, than the examples shown. If in doubt, ask a surveyor for an 'estimate of the reinstatement costs'. He or she should not charge a lot for this, if you request it when arranging the survey.

Bear in mind that in the case of an older house in a terrace, or in a street of houses of similar types, if yours is destroyed by fire, the planning authority would almost certainly insist that the replacement should be as much like the original as possible, at least the façade. So, even a small Victorian terrace house, with a stone bow window, could be very expensive to replace.

Nowadays, nearly all insurance companies issue index-linked policies, with the sum insured linked to the house rebuilding costs index and changing automatically as the average cost of rebuilding changes, although the premium you pay does not change until renewal.

You should hold on to the buildings policy for the house you are leaving because you remain liable under the Defective Premises Act: most policies will cover this liability for seven years after the sale.

Contents insurance

If your buildings insurance is now with a different insurance company because of the building society's requirement, it may be practical to transfer the contents insurance to the same company. (This would simplify matters if you should have a claim involving both the building and the contents policy, such as a burglary claim.) You should claim a refund of the unexpired part of the premium – if the unused part of the insured term makes this worthwhile.

The sum for which you insure the contents may have to be adjusted if you are buying a lot of new things for the new house or are selling a lot on moving out of the old one. The premium you have to pay may also be different because of the different area and type of house to which you are moving.

Motor insurance

Your motor insurers will have to be informed of the new address and whether or not the car will be garaged, which may affect the premium.

Council Tax and water charges

Council Tax on a property in England or Wales depends on the tax band in which the house has been put and the tax charged per band. Information is available from the local authority for the area where the house is situated.

Water

Water charges are levied by the relevant water authority, not by the local authority in England and Wales (in Scotland, water rates are paid along with ordinary rates). For domestic consumers, the charges are generally based, at present, on a percentage of the property's rateable value; if metered, they are based on exact consumption plus a standing charge.

A move to a new house may be the moment to change to metered water consumption if you calculate that this would be financially advantageous. The water authority for your new area will be able to give you information about their charges.

Even if your water consumption is metered, you have to pay a charge for sewerage and environmental services, at present based on the rateable value of the property. A sewerage charge is not payable if there is no connection to the public sewer.

Apportionment

The seller is responsible for Council Tax and water charges for the part of the rating year before the completion date, and the buyer for the part after the completion date. For example, if completion takes place on 1 July, the seller must bear the liability for the 92 days which make up the months of April, May and June, while the buyer must accept liability for the remaining 273 days of the rating year. It used to be a convention for rates and water charges to be apportioned on a day-to-day basis, not weekly or monthly. Nowadays, the local or water authority prefers to make the necessary adjustments, as this helps it to keep its records up to date.

Accounts

Your bank account or accounts may need to be transferred to a branch in your new area. If you have not already noted the address of the one nearest to your new home, your present branch will be able to find out for you. Your bank manager may require a formal letter asking for the transfer to be made on a certain date. You can arrange this by visiting the branch you wish your account to be transferred to. You will be given a standard 'transfer' letter to sign. Ask for the new branch's bank-code number and your new account number(s) so that you can notify anybody who pays directly into your account or debits it directly. You can go on using your existing cheque book and card until you get the new ones.

With a bank deposit account, it is important that there is continuity so that no interest is lost. Check in due course that the closing date at your old branch and the opening date at the new one are the same.

Even if you do not need to move your account, you will have to notify the bank of your new address. This applies generally to all savings accounts – such as building society or National Savings.

Charge accounts

If you have accounts which are paid weekly or monthly by post or personally with retailers in the area, write or telephone a request for these to be closed and any outstanding accounts to be sent to you, either to your old or your new address.

If you intend to continue to use a monthly or budget account at a large retail store, you will have to notify your new address, so that the accounts will be sent to you at that address. An inadvertent lapse on paying an outstanding bill (sent to the wrong address) may get you on to a computer record as a bad risk without your realising that this has happened. You should also notify any credit card company of your change of address.

Hire of TV

If you hire your television set and/or video recorder, check with the rental firm whether you can take it with you to your new home: if necessary, have your account transferred to another branch. This would be worth doing if you have been paying a reduced rent for an older set. Otherwise, turn in the set and take out a new contract locally for another one.

It is more usual to include a roof TV aerial in the sale of a house – also more sensible. But if you have decided to take it with you, you will have to arrange to have the aerial taken down off the roof (the removal men will not do this) and then to have it put up on your new roof – and will have to pay someone to do this.

Forwarding mail

You can collect from any post office a form requesting redirection of mail, to fill in and return to your local sorting office with the appropriate fee. The post office will re-direct your letters and parcels as follows:

● letters – for an initial charge (£6) for a period of up to one month, followed by a further charge (£13) for any period up to three months, or up to one year (£30)

- parcels – a charge equal to the original postage is generally payable on each parcel on delivery to the new address (only inland parcels will be redirected).

Seven days' notice must be given before the date you want the redirection to start. The request form must be signed by all those in the household who want their mail redirected, and a separate fee is payable per surname if there is more than one. (As an added precaution, make sure that the new owner knows your new address, and ask him or her to redirect any mail that comes for you.)

The same form contains a section for you to complete for notifying the National TV Licence Records Office in Bristol of your change of address.

Change of address notification

If you intend to have your own change-of-address cards printed, arrange this far enough in advance to allow time for the printing to be done. It is advisable to include both your new and old addresses on it because if you are notifying organisations which keep geographical lists, they will only be able to trace you by your old address. Some removal firms supply cards free.

To help you estimate how many change-of-address cards you will need, make a check list of organisations you may need to advise and then tick off each one as you send the notification. After your move, you can check against your list any incoming mail which has had to be redirected by the post office and, if necessary, notify any sender you may have forgotten or remind those who on their side have forgotten or not noticed.

One thing that may hold up your preparation for change-of-address cards is having to wait for your new telephone number.

Do not get change-of-address cards printed till contracts have been exchanged.

The following is a basic check list for change of address notification.

Finance

- bank: if moving to another area, authorise transfer of accounts to new branch, cancel any standing orders no longer needed

- Girobank: ask at the post office about procedures
- building societies: take your account book to any branch
- pension/benefit book: notify your local social security office; nominate a new post office or give the new number of an account for paying in; if your pension is sent quarterly, tell DSS Central Pensions Branch, Newcastle upon Tyne NE98 1YX
- National Insurance: notify your social security office of the old and new address, giving your National Insurance number (as on your pay slip). If employed, your employer will do this for you
- Inland Revenue: tell your inspector of taxes
- Premium Savings Bonds: complete the notification card attached to your holder's card or form P2767 at a post office and sent to Bonds and Stock Office, Lytham St Annes, Lancashire FYO 1YN
- National Savings Certificates and Save-As-You-Earn: send old and new addresses and holder's number to Savings Certificate and SAYE Office, Durham DH99 1NS
- stocks and shares: write to the registrar (details on share certificate and dividend vouchers); give new bank details if dividend paid directly. Also, inform your stockbroker
- credit card companies, hire purchase company, local authority (Council Tax), water authority: amend standing order for payment by instalments

Insurance
- broker/agent
- life insurance company
- any other insurers

Car
- vehicle registration: complete the section on your vehicle registration document and send it to DVLC, Swansea SA99 1BN
- driving licence: complete the section on your present licence and send it to DVLC, Swansea SA99 1BN
- motor insurers (premium may change)
- AA, RAC or other motoring organisation

- NHS or private doctor/dentist, private health insurers
- National Blood Transfusion Service: if you are not moving out of the area, notify your present centre
- hospital, clinic or day centre

Work and leisure
- employer
- firm's (and previous firms') pension fund
- trade union, professional association
- TV licence records office: Barton House, Bristol BS98 ITL (can be done via post office or on mail redirection form)
- VAT office (if you pay VAT)

Others
- children's school(s)
- clubs, societies or any organisation you belong to, magazine or book club, football-pools company
- charities to which you regularly donate money
- public library (and return all borrowed books)
- mail order firm(s)
- theatre, concert or other mailing lists
- *Which?* (complete the address slip in the latest *Which?* and return it to Castlemead, Gascoyne Way, Hertford SG14 ILH) and other subscription publications

Do not forget to add relatives or friends whom you want to inform – and any individual or organisation from whom you are expecting a communication. For instance, if your children have been offered provisional places at university or college (pending A-level results or similar), make sure UCAS or the college knows (ask for an acknowledgement), lest the places get filled for lack of prompt reply.

Also, leave a change–of–address card or two for the incoming occupant with a request to forward mail and redirect telephone calls (and leave behind any headed stationery you may have left over).

Arrangements for new schools

If you are moving into a new area and want to find a new school for your child, send details of him or her to the local education authority of the area you are moving to and ask for help in finding a place. The authority should send a list of all available schools in the area, and may send prospectuses of individual schools. You can write direct to the schools for information and to arrange a visit; do not commit your children to a school until you have visited it.

The Education Authorities Directory and Annual and *The Primary Education Directory*, published by the School Government Publishing Company★, give information about state schools. The Advisory Centre for Education★ also produces useful publications.

If you want information about private schools, contact the Independent Schools Information Service (ISIS)★ or the Regional Director, ISIS (Scotland)★. ISIS has published a book *Choosing Your Independent School*. The Scottish Education Department★ can provide a list of independent schools.

A number of education yearbooks and guides give information about independent schools (for example, *The Independent Schools Yearbook* in two volumes, one for boys' and one for girls' schools, published by A & C Black; *Which School?* published by J Catt Educational; Gabbitas *Guide to Independent Schools* published by Kogan Page); all should be available in public reference libraries.

Information about approved pre-school playgroups and private nursery schools is obtainable from the local authority's social services department, and information about maintained nursery schools and nursery classes at primary schools from the local education authority. Information about nursery, primary and secondary schools in Scotland is available from education departments at relevant regional council offices.

The Pre-school Playgroups Association★ can tell you about any playgroups in an area.

Telephone

It is worth liaising with your seller (and a kindness to do so with your buyer) to save unnecessary disconnection and reconnection

191

charges or having to be without a telephone for any length of time. The telephones at the new address may be owned by the previous occupant, the seller, who may unplug them and take them away. You would then have to make arrangements to buy or rent the telephones you would like to have.

Giving up your existing telephone

Notify the sales office of your local telephone area at least seven working days in advance that you will be moving out. The number to ring is in the front of the telephone directory. Give the date when you want to stop renting and being charged for the telephone, and give the address to which your final account up to that date should be sent. At the same time, say if the buyer of your present house or flat wishes to take over the telephone from you, so that the line will be left for him or her (he or she will have to apply to take it over). The rental charge will be apportioned between you on your next telephone accounts.

Getting a telephone at your new address

Contact the sales office in your new area as soon as possible, by letter or telephone (if you are moving out of the area, dial 100 and ask for the appropriate number to ring in the new area). Explain what you want: either to have a telephone installed at the new address or to take over the existing line there. Whether this can happen and when depends on the availability of telephone lines in that area.

If you do not want any of the extras that the previous occupant had – such as extensions or coloured or special telephones – ask for them to be taken away. This will save on the quarterly rental.

If you own your telephone, you can take it with you if the new house has modern plug-in sockets. If it does not, new sockets (or at least one) will have to be installed. If you do not own a telephone, this may be the time to buy one; but there is no reason not to continue renting.

When you are taking over an existing telephone and number and the line remains unbroken, there is no takeover charge, but if the line is unconnected, even for just a day, there will be a charge.

If you are moving within the same telephone exchange area to a new address, it is usually possible to take your existing number with you if you want to, but you will be charged for doing so.

If you are to have a new telephone line, ask what the likely delay is. An engineer may have to come and see how the wiring is to be brought into the house. There is an installation charge – BT's present maximum is £116.33 including VAT for a new telephone customer, less for someone who has previously been a subscriber. The number is not usually allocated or confirmed in advance of the actual installation – this may hold up your change of address notifications.

A BT booklet *In touch*, with details of the features of phones and systems available for renting or buying from BT, can be obtained from BT shops or by dialling 150. You can also obtain pricing and bill-paying information by phoning the same number.

Gas and electricity

In a newly built house, the builder is almost always responsible for paying to have mains supplies laid on, but you must still make an application direct to the relevant authority for the supply (gas/electricity/telephone) to be connected up and for you to become responsible for payment.

You cannot make definite arrangements until contracts have been exchanged and a date fixed for completion, but subject to this, contact the suppliers of household services well in advance of your moving out and moving in date so that you can give sufficient notice to book the work to be done on the day and at the time you want. Meters can be read at fairly short notice, but if you want a fitter to connect or disconnect appliances or turn on or off supplies at an appointed time, give at least a week's notice, preferably more. And confirm the day before that someone is coming at the right time.

If the house you are going to has been previously occupied, the owner should, on his or her part, tell the local gas and electricity companies that he or she is going and that you are moving in. But some people leave without informing the gas or electricity company and arranging for the meter to be read, so it would be best to have them read on your arrival, too.

Gas

If you are going to the area of a different gas company, ask at your present service centre for the address and telephone number of your new one. Then, get in touch, either personally or in writing, well in advance, so that you can sign an application form for taking over the supply and make arrangements for the meter to be read and, if necessary, can have the supply turned on, on the day you move in. At the same time, you can arrange for a service engineer to call to connect any appliance and to alter the gas supply pipe to fit the incoming appliance, if necessary. The charge for connection is normally slightly more than the disconnection charge.

Gas cookers can be fitted with a plug-in flexible hose instead of rigidly, so that the cooker can be easily moved for cleaning. You may want to have this fitted to your cooker when you take it to a new house.

A deposit is not usually asked for when taking over a gas supply unless a customer is known to have been a bad payer or has previously not had a gas account and cannot give an acceptable credit reference or guarantor.

Electricity

To arrange for your meter to be read on leaving, you should notify the local electricity company, giving as much notice as you can. You may be asked to fill in a form of notification of removal, giving your old and new address and details of your date of departure, and the name and address of the incoming consumer (if you know it at this stage).

Ask for a meter reader to come on the day of your move before you leave. (There is no charge for this.) Telephone the day before, to confirm the time that he or she is coming.

You have to make formal application to the electricity company where you are going, for a supply to be made available. There is an application form to be completed. If you are not able to visit the local showroom in advance, write or telephone and ask for the form to be sent to you beforehand, together with details of its tariffs. You can get the address or telephone number from your local (where you are now) showroom.

The application form usually asks for the approximate total wattage you expect to use, so that the electricity company can check that the installation will be large enough to cope with your maximum demand. Ask the showroom for advice or put down on the form the total number of watts your appliances would use if they were all switched on full. (The wattage is usually marked on a plate somewhere on each appliance.)

The form also asks which sort of tariff you want to be on. If you are going to install storage heaters and off-peak water heating, or if you run a washing machine, tumble dryer and dishwasher in the night, you will want the Economy 7 tariff instead of the standard tariff.

You could be asked for evidence of your past record of paying, or asked for a deposit. If you have to pay a deposit, this earns interest, credited to you once a year, and will normally be refunded when you leave the company's area or have established credit-worthiness by paying bills promptly. You will not be asked for a deposit if you agree to pay a regular amount each week or month, have a slot meter put in, or give an acceptable credit reference or guarantor.

If the house is to be empty for a period, the company may ask you if the supply is to be left connected or not (there is no charge for disconnection and reconnection in these circumstances). This may depend on whether you are having any work done before you move in, when the workmen would need an electricity supply for lights, heating, electric drills or other tools. Also, if during the winter you want to keep the central heating on low, it needs electricity to run it, even if it is gas or oil-fired heating.

Lighting and sockets
Ask the present owner to show you where the electricity main switch and the consumer unit and fuses are.

You may need additional or replacement light fittings if the seller is removing any that he or she is entitled to. He or she must not remove lamp holders or sockets or leave bare wires. There is no basis for the belief that one electric bulb must be left for the incoming owner: you should be prepared to find none and should be armed with a supply.

Compare the number of socket outlets in the house with the number of appliances you have. If you have many more appliances than there are sockets, you will need adaptors to begin with but must be careful not to overload the electrical circuits and should consider installing more socket outlets. Where sockets are in places that would make it difficult to use your appliances, you may have to fit longer flexes on yours or buy an extension lead.

The heating system

Find out from the present owner as much as you can about the operation and maintenance of any central heating system and water heating, and ask him or her to leave you any instruction booklets there may be.

If the system uses oil or solid fuel, check how much fuel is being left and confirm how much you will have to pay for it (if anything), and what the arrangements have been for delivery.

Ask for the name of a local plumber and electrical contractor and get details of any maintenance contract there has been, and when a service was last done. Discuss the possibility of taking over the contract.

Measuring for curtains and flooring

Check what kind of curtain rails there are (if they are being left) in case you need to change the hooks and attachments on your curtains. Have any curtains cleaned before rehanging them.

When you measure for new fitted carpets so that you can give the carpet shop 'approximate' details, take the measurements from skirting board to skirting board and explain to the retailer when ordering the carpet that you have not allowed for the turnings required for the edging strips now normally used for fixing fitted carpets. Do not assume that opposite walls in a room are parallel: not all corners are an accurate 90 degrees, nor is every chimney breast the same thickness. The carpet supplier will be responsible for accurate measuring and fitting.

The kitchen, too, needs careful measuring if you intend to put down new tiles or other floor coverings. An accurate floor plan will also help you to work out where your present equipment will fit in and, if you are getting a new cooker, fridge or washing machine, what size and shape to order.

When you have measured, chosen and ordered any new curtains, carpeting, floor covering, bathroom or kitchen fitments, get them delivered, where appropriate, to the new address, on or after completion day.

On completion day

On completion day, all the weeks and months of worry and preparation will reach their climax.

The money

On the day of completion, the buyer must be able to pay the remainder of the purchase price. The money for this may come from various sources:

- anything left over after discharging your own mortgage from what your buyer (or his or her building society) pays for the house you are selling
- your new mortgage loan (the building society or other lender's percentage of the purchase price of the house you are buying)
- any top-up loan
- a bridging loan if you have not completed your sale or there is a temporary shortfall
- your own cash from savings.

From the total mortgage loan, the lender may deduct:

- the amount of the first premium for the buildings insurance policy
- the premium for a mortgage indemnity policy if you had to take one out
- the lender's solicitor's charges (if the same solicitor is not acting for you and the lender).

197

If the same solicitor is acting for you and the lender he or she may deduct from the amount of the advance his or her own fee and any disbursements – the charges he or she pays on your behalf, such as stamp duty and Land Registry fees – where applicable.

It is normally a condition of a mortgage that the solicitor should have in his or her hands on completion sufficient money to pay the stamp duty and Land Registry fees.

In case the remaining amount will be less than is needed to complete the purchase, ask the solicitor or conveyancer in good time what the deductions and final amount will come to, so that you can make arrangements to finance the shortfall.

You may be charged interest from the date on which the loan leaves the lender (or, with some, the following day), even if it is not used for a few days. With other lenders, interest is charged from the date of completion, which your solicitor specifies in the request for the money. Whichever procedure the lender follows, your solicitor should not get the loan money too early.

If you are getting an endowment mortgage, you may have to pay the first premium on the endowment policy. Make sure that the policy is put on risk at the right time.

If any part of the money is not coming from a mortgage, your solicitor or conveyancer will ask you either for a cheque in sufficient time to have it cleared so that he or she can draw a cheque on the firm's account for the money, or for a banker's draft. A banker's draft is a cheque signed by a bank manager, or one of his or her staff, on behalf of the bank instead of the customer; it cannot be stopped as a cheque can be and so is treated in practice as being equivalent to cash.

Usually, on completion, your solicitor will make the final payment to the seller's solicitor by sending the money by telegraphic transfer from one bank to another. The fee for this is around £20 + VAT.

When the final payments are made, the deeds will be handed over, including the conveyance or transfer to the buyer. You do not, however, get the title deeds of the property or a land certificate if you have a mortgage: the relevant documents are kept by the building society, or whoever is the lender, as security for the money being lent.

It is not usual for either the seller or the buyer to attend personally at the completion (unless they are doing their own conveyancing without a solicitor or conveyancer).

In the days leading up to completion, stay in touch with your solicitor or conveyancer, but get on with the move and let him or her take care of the rest.

Timetable and check list for moving
Tick when done

About four weeks to a week before:

☐ Get 3 removal firms' estimates and/or quotes for d-i-y van hire charges (the earlier the better for this)

☐ Choose firm; confirm arrangements

☐ D-i-y: alert friends/family for help on the day (packing, driving, providing meals, cleaning up, being available)

Old address

☐ Arrange for meters to be read

☐ Arrange for disconnection of cooker, washing machine, dishwasher

☐ Arrange for carpets to be cleaned if required

New address

☐ Arrange for taking over gas, electricity

☐ Arrange for reconnection of cooker, washing machine, dishwasher

☐ Arrange for carpets to be laid

In general

☐ Notify telephone sales office of date account to be closed

☐ Apply to take over telephone or request new telephone to be installed at new address and extra sockets if required

☐ Change-of-address cards – buy, or order printing (after new telephone number known)

☐ Arrange insurance of contents at new house from date of moving and during removal

☐ Start sorting and throwing out things, getting rid of surplus

☐ Arrange extra rubbish disposal

☐ Get boxes, packing material, strong string

☐ Buy stick-on labels

☐ Arrange any hotel booking that may be needed

☐ Children – arrange to leave with relatives/friends

☐ Pets – book kennels/other arrangements to be made

One week before

☐ Prepare diagram of new house with location of furniture

☐ Send off change-of-address cards

☐ Bank etc. – arrange for transfer of account

☐ Post office – apply for redirection of mail

Old address

Arrange cancellation of deliveries and settlement of accounts:

☐ milk

☐ newspapers

☐ laundry

New address

☐ Arrange deliveries, e.g. milk

In general

☐ Put valuables and documents in bank/safe place

☐ Tell police of imminent move

☐ Check arrangements for hiring van/borrowing car

☐ Get own car serviced

Confirm arrangements and timings for meter readings and disconnection/connection at old/new address:

- [ ] electricity

- [ ] gas

Arrange with seller and buyer about leaving off/on:

- [ ] electricity

- [ ] water

- [ ] heating

- [ ] Arrange to leave keys at old address

- [ ] Check arrangements for collecting keys at new address

- [ ] Finish packing and labelling

- [ ] Prepare survival kit

Day before

- [ ] Pack personal overnight case(s)

- [ ] Organise meals/drinks for moving day

- [ ] Switch freezer to maximum (if moving it with contents)

- [ ] Take children to relatives or friends to stay

- [ ] Deliver pets to kennels or elsewhere

- [ ] Get supply of cash (e.g. for tips, meals, petrol, coins for emergency telephone calls)

- [ ] Defrost refrigerator

- [ ] Go to bed early

Moving house

Fixing the date of your move

IT IS important to realise that once contracts are exchanged and you have agreed on a date for completion, you must move (or at least pay for your new house if you are not selling one) on that day or risk having to face large claims for compensation and court proceedings.

Most people try to arrange for the completion of their sale and purchase to take place on the same day. This means that your old home must be vacated on the day your buyer hands over the purchase money to you, and you must be prepared to move out on that day.

When settling on a date, check the day of the week. Completions are often on Fridays at the end of the month. But Friday is not necessarily the ideal day on which to move. Even though this would give you a weekend to settle in, if you arrange delivery of goods or the connections of any services – gas, electricity, for example – for Friday afternoon, if anything should go wrong with any appointments, you could find yourself without a cooker or power for three days. Similarly, if you need professional help in an emergency – a plumber, say – it is going to be more difficult (and probably more expensive) if it is a weekend. For the same reason, you should avoid bank holiday periods. (Scottish holidays do not necessarily coincide with bank holidays in England and Wales.)

If you are moving some distance away, allow for the fact that the move will have to be spread over two days, with an overnight stop somewhere. Also, if a long-distance removal is involved – say, from the south to Scotland – you would have to pay overtime for the remover's staff to travel back on a Saturday. Moreover, there are tight restrictions on the hours a driver of a heavy goods vehicle may legally drive in the course of a day or week, so you may have to pay for weekend accommodation.

Removal firms tend to be heavily booked at the beginning and end of the month, so you may stand a better chance of getting the firm you want on the day you want if you pick a day in the middle of the month. And if you are able to move during a period outside the peak moving periods (school holidays, particularly the summer), the cost may be less.

It is not possible to predict whether the previous owners are the kind of people who will leave their home spotlessly clean on vacating it – or at least clear of unwanted rubbish. As well as allowing yourself sufficient time for clearing up your house on leaving it, you should be prepared for the probability that you will have to clean your new one before putting your possessions into it. If you move on the day of completion of your purchase, you will have no opportunity for preliminary cleaning. You could find the floors need cleaning before any carpets you have brought with you can be laid.

If you want a little time to clean up, lay the carpets, prepare the house and generally relieve the pressure, you should assess whether it would be worth completing your purchase a few days before the day of completing your sale – with a bridging loan to tide you over.

If it was your buyer who chose the date because it suited him or her to move in then and you accepted this, you may not have a new home, or not be able to move into it, on the day you have to vacate your old one.

Particularly where a newly built house is concerned, there is a serious risk that it will not be completed by the promised date(s) due to over-optimistic calculations by the builder.

If you cannot move straight out of the old home into the new one, it may be necessary to put your belongings into store and to find a temporary home, perhaps in rented accommodation, a hotel, or with relatives or friends. These extra expenses can add considerably to the cost of your move.

Putting furniture into store

The expense of putting furniture into store is based on:

- the cost of getting it packed up and taken to the depository
- the charge per cubic foot for the time it has to be in store
- the insurance
- the cost of getting the furniture out of storage
- the cost of delivering it to the new house.

Removal firms with storage facilities can be found in the *Yellow Pages* or similar local directory, or by asking the British Association of Removers (BAR)★ for the names of three members based in your area. Unless there is no choice in the area, you should preferably get more than one estimate.

Storage firms accept the whole contents of a house with the exception of perishable goods such as food and plants, and of flammable goods such as matches, fuel or paint. They recommend that carpets and rugs be cleaned first and some will arrange this for you. Clothes and blankets should be treated with a moth deterrent – storage firms do not accept responsibility for moth damage.

Generally, goods are stored loose, covered but not encased, in a space allocated to you in the depository. You can inspect your goods in the warehouse (sometimes for a small charge), unless they are housed in containers.

Containerisation is now becoming the accepted method of storage: goods are packed into sealed containers at your home and these are stored untouched in a warehouse until required. The advantage is that the risk of damage by movement or careless handling during transit and warehousing is greatly reduced; also, there is much greater protection from dust and dirt and a lower possibility of loss.

You should have an inventory (and, if in containers, a note of what has been put into each one). Note the value of all items. Insurance premiums are often based on the total declared value; storage charges are more likely to be based on the space required.

Storage insurance

Insurance cover can be arranged through the storage firm, or your household insurers may give you special cover for these circumstances. Make sure it is for a sufficient sum and for 'all risks', including fire, flooding and any other loss or damage. Insurers usually charge an all-in premium covering transit from your house to the warehouse, storage for a given length of time, and transit from the warehouse to your new home. (If you later find that you need a longer period of storage, the cover can be extended by paying an additional premium.)

There may be an individual limit on specific items (of crockery, for instance), but if one item gets broken and that style is no longer made, you would have to replace the set; make sure that the insurance cover is sufficient for such a situation (the premium may be high). Check any policy carefully for exclusions and excess clauses (an excess is the amount of any claim you have to pay yourself).

Getting goods out

If you think you will want to take some items away earlier than others – for example, carpets or cooker – you should advise the storage firm at the start so that these can be labelled and stored as 'keep forward' items, accessible for collection when required. If the storage firm delivers these, there will be a charge per delivery. Written authorisation is usually required if you want someone else to collect any of your goods for you.

Find out how much notice is required for getting your goods out of store when you eventually need them. If the delivery is not done by the storage firm, you may have to pay a handing-out charge.

When all your goods are delivered to you, check the inventory as soon as they arrive. Without any attempt to steal or defraud, one packing case might be left behind at the warehouse; it is easier to trace if this is notified at once, rather than some weeks later when the warehouse space may have been filled and the premises rearranged. Your insurance may stipulate that any claim must be made within a set period.

Renting storage space

In some places, there are 'self-access' facilities for storage of possessions in specially constructed steel-walled compartments or units, in a secured building or a 'mini-warehouse'. You are the only person who has a key to the compartment you rent or who is told the control code to gain entry, and you are free to go at any time within working hours to get your possessions. There is an initial refundable deposit, and you then pay monthly, according to the space taken and the period booked. You have to arrange your own insurance cover.

Arranging the move

Using a removal firm is a more expensive way of moving than borrowing or hiring a van and doing your own removal with the help of friends or relatives.

A lot will depend on how much stuff you have to move. If you have a considerable quantity of furniture or belongings, or a number which are large, heavy or awkward to move, or if there are any difficulties of access (flights of stairs or long distances to carry furniture out or in), do not do it yourself unless you are very strong and prepared for really hard work.

The preparatory work of clearing up before leaving a home, plus organising and preparing the new one, can be extremely tiring. If this is then to be followed by one or two days of hard physical work, lifting and carrying for hours on end, the effect can be cumulatively one of total exhaustion.

If you are working full-time, or if you are elderly or unfit, pregnant or have small children, you may think it worth the cost of paying for all the packing and moving to be done by experts, so that all you have to do is the supervisory work, plus transporting yourself (and your family) from one place to the other. Even with a removal firm, the actual day of the move is a tiring one.

Removal men are usually experienced, and pack and move quickly – much quicker than you could. They may not seem to be as careful with your belongings as you would be but a professional remover is used to handling articles in a way that avoids damage.

If you are moving further than a short distance, particularly if you have a lot of furniture, using a removal firm will be more practical than hiring a self-drive van with which you would have to make several journeys (plus one more in order to return the van to its owner).

Using a removal firm

If you decide to pay for a firm to do your removal for you, you should set about choosing one well in advance. Find out the names of local firms as well as the large national firms and ask friends and neighbours for recommendations and warnings.

The BAR will give the names and addresses of three members and send you helpful leaflets if you send an s.a.e. Many firms who are members of the BAR provide similar leaflets – or a whole kit of them – for potential customers.

Prices vary considerably, so you should get at least two, preferably three, estimates. These are usually given free. If you are moving to a different area, consider getting a quotation from firms in the area you are moving to.

Getting an estimate

As soon as you have some idea of the date of your move, ask the removal firms to send a representative to give you an estimate. It is not wise to accept an estimate given over the telephone: you may find yourself supplied with too few men or too small a van when the day comes (or too large a van – and bill).

When the estimator arrives, he or she should inspect your whole house and garden to see the quantity and type of furniture and belongings involved. Do not forget to include the contents of any loft, garage or garden shed. Also, point out if any items are to be left behind, have to be picked up from some other place or are being bought before the move, so that these are taken into account in the estimate.

Charges may be calculated according to the quantity and type of belongings to be packed and moved. The firm's estimator can judge how many van loads and how many men will be needed. He or she will take into account whether the move is a local one, which can be completed in one day, or, if it is a long-distance move, the length of time it will take and how many overnight stays there may have to be.

Or, charges may be estimated according to the time taken over the packing and move or may be based on an hourly rate (not suitable for a move of any distance), by half a day or a whole day. Check what the hours concerned are: when does morning/afternoon begin and end? Is a day 8 hours, 12 hours or 24 hours? Does the rate per hour vary according to the time of day? When would overtime start, and at what rate? (If you do not get access to your new home until, say, after lunch, you could be involved in overtime.)

Hourly charges are normally based on a depot-to-depot principle, but meal times are usually excluded from the charge. Charges may be more (or less) expensive for a move on certain days of the week, but this would not help you if you are committed to move on a certain day because of your completion

If you are able to reduce the quantity to be packed by doing a lot of it yourself beforehand, you could reduce the cost. If you are moving only a short distance, and have access to your new home before the day of the move, you can transport small loads yourself in advance.

Things to discuss with the estimator

Removal firms do not generally accept responsibility for damage to any items which have not been packed by them, and nor do their insurers.

_ You should point out to the estimator any of your belongings that may need special packing, or may present problems in handling or transporting, such as:

- pictures
- audio equipment, records
- collections of valuable objects
- antiques, fragile items
- books, if a large quantity or of special quality
- freezer, home safe
- wine

- plants, animals
- any heater or appliance fuelled with LPG.

Things to discuss with the estimator

You may ask the firm	Pro	Con
to pack everything	important if you work full time/are elderly/unfit/have small children	more expensive
to pack only your crockery and glass for you	cheaper	needs effort and plenty of time in advance to pack contents of wardrobes, cupboards, bookcases
to provide chests, crates or purpose-made cardboard cartons for you to do packing	even cheaper	needs time in advance, effort and skill in packing breakables properly; if you pack and they carry, you may have difficulty in getting compensation for any breakage
to do the unpacking for you	important if you work full time/are elderly/unfit/have small children	more expensive; need to know at once where in new house items are to be unpacked (tiring exercise at end of moving day)
to do no unpacking and collect cases at later date (may not be possible for a move to an area some distance away)	unpacking can be done at leisure; cuts cost, especially if charge is on hourly basis (unless there is a charge for collecting later)	needs somewhere to store emptied cases to await collection; deposit payable for cases left, may be only 50% refund on collection
whether the move needs to be spread over more than one day	possibly less wear and tear/ pressure	extra expense (including overnight accommodation)

Point out any built-in cupboards or shelves that will need dismantling to get them out (but they may not be designed to be dismantled and reassembled – some of the cheaper chipboard systems will not fit together again satisfactorily).

For pictures and mirrors, there are corrugated packs which the removal firm might offer to supply; mattress sacks are also available.

Some firms offer special cardboard carton or 'travel boxes' for use with an inner paper sack or liner (which can be filled separately) that fits into the box. The advantage is that the paper sacks can be sent by post to the client who can fill them ahead of time, and they are then left to be unpacked at leisure after the move. The cartons are less likely to snag the carpet or scratch the floor than the old-fashioned tea chests, and can be carried by one person.

Piano Some firms have special trolleys ('shoes') and webbing for transporting pianos and are accustomed to handling them. Others sub-contract to a specialist transport firm, particularly if there is any difficulty about getting an instrument in or out of a house or flat – through a window, for instance. Check with the estimator and, if your piano is a valuable one or there is any problem about moving it, consider engaging a specialist firm. Look in the local classified telephone directory or contact any local concert hall, theatre or piano retailer for advice. (Allow a piano time to recover from its journey before having it retuned.)

Carpets If any are to be moved, discuss whether the men will lift and re-lay these, will only spread them out on delivery, or will simply unload them. Lifting and re-laying, particularly of fitted carpets, may incur extra charges.

Clothes Ask whether clothes, linen, or other contents can be left in drawers, and whether the removers can provide 'wardrobe' packing cartons to hang clothes in (these are large, collapsible cardboard cartons in which there is a clip-on plastic rail on which clothes can be hung straight from a wardrobe). Some firms will leave these for collection later, so that the cartons need not be unpacked immediately.

Access If the approach to your new home (or to the present one) is at all difficult, mention this to the removal firm's estimator. A steep drive might be too much for a large van, or a narrow entrance or approach road could mean having to use two smaller vans. Many houses do not have direct access for a van, so if belongings will have to be carried a long distance from van to house, tell the removal firm's estimator.

If there are parking problems at either end – for instance, restrictions on parking during certain hours – you will be expected to make arrangements with the local police for permission to load or unload, or pay to have a parking meter suspended. The removers may ask you to reserve a parking space if possible the night before.

Go over the layout of your new home in your mind and assess whether there could be any problems about getting any of your furniture into it. Narrow staircases or awkward corners, for example, could mean temporarily taking a window out in order to get access to a room, and the removers might need to bring special equipment to deal with this. Do not leave it until the day of the move but warn the estimator when he or she is with you – otherwise, you could be faced with extra charges for difficulties in unloading.

Do not think that if you say nothing about likely difficulties they will not add to the cost. On the contrary, if there is any serious delay, you are likely to get an extra bill.

If anything is not absolutely straightforward, confirm your requirements in writing so that the firm has no excuse to say that it was not agreed or included in the estimate.

Acceptance of the estimate
The firm's estimate is likely to be on a standard form which incorporates the terms and conditions. Study carefully the small print concerning claims, exclusion clauses about liability (even though, in law, they may not be enforceable) and insurance cover. If a removal firm is a member of the BAR, it will probably use a standard contract, the clauses of which have been drawn to protect the firm. You may be able to add terms of your own or ask for unacceptable ones to be deleted.

Although the terms and conditions are usually the same, prices can vary considerably from firm to firm. Many firms ask for payment to be made in advance; you may be able to arrange to pay on the day of the move. Some firms accept credit cards: this can help to spread your outgoings.

When you accept an estimate, you are expected to give a firm date for the job and, having booked a date, you would have to give reasonable notice if you want to change it – otherwise, the firm may well charge a cancellation fee.

The removal men

The estimator's principal job is to assess how much the firm should charge you, rather than make arrangements for the practical aspects and convenience of the move. He or she will not be there on the day and should pass on any messages or warnings about what is involved and any special requirements of yours direct to the foreman of the team which arrives. But do not rely on this: write down all the relevant details and send them to the firm in advance, to be given to the foreman.

Ask how many men will be provided. There should be at least three if the removers do all the packing, so that one person can be packing china, glass, kitchenware, etc. into containers while the others carry and load large items. Ring up on the day before the move to confirm the time when the men and van(s) are due to arrive.

Insurance for the move

While the contents of your home are being moved from one building to another, they may automatically remain insured by your household contents policy. (If your contents policy includes 'contents temporarily removed', do not assume that this covers a household removal: check with the insurers.) If not, most insurers will extend an existing contents policy to take in the increased risks of a removal, at an additional premium (likely to be at least £25). Insurers are unlikely to be willing to issue a separate household removal policy if you have no existing insurance with them.

Provided you are going to have the removal undertaken by a specialist firm of removers, you should have little difficulty in getting insurance. The cover offered is usually on the basis of what is called 'all-risks' insurance for loss or damage, and includes accidental breakages, but excludes scratches and dents. Very often, you are expected to pay a part (which may be £50 or more) of any claim (the excess).

Ask whether you would get the replacement value for any article lost, or the value at the time, allowing for depreciation and wear and tear. Make sure that you insure for the maximum value of your goods: if you are under-insured, you may receive only a proportion of the amount of your claim.

Watch out for the 'pairs and set clause' which means that the insurers will not pay for the cost of replacing any undamaged item forming part of a set when replacements cannot be matched – this could leave you with an odd one out.

Tell the insurers if your removal necessitates overnight storage in the van, to make sure that the policy will cover this. A householder's policy does not cover storage at the removal firm's depot; other policies can be extended to do so.

Removals insurance generally excludes loss of or damage to bank notes, shares, bonds, deeds, stamps, securities; also, loss or damage due to atmospheric or climatic conditions, strikes, delay, the nature of the goods insured. There are likely to be other exclusions, depending on the insurers. Melamine furniture, for instance, is not likely to be covered.

Consequential loss is also excluded: removals insurance does not cover any additional expenses you may incur due to the loss of your furniture or belongings. For instance, unlike a householder's contents policy, you cannot claim for having to stay in a hotel or for the expense of making arrangements for new furniture to be bought.

Check the time limit within which a claim must be made in writing both to the insurers and the removal firm – within three days of the delivery to the property sounds reasonable enough. But, if for some reason you are delayed or arrangements have to be made for delivery in your absence, it could technically invalidate a claim later.

It is also advisable to find out whether the policy is restricted to goods that are professionally packed – which most policies are. If so, remember to allow the removers to pack everything. Do not help them do it, even if it means you have to stand around and watch all day, because if you help and something gets broken, the insurers will be able to repudiate your claim because you did not comply with the condition. Remember also that, for the same reason, the removers must themselves unpack everything.

Insurance through the removal firm
If insurance is part of the removal firm's contract, there may be a specified (low) limit on what will be paid as compensation.

Members of the BAR have to undertake to provide a specified minimum standard of insurance cover for their customers.

Ask what the payment would be for the amount you want to insure and what the maximum premium would be for any one item. Insist on seeing in writing exactly what is covered, the time limit for making a claim, how much of each claim you will be expected to bear and all the principal exclusion clauses before paying the premium and accepting the insurance.

A do-it-yourself move

The advantage of a d-i-y move is that it is cheaper than a professional move: the basic cost is the hire of a van plus petrol, or only petrol if a van can be borrowed from a friend who owns one, or from your employer.

If you can take the opportunity to help someone else with a d-i-y move, you will learn a lot about the knack of negotiating stairs and doorways with pieces of furniture, also about packing a van to make maximum use of its capacity.

The disadvantages of a d-i-y move are that it:

- is physically very tiring
- needs strong and willing helpers who can be available on the day(s) of the move
- needs plenty of time in advance for pre-packing since the day(s) of the move will be spent carrying and loading
- is not easy if you have a lot of things or heavy equipment to move and they have to be carried up or down stairs or where there are difficulties of access – for example, where the house is in a pedestrian court
- is only practical for moves of short distances – say, not more than 50 miles; a number of journeys with a small van over a greater distance adds to the time and cost, and the hired van has to be returned to its depot at the finish
- requires providing your own packing cases and packing materials, rope or webbing to secure items in the van, blankets or other protection for polished surfaces.

Hire of a van

Before you decide on a self-drive van, you should be sure that you could cope with driving an unfamiliar vehicle. One that is larger than a private car can take some getting used to, and parking a van which has restricted rear vision may also be quite difficult. But an experienced car driver, even if unused to handling any type of van, can probably cope with a laden 18-cwt van.

A self-drive van may be hired from nationwide companies specialising in this type of hire or from a local hire firm. Look in the *Yellow Pages* or the small ads columns of your local paper, or ask friends or colleagues for recommendations.

The bigger firms may have several sizes of vehicle which can be driven on an ordinary driving licence. For trucks or lorries above 7½-tonnes laden weight, an HGV (heavy goods vehicle) category licence is necessary. You are allowed to drive small goods vehicles (up to 3½ tonnes laden weight) from the age of 17, between 3½ and 7½ tonnes laden weight from the age of 18.

Hire firms may stipulate any other minimum age limit, or that a licence has been held for at least a year, and is a clean one. When you hire a self-drive van, the company will want to see your driving licence, so do not send this off to the licensing authority to notify them of your change of address until you have completed the move.

If you prefer to hire a van plus driver – which will probably cost a bit more – find out whether the driver will help you with the loading and carrying or not. Whatever the size of the van, the driver will be subject to the regulations on goods vehicle drivers' hours – he or she must not drive for more than nine hours in the course of one day and must take the stipulated rest breaks.

Size of van

The hire firm will give you the dimensions and cubic capacity of the various vehicles. It is difficult for the amateur to estimate from the capacity of a van what loads it will take and, therefore, the number of journeys that will be necessary. Because you will not be experienced in loading economically, work on the basis of needing more capacity and making more journeys than you may at first think.

The size of the door-opening of different makes of van varies, so if you have large items of furniture, measure these first and choose a van with sufficient door size. This is especially important if a fridge or freezer has to be moved because these should always be kept in an upright position.

A van with a low kerb height or a let-down tailboard can be very useful; a truck with a hydraulic tail lift is invaluable for loading and unloading your cooker, wardrobes or other bulky furniture. Alternatively, see whether some form of ramp can be built up into the rear of the van. Find out about hiring or borrowing a trolley or a wheeled platform for moving a cooker, fridge, washing machine, and other heavy items.

Cost of hiring a van

Charges may be either a fixed sum per day or week for unlimited mileage during the period of the hire, or a smaller fixed sum per day plus a mileage charge, or an allowance of free miles followed by a mileage charge. Ask whether VAT is included in the charge, or will be added.

Work out whether it would be cheaper to pay a higher daily rate and nothing for mileage, or a lower rate plus mileage costs. To make this comparison, you need to have some idea of how many miles you will be driving during the period of hire. Subtract the lower rental charge from the higher one and divide the answer by the charge per mile. The result will give you the break-even point: if you drive more than this number of miles, the firm offering unlimited mileage is probably cheaper; if fewer miles, the firm charging so much per mile will be cheaper.

Check the exact hours of hire and what happens if the van is returned late – there could be a penalty charge, or you may be charged for another 24 hours' hire. If you know you are going to be late, let the firm know – if only for the sake of the next hirer waiting.

Find out when a day starts and ends (whether it is 24 hours, or perhaps 9 a.m. to 6 p.m.). Consider whether it is worth starting the hire on the day before the move, so as to be able to get most things packed up, ready for moving off early the next morning (after a good night's sleep). But do not load a van the night before a move unless you can lock it securely and park it safely, or put it in a lock-up garage.

You will have to return the van to the hiring place, so you have to take account of the cost of the extra mileage and time. It may be more sensible to hire in the place to which you are moving, so as not to have the return drive at the end of moving day (plus an extra return journey thereafter).

Find out what insurance is included and what is excluded. There may be an excess of £200 or more which you would have to pay towards the cost of any damage to the vehicle. It may be possible to pay a small extra premium to have the excess clause waived. Some van hire firms will arrange goods-in-transit insurance cover, if required.

You will be asked for a deposit when hiring the van, but will get it back when you return the van. Some hirers ask for a deposit to cover the amount of the insurance excess.

In your calculations of the cost of petrol to cover however many journeys you think you will make, remember that an 18-cwt van does no more than about 20 mpg. Ask what the tyre pressure should be for the van when laden, so that you can check before driving with your load.

Loading a hired van
Remember that the order in which the items are put into the van will be the reverse when unloading. You will want to off-load any carpets first, so these should go in last. Also, any heavy items that will be upstairs in the new house should be loaded near the end so that, at the unloading stage, the toughest work can be done at the beginning. But keep in mind the stability of the van – heavy items should be packed low down and distributed overall.

When stacking the van, try to make flat surfaces and use rugs or blankets on top of pieces of furniture to protect them from scratches. Damage can be caused if the furniture moves about while in transit, so make certain everything is wedged firmly to prevent this. The contents of the drawer of a chest of drawers can be left inside, covered with newspaper or towels. Remove the drawers while loading the emptied chest on to the van, replace them for travelling, and reverse the process when unloading. It may be wise to code the drawers as they are not always interchangeable. Cupboards and wardrobes can be filled with small boxes when they have been loaded into the van.

There may not be enough space for your helpers to travel in the van once it is loaded, so remember to arrange separate transport for them if you want the same team to help you unload at the other end.

Preparing to move out

Allow plenty of time to sort out your possessions and, if you are going to do so yourself, to pack them. How long to allow for preliminary sorting will depend on how much you have accumulated, and this will probably be related to how long you have spent in your present home and whether or not you are moving to a smaller place. Far too many of us keep junk stored in the loft, garage or garden shed. Tackle these hoarding places as early as possible – months ahead, if you can – because they take longer to sort and clear out.

If you want to delay a decision on some things in case you would regret discarding them, ask friends or relatives if they would like to house any item while you think about it, making it clear that you might ask for it back.

It will help to draw scale plans of each room in the new house or flat, then cut out shapes to scale (as far as possible) for each piece of furniture, and see how they will fit into the room. (Remember to allow for the position of electric sockets.) This will not only enable you to see which items to keep but, when you come to the day of the move itself, you will be able to direct the operation so that no pieces of furniture finish up in the wrong room.

Once you have worked out where everything can go, list it room by room so you can direct the removal men (they come thick and fast when they are unloading). Mark the furniture with a code for each room – perhaps with coloured stickers (red for one room, green for another).

Be ruthless about parting with any surplus furniture or equipment – you will not do it once you have moved. Make each member of the family do this, particularly the squirrel-type hoarders:

Disposing of things

Sort unwanted possessions into groups of what you think are saleable items, those which could go to charities or jumble sales, and those of no value to anyone. Disposing of things takes time and can be difficult – another reason for allowing yourself plenty of time to make any arrangements.

Saleable items
Do not get rid of things without checking whether the incoming buyer might want to buy them at a reasonable price.

Classified advertisements
The local papers (weekly or daily) will serve as a guide to the types of things which are wanted and to current prices. Some localities have publications dealing only with articles 'For Sale' and 'Wanted'.

Find out the advertising rates for your local paper and whether there are any 'free' ones. *Exchange & Mart*, the weekly paper for advertising second-hand goods, has a wide coverage; it is used particularly by advertisers and readers in London and the south of England.

If the article is a piece of special equipment, it might be worth advertising it in the appropriate magazine on the subject. It can take weeks to have an advertisement included in some magazines, so check this.

You will have to be in to answer the telephone and show the items to prospective buyers. Make sure you get paid before you let any item go.

Auction rooms
Some towns have permanent auction rooms where regular sales are held. Look in the *Yellow Pages* and for advertisements in the local press.

Go along to the auctioneers and explain what you want to sell. Some auctioneers divide goods offered for sale into groups according to quality, or handle only those of a certain standard.

If they think your goods are not suitable for their auctions, they may refer you to a secondary, or chattel, sale room which deals in miscellaneous selections of lots.

Remember to find out what percentage commission (plus VAT) will be deducted from the sale price by the auctioneer. If any items are fairly valuable, discuss whether you should place a reserve figure on them – that is, a sum below which you do not want an item to be sold. You will have to arrange for the goods to be delivered to the sale room, and collected if not sold.

Second-hand shops and dealers

Local knowledge is probably the best way of discovering dealers. (Some removal firms are also second-hand furniture dealers.) Before approaching a dealer, try to gauge current second-hand prices by keeping an eye on advertisements or second-hand shops.

Ask a dealer (or two) to call to inspect what you wish to sell. It may be helpful to have someone with you when he or she comes, to give you moral and factual support. You may be more diffident about bargaining when you feel you are not being offered a good enough price. The dealer will probably collect the items from you if he or she agrees to buy them, and you should take this factor into consideration. If your problem is to clear your bulk, do not let the dealer pick out selected bits and pieces – insist that he or she takes the lot. Otherwise, you will be left with the unwanted residue.

Books, particularly non-fiction books, may have a saleable value to collectors or specialist second-hand dealers. You may find one through local knowledge or the *Yellow Pages*; ask the dealer to call and make you an offer.

You can organise your own sale by putting the things into the garage or on the lawn, with prices clearly marked, and advertising the fact that they are for 'Sale on Sunday between 2 p.m. and 6 p.m.', or whenever.

There may be a 'car-boot sale' location near you, where you offer whatever you want to sell from the back of your car. You should decide beforehand what prices you will charge – and be prepared to come down (or not). It will take a day out of your pre-move weekend and timetable.

Items for charities and jumble sales

Some articles which are not worth selling, but which could not be considered rubbish – for instance, old clothing, curtains, bedding, toys etc. – can be donated to charity shops or jumble sales. Consult your local telephone directory, or ask at the Citizens Advice Bureau or council for voluntary services.

Local private housing associations or homes are sometimes grateful to be given unwanted furniture, carpets or curtains. You could also try the local branch of the Salvation Army if there is one, or your local church, social services department, British Red Cross, or other voluntary organisations. Some voluntary organisations run a 'charity auction': donated goods are auctioned in the conventional way, half the price going to the donor, half to charity.

Items of no value

If you finish with a residue of undisposable items – rubbish – you may have to make a special arrangement with the local authority for this to be taken away. There may be a charge for a special collection of this kind. Ask your dustmen first, and if they are unable to collect it as normal domestic refuse, telephone your local council offices and ask what to do.

Some local authorities have established dumps where unwanted household waste, old appliances, mattresses or broken furniture can be taken by householders free of charge. The authority then disposes of them.

For large quantities of rubbish, and where no local authority facilities are available, it may be necessary to hire a container or skip from a commercial firm. Look in the *Yellow Pages* under 'Waste disposal services' or 'Skip hire'. Containers of varying capacity can be hired for the day or for a number of days – over a weekend, for example. It is wise to book ahead. The firm which delivers the skip also comes to collect and get rid of it. The cost varies according to how near you are to a disposal site. Payment is usually required on delivery of the container.

If the container or skip cannot be left in a garden or driveway and has to be deposited on a public highway (that is, any road), a licence is required from the local authority. It is free and should be applied for a few days ahead. There are regulations concerning the placing of warning cones and, if the container is parked overnight, red warning lights. These can be hired from a local hire shop.

A parked skip can be an invitation to two-way transactions. You may find it the next morning filled up with neighbours' junk – or that some of your discards have disappeared.

Your car

With so many additional problems to cope with at this time, the servicing of the family car may be neglected – you may have mentally added it to the list of things to be done later, but if you will be transferring goods in your car over the period of the move, or even just ferrying yourself and your family with personal luggage on the day, be sure to take precautions beforehand in order to avoid a breakdown on the way: check oil level, battery, water and so on. The car may be carrying a lot more weight than normally, so check the brakes and, if necessary, adjust the tyre pressure. If there is anything about the car that has been worrying you, get it seen to before the move.

If you do not own a car, try to borrow one for the day of the move. It may even be worth hiring one. Find out about insurance cover.

Packing

Both sorting and packing take longer than most people estimate and they find that they have too much still to do on the actual moving day. So, start packing well in advance, particularly if you will be doing the move yourself or the firm of removers will not be packing and unpacking everything. The advantage of pre-packing items which are not in daily use is that they can be stored in their containers somewhere until you move, and in the new home can be left to be unpacked at leisure later.

Lifting and carrying
Many a physiotherapist has patients who have come for treatment for muscular strain after a move, as a result of the unaccustomed lifting and carrying of heavy weights, often done incorrectly.

Here is some advice to help you avoid back trouble when lifting, shifting and carrying.

- You should always try to anticipate and size up the job. Think before you move: how heavy is the object? can levers be used to reduce the stress? is the floor space clear to move about without kicking or stumbling over an obstruction? is the floor slippery? where are you going to put the object? where can you grasp it? is it a two-person job?

- When you lift or shift an object, get as close to it as possible, with your feet around it rather than to one side or behind it. Position your feet so that you are firmly balanced, one foot ahead of the other, ready to move off in the right direction. Keep a straight back: do not tackle lifting jobs with your back rotated, twisted or bent sideways; your shoulders and pelvis should be facing the same direction. Bend the hips and knees until the object can be reached. Grasp it firmly. If there is nothing by which to hold it, use a sling or ropes.

- Lifting, heaving or carrying with arms outstretched throws needless strain on the chest, upper back and shoulders. Keep the load close to your body; the farther from the body you hold it, the greater the stress – hence the risk when lifting a box out of the car boot. Whatever you are lifting and carrying, keep its centre of gravity as near as you can over or under your own centre of gravity.

- When dealing with something large and heavy, lift it first at one end only, and get it on to a higher level before you take the full load. This halves the stress. Rather than carrying a heavy load, pull it on a trolley. If that is not possible, divide it into two smaller loads, one for each hand – or make a second journey, if need be.

- When putting things down, if you cannot safely drop the object (which is the best way), put the lifting drill into reverse. Keep the object close to your body, and put one end down first.

Packing containers
Start in good time to collect plenty of boxes and other containers and newspaper.

Chests, crates or cartons may be provided ahead of time by the removal firm. (Tea chests are becoming hard to obtain and, in any case, are heavy when full.) Some removal firms may send you a batch of paper liners for the crates and boxes they use for you to fill (with non-breakables). The paper bag is shaped to fit into the box, to be lifted into it and carried away for transporting by the removal men on moving day.

Try the local supermarket, food shop or off-licence for cardboard cartons and discarded boxes; the partitioned kind are ideal for packing food jars, bottles or breakable vases, and suchlike. Remember that cartons will get stacked on top of others, and that the bottom carton in the pile will collapse if it is not strong enough to take the weight.

For transporting larger breakables, ask electrical retailers and china shops if you can have cartons with the straw or shavings or packing materials in which goods have been delivered to them. Obviously, use all your own suitcases, trunks, holdalls, and borrow more from friends and relatives (tie on a label straightaway to identify the lender – you will have to return the empties eventually).

Wearing gloves while you do the packing will protect your hands (you will be surprised to see how dirty they get).

When wrapping china and glass, it is not so much the paper that protects them as the resilience of crumpled paper. When packing china in tea chests or boxes, first put in a thick bottom layer of crumpled-up newspaper. Large plates and lids should be individually wrapped and can be packed vertically round the sides of the box or chest, or be held in place by other items. If you are packing fragile items for transporting, it is sensible to label these as 'fragile' or 'this way up'. Do not – obviously – put heavier items on top of breakable smaller ones.

Do not fill chests or boxes too full, particularly with heavy items, such as books; otherwise, they become impossible to lift or carry any distance. Instead, use a greater quantity of smaller cartons, and tie them with string to make them easier to carry.

Labelling
It is essential to label boxes and cases as you pack them, to identify the contents. You may think you will remember what

each contains – you will not. Also, keep a list of the contents of boxes or containers which are not going to be unpacked straightaway, identifying the room to which they belong.

People devise their own systems of labelling: per room or per type of contents or for unpacking chronologically. Choose whatever method appeals to you.

Containers which are to be emptied immediately need only be labelled or numbered to identify in which room in the new home they are to be deposited. Provided you put up a correspondingly labelled or numbered plan in a prominent position in the new house or flat, everyone should be able to see where things are to go. Some people use a colour code or a letter code – allocating a colour (or letter) to each room in the house and sticking the appropriate coloured sticker or letter on each door and on the furniture and containers.

Preferably, put the labels on the side – not the top – of boxes, so that they can be seen when stacked one on top of the other. Be careful not to put a self-adhesive label on a polished surface, or on any normally visible surface: after a day or so, the fixative may harden and then you may not be able to get it off without leaving a mark.

Some removal firms will supply labels free of charge. Stationers sell packets of adhesive labels of various sizes, also coloured stickers. Buy about twice as many as you first think you will need.

Put labels on items not to be removed from the house as well, so that they are clearly identifiable on moving day.

Keys

Sort out all the keys to rooms, cupboards, garage, outhouse, as well as sets of front- and back-door keys, and label them. It will be an act of kindness to the incoming owner, and may avoid any unnecessary queries later, if you make a list of how many keys exist and which, if any, are missing. Make sure that all the keys are duly rounded up eventually – husband and wife have their own set, the children may have keys, near or distant relatives, trusted neighbours, the 'daily' help.

Make sure you tell your buyer where you are leaving all the

keys but do not let him or her have them until you know that completion has taken place.

Furniture and other items

If you have any furniture that needs renovating or re-upholstering, or you want carpets cleaned, it can be a good idea to get the firms to collect them before you move and to deliver them to the new home. This is a good time to get all these jobs done, while you are living in chaos anyway, and it means that someone else is doing some of the removing for you. It is, however, only practical if you are moving locally.

When pieces of furniture, shelving or kitchen appliances have to be dismantled, any screws and fittings should be kept with the items to save time when re-installing. Tape them to the piece of furniture, on an inside surface with adhesive tape, or ask the removers to do so.

Label all the keys to cupboards, chests of drawers, wardrobes, etc. and keep them together in a clear polythene bag; some removal firms provide key bags.

Ask the removers whether they prefer any drawers to be locked or left unlocked – this could depend on the weight of the piece of furniture. Drawers can be used as packing containers: cover the contents with rugs, old sheets or polythene sheeting.

Beds
Bedsteads are usually dismantled by the removers. Check if they will also put them up again at the other end (make sure the bedstead spanner stays with it). Put identifying labels on mattresses and bedsteads or bases for matching up at the other end. Some removal firms provide special mattress sacks.

Carpets
Carpets should be rolled, not folded, to prevent creasing. Label the pieces of underlay (with a stick-on label) to identify which carpet they belong to. Some of the foam varieties of underlay may be found to have disintegrated into dust, particularly where there has been much traffic (on the stairs, for instance), so you may find nothing to take away and will need new underlays at your new home.

Valuables
If the move is a local one, valuables could be lodged with your bank for the period of the move. If you have to take them with you, consider packing jewellery and other small valuables discreetly among your clothes. But remember to make a note of where you put them.

Clocks
You will have to immobilise any clock that has a detachable pendulum or weights. If you are unsure how to do this, consult a local clock repairer before attempting to remove any weights. Some removal firms specifically exclude responsibility for any internal damage to clocks.

Flammable items
Run down or remove any fuel remaining in oil heaters, oil lamps or a lawn mower. The removers will not accept them with fuel, nor half-used tins of anything volatile.

Children's toys
If you have small children, do not forget to keep out a selection of their favourite toys and games and books to have at hand over the period of the move.

Tools
Before packing up your workshop, garage or tool cupboard, prepare an emergency tool kit to take with you, readily accessible. Include such tools as screwdriver, pliers, sharp knife, adjustable spanner, nails, hammer, screws, hooks, fuses or fuse wire, adhesive, tape, rope, string, light bulbs, plugs and torch.

Dustbin
The dustbins at both houses are likely to be overflowing by the day of the move. Invest in a new dustbin, and liners, and take these – kept empty – for use as soon as you arrive at the other end.

Moving household appliances

Do not forget to check that there are sockets for portable electrical appliances and fuse connection units for stationary appliances in convenient positions in your new home. There should be a socket outlet or connection unit within 1.8 metres of all likely locations of electrical appliances.

Cooker

Remember to switch off the electricity supply at the mains position before disconnecting the cooker.

Freezer

Ideally, run down stocks before moving; defrost and dry out the cabinet.

Freezers are not designed with the strength needed to be transporting containers. Some removal firms will not take a freezer with its contents, mainly because of the extra weight. The vibration during a move and weight of the contents can damage the pipework.

If you must move it with frozen food inside:

- reduce stocks to no more than 25 per cent of the freezer's capacity
- switch to 'maximum freeze' for at least 24 hours before removal
- do not open the door or lid after refrigeration is switched off.

A risk in moving frozen food is the possibility of thawing: refreezing partially defrosted food can spoil its taste and can be a health hazard if it has been left long enough for it to go off.

Even when the freezer is empty, it is vulnerable to damage during the move. If it is tipped more than about 30 degrees – to come down some step, for instance, or when negotiating doorways – this can cause an airlock in the cooling system. A freezer that has been moved must be left to stand in its final position for a minimum of two hours before it is switched on.

Fridge

Defrost just before the move, and leave the fridge dry and empty. Pack any remaining perishables in an insulated picnic bag or wrap them in plenty of newspaper and put them into thick cartons.

Remember that fridges must be carried upright.

Dishwasher and washing machine

A plumbed-in dishwasher or washing machine with a stop valve on the supply pipe does not need a plumber to disconnect it. (Leave a label telling the new owner 'this is a water supply pipe'.) But you may need a plumber at the new house for fitting a stop valve to the supply pipe there.

If the washing machine has a revolving drum, this should be immobilised before moving it. Ideally, find the restraining bars which came with the machine when it was new. If you cannot, consult the manufacturer or a local retailer for advice. Tilting a front-loading machine can cause damage to it. Some machines have bearings or gear boxes with an open reservoir of oil – if the machine is not kept upright, you will have an indelible dribble over everything.

Home computer

Computers are vulnerable to damage – from damp, dust and magnetic waves. It is also possible to damage the recording heads by rough handling.

Ensure that your computer is sealed in a plastic bag and handled gently. You may prefer not to use the removal men for this. Disks should be kept away from sources of magnetism – such as radios, telephones and some children's toys. With hard disk computers there is often a 'park' utility to ensure that the computer can be moved safely.

Survival kit

Before packing up the contents of the kitchen, you would be wise to prepare a survival kit to be taken with you in your car, or in the van if you are travelling with it.

If you are moving over two or more days, you will also need an overnight bag of personal belongings for each member of the family.

The kit should contain:

- kettle and its flex
- can opener
- teapot
- tea and/or coffee
- milk (longlife, tin or powder)
- sugar
- disposable or plastic cups/beakers, plates and cutlery
- saucepan (and camping stove if there's no working cooker)
- teaspoons
- washing-up liquid and brush/cloth
- bedding and towels
- soap
- notepad and writing implements
- any regular medication
- lavatory paper
- candles, matches
- corkscrew
- first aid kit, including sticking plaster, scissors, aspirin
- cash
- coins and phone card for telephone from a public call box (and the telephone numbers of the estate agents, your solicitor, the seller, your buyer, electricity company, gas services)
- cheque book, bank and credit cards
- things to amuse the children
- clean clothes (and slippers)
- plugs and adaptors
- self-sealing plugs for sinks and basins
- hot water bottle
- basic tool kit
- torch
- driving licence, motor insurance document
- removal contract
- champagne, G&T etc.

Children on the move

Most adults find moving house a traumatic business. Children can find it disturbing, too – which, in turn, will be an added worry for the parents. So, it is important to protect the children as much as possible from the upheaval and to settle them down in the new surroundings as smoothly and as quickly as possible.

Older children should be encouraged to look forward to a move and to feel involved in it. If it can be organised, take them to see the new house beforehand. Let them have an opportunity to imagine themselves in their future surroundings, to inspect their new bedroom and perhaps to choose their own decorations for it.

Even if the children are very young, talk to them well in advance about what is to happen; they may not fully understand what it is all about, but they will be getting some warning of what is to come.

A baby in a carry cot can be less trouble than an older child, provided you take with you enough milk, baby food, drink and nappies.

If it is practical, it may be better to 'farm out' a toddler or small child with relatives or a neighbouring family with children over the day or days of the move.

When the time comes to collect the children from relatives or friends for their first night in the new home, arrange this so that there is sufficient time for them to find their way round it, and to explore a little, before it is their bedtime. If there is any spare time or energy left, use this to make their bedroom as familiar as possible by putting out their toys, clothes, and so on. They are at first going to feel insecure in the strange new surroundings, so anything which can be done to reduce this – such as providing them with their favourite toys – will help.

As soon as possible after the arrival in a new area, make it a priority to locate any neighbouring children of the same age for yours to play with. Your children will miss their former friends considerably, and will need new ones quickly if they are to enjoy the change.

Moving pets

The societies for the prevention of cruelty to animals are ready to give advice on any problem to do with animals.

Dogs

Whether you would be wiser to put the animal into kennels or not depends on the kind of move, the distance, the protractedness of the changeover – and on your dog. A good guard dog might find the comings and goings of workmen or removal men a strain, in which case it would be less harassing for dog – and owner – if it were not about the house. And if there is any chance that your dog might escape and run off while doors are left open during loadings of the furniture van, or that it would continually get under everyone's feet, it would be kinder and safer to board it out for this stage of the move or to ask a neighbour to have it for the day.

If you can leave the dog for the day with a relative or friend, so much the better, but it may be necessary to put it into kennels for a day or so if you are involved in a lengthier operation. If you do not know of a local kennels, consult your vet or look in the *Yellow Pages*. If you are moving some distance away, it would be more practical to find kennels near your new home if arrangements can be made for the dog to be delivered there beforehand. Good kennels get booked up in the holiday season so make your booking as soon as you know the date of the move and get any required injections done; a recent certificate of vaccination will almost certainly be required.

Do not forget to check the new garden (if there is one) to make sure that it is dog-proof before releasing your dog into it.

Cats

A cat can be more of a problem, particularly about settling into the new home. It is probably best to take your cat with you in the car in its travelling basket or carrier; some removal firms provide cardboard pet-carrying cartons.

If your journey is to be a long one – say, over four hours – or a disturbing one, ask your local vet whether he or she would consider prescribing a tranquilliser. This would depend on the age, size and fitness of your cat, and how accustomed it is to travelling.

Immediately on arrival, choose one of the rooms as the cat's temporary quarters and release it in it, keeping the windows and door shut. Warn everyone, or even lock the door, to avoid the cat being released accidentally, and leave it there with food, water and a litter tray (and perhaps its favourite chair or cushion) while the unloading goes on. At the end of the day, close all the windows and doors and then allow the cat the run of the rest of the house. Do not let it out until at least 24 or even 48 hours later, and then only do this just before its feeding time. (It may have taken refuge in a safe corner – under a stack of packing cases, perhaps – and may need to be coaxed out.)

For the first week or so, just to be on the safe side, put a collar on the cat, with a tag giving your name, address and telephone number.

Small caged birds

Birds should be no problem because they can be transported in their cage covered with a cloth. Make sure that there is adequate ventilation and remove any loose articles that could move around inside the cage. Birds are susceptible to changes in temperature, so be careful not to leave the cage in a draughty spot during transit or in the new house while everyone is occupied with moving in. Empty the water and seed containers and remember to fill them again after you arrive. Alternatively, use non-spill containers.

Other small pets

Mice, guinea pigs, gerbils, hamsters and rabbits should be transported in 'chew-proof' well-ventilated containers. Water should be provided in a securely fixed inverted bottle with a drip tube, making sure that the end of the tube is at a convenient height for the animal to drink. Some food and bedding (not the synthetic variety) should be provided in the container.

Fish

For fish being moved from a pool you need a non-spillable, well-oxygenated container: for instance, a large polythene bag quarter-filled with pool water, placed in a bucket for protection and support during transit. Polystyrene chips can be used to cushion the bag and will also help maintain the temperature of the water.

For tropical fish, get the advice of the local aquarium expert or pet shop about maintaining the correct water temperature, and tell the removers.

The day of the move

Have a good night's rest and start the day with a proper breakfast, since the next meals may not materialise when most needed. You could try enlisting the help of one very good friend to be responsible for making the innumerable cups of tea or helping with last-minute packing or cleaning and generally giving moral support.

Last-minute jobs will be the stripping and packing of beds, and the final clearing and packing of foodstuffs in the kitchen. Prepare any packs of sandwiches or snacks you have planned, and fill a thermos (or two) with soup or hot drinks or just hot water for making drinks with.

Wear sensible clothes, with large pockets (tuck a notebook into one of them) and comfortable shoes: you will be doing a lot of running about and standing around. Keep out a stool or folding chair to sit on during the day whenever you can.

Arrange to keep to one side the vacuum cleaner or a broom and dustpan and brush, and any other basic cleaning equipment, to be loaded among the last lot, so that they can be used at this end for a final clean-up if needed, and will be readily available at the other end.

Collect your survival kit to go with you in the car (do not let it go with the removal van in case it does not reach your destination as quickly as you do). Decide where you will put any documents you may need on the day, and your valuables. Do not leave cash or jewellery around on moving day. There is no need for absurd security, but it's always best to take common sense precautions.

You may need to cash a cheque unexpectedly during the move (to have the money for tips, for instance, or to buy fish and chips or a dozen light bulbs) so keep your cheque book and bank card handy.

If arrangements go according to plan, the servicemen from the electricity and gas companies will call early in the day to read any meters and disconnect any appliances you are taking with you. (This may mean no more hot water or hot food for you there.)

When the removal men arrive, show the foreman round, not forgetting any loft, garage or outhouse. Explain the labelling system you have adopted and indicate which items are not to be removed. Check whether the requests you made to the estimator have been passed on to the foreman. If they have not, telephone the management right away, or get the foreman to, so that it can be sorted out as soon as possible.

Carpets in the entrance hall should be protected with druggets, plastic or dust sheets, especially if it is a wet day. Be prepared to provide these coverings in case the removal men do not bring their own. See that they are brought away in the van.

If the removal men are to do all the packing and loading, leave them to it at this stage. As far as possible, keep out of their way, and only give further instructions to the foreman. Cups of tea or coffee will be welcome several times.

When all is loaded on to the van, make a final tour of inspection both inside and out, to check that nothing has been left behind (look into built-in cupboards), but that all items included in the sale have been left.

Check that you have left the heating system on or off according to the arrangement made with the new owner, and turn off the mains water if this has been agreed. This could be important if the house is to stand empty and unheated for any time in winter. Close and lock all windows and doors, and leave the keys wherever you have arranged with the new owner.

Before the removal men leave with the van, check that they have the new address, and give clear instructions how to find the house if it is at all difficult. Make sure you have made arrangements about what they should do if they should arrive first – you could be delayed en route for some reason. (An emergency contact telephone number might also be useful.) But try as far as possible to be at the new house in time to supervise the unloading, or arrange to have a reliable friend or relative there to do so.

Completion and handover of keys

While you are moving out, your solicitor or conveyancer should be dealing with the legal (and financial) side of completion. Unless you are doing your own conveyancing, neither the buyer nor the seller is there. The crucial factor of completion is the handing over of all the money.

Normally, the keys of a house are not released until the purchase money has reached the seller's solicitor. Strictly, the seller should get a set of keys to the solicitor, who will hand them over to the buyer's solicitor, and the buyer then gets them from him or her. This can be physically difficult, and complicated by the venue where completion takes place.

It may be more convenient for the keys to be handed over by the estate agent. The seller's solicitor will then authorise the estate agents to hand over the keys as soon as completion has taken place. In practice, the buyer and seller often make their own arrangements for the handing over of the keys.

Delays in the money reaching the solicitor or in the estate agent being notified of completion will delay the buyer being able to get hold of the keys and can cause a hiatus in the moving-in operation. Waiting outside your new home for some time before you are able to start unloading could prove expensive if your removal is being charged on a time basis.

At the new home

Before any furniture is unloaded, see that the carpets in the entrance, hall, or stairs are protected with coverings of some kind. These can get very dirty, especially on a wet day or in a house on a new estate where there is still a lot of mud on the site.

If you have adopted the method of labelling each item with a colour or number corresponding to the room in which it is to be put, label the rooms accordingly and stick the plan in a prominent place by the front door. Or, you may prefer to position yourself there and to indicate the correct room as each item is unloaded. Remember, with the heavier pieces of furniture you should specify exactly where in the room each should be put – you should have worked this out beforehand – to avoid finding yourself having to heave them about later.

When the foreman tells you they are ready to go, have a look inside the van, just to make sure that nothing has inadvertently been left there.

The removal men will expect a tip. If you feel they deserve one, you can give a sum to the foreman for distribution or give individually to each man (and the driver). But if you are not satisfied, say so. If you give a tip without comment, it can sometimes lead the removers to suspect that any claim you may subsequently make is exaggerated or even false.

You may be asked to sign a discharge document that the job is completed. (It may incorporate a receipt for payment, if you pay at the end of the moving operation, not ahead of time.) This is the document on which to write down if you have any reservations about how the work has been carried out. If you have not yet inspected your belongings, sign as 'unexamined'.

Switch on the water heating. Make up the beds as soon as they are unloaded, so that they are ready to be collapsed into when needed. If it is possible to hang curtains in the bedrooms, do this as well.

Unpack only essentials – not only because you may want to clean any fitted cupboards and shelves before putting your belongings into them, but because you should not tire yourself out on jobs that can wait. Also, the more items that can remain packed in boxes or containers, the less chaos. But, you will have to empty the chests or containers that the removal men will want to take away.

Be prepared for:

- a lot of discarded packing materials
- emptied containers waiting for collection/disposal
- piles of books unloaded but not put on to shelves
- pots, pans, crockery everywhere on the wrong surfaces
- debris and dirt.

Do not expect to be fully organised at your new house straightaway. If you try to be, you could be heading for a nervous breakdown.

There may be a kind friend or neighbour who will feed you. But if you are planning to prepare some sort of meal the first evening, you will have to locate crockery and food. If you find you are too exhausted to want to prepare a meal at this stage, find a café, take-away or fish-and-chip shop.

Claiming for damage or loss

If anything gets broken or damaged, try to make a written note of it at the time, and ask the removers' foreman to sign or initial it. Such an *aide-mémoire* should not be altered or amended after signature. Keep your copy carefully, to support any claim.

You may not spot deficiencies, loss or damage in all the hurly-burly straight away. Make a list of anything that has been broken or damaged as soon as possible, and notify the insurers and the removal firm's head office that there is a likelihood of a claim on the removal insurance policy.

If something prevented you from being present when the goods were unloaded, or everything is not being unpacked immediately, tell the insurers (and the removers) at once that you are unable to comply with a claims time limit.

If damage is caused to your goods as a result of negligence on the part of the removers, they should, as far as possible, put it right by repairing or replacing it or compensating you financially. Take the advice of your solicitor. Many solicitors will not charge extra for sorting out the odd problem after completion if you have to claim on your insurance.

The claim form you receive will not have been designed specifically for this type of insurance: many questions may be irrelevant – or missing. Describe the circumstances as precisely as possible in the blank space provided. If only a few articles have been damaged, you should list each item. Depending on the extent of the loss, the insurers will either ask you for further details before taking up the matter with the removers or send you a cheque rather than waste time and money with enquiries about a small sum. Keep any bills or receipts for repairs or replacements to produce in support of your claim.

If a lot has been destroyed (by fire or a major accident perhaps), the insurers will arrange for a representative to call to formulate some idea of what has been lost and what can be salvaged, and the value. Do not agree to a figure if you think it is too low.

After the move

Security

It is wise to have the locks of the outer doors changed. There may be unaccounted-for keys: you never know who else had keys from the previous owners.

Consider fitting door and window locks, an alarm system or security lights. See the *Which?* report entitled *Burglary: who's next?*, November 1993, which includes test results on d-i-y burglar alarms; see also *Safe and Secure, Which?* November 1994 and pages 114–5. You can get advice from the crime prevention officer at the local police station.

Safety

Consider also the safety of your new home, particularly if there are young children or elderly people involved.

Safety checklist:

- Are there any holes or worn places in the carpets or other floor coverings. Are any not fixed securely (especially stair carpets)?
- Are there adequate smoke alarms positioned in the right place? Do they work and are their batteries in good condition? Consider getting inter-connectable alarms.
- Are there fire extinguishers – appropriately located?
- Are safety gates (top and bottom) needed on the stairs?
- Are there any locking cupboards which cannot be opened from the inside?
- Are there any stoves or open fires which need guards?

Documents

You should keep safely in one place all the documents, certificates, policies, guarantees, and other paperwork connected with your purchase. In spite of probably feeling that you will never move again, some of these papers would be required if you did so at any time in the future. If any papers are being kept by your solicitor, bank or mortgagee, make a note of this in the file.

CONVEYANCING (THE LEGAL SIDE OF BUYING AND SELLING A HOUSE)

'CONVEYANCING' is the popular word for all the legal and administrative procedures involved in transferring the owner-ship of a house. The system's checks and balances are designed to ensure that the buyer gets a 'good title' (i.e. the legal right to possession) to the house with all the rights that go with it – and none that shouldn't. Pitfalls for the unwary can range from undisclosed mortgages, the seller's bankruptcy, or Granny refusing to move on completion day, to difficulties over rights of drainage, disputes over fences or ancient common rights. The conveyancing process should unearth and resolve such problems.

Changes in the wording of obligations for those selling houses were introduced on 1 July 1995. Transfers now include an under-taking that the seller is selling 'with full title guarantee', i.e. that he has the right to sell the property, is transferring it free of any mortgage or other third-party rights created by himself or his predecessors (other than those disclosed before contracts are exchanged), and will if called upon to do so at his own expense take all necessary steps to complete the transfer of the ownership to the buyer.

A little legal background

Historically, ownership of property has been divided into two groups: real property and personal property. Real property is confined to freehold ownership of land (hence the American expression 'real estate') and everything else is personal property (including leases). The distinction between the two types of property is less than it used to be, before the ownership of land was reformed in 1925, but it still has some relevance in tax and inheritance law. So, if in your will you leave all your realty to Nicholas and your personalty to Sophie, Nicholas will get your freehold properties, and Sophie will get your personal possessions, and any leasehold property you own.

What makes buying a house unlike buying a car or washing machine is that you are acquiring something which is permanent – built on land which has always existed and may be affected by things which happened years ago. For instance, any land can be subject to easements or common rights or even to ancient ecclesiastical rights. 'Land' includes all the buildings on it and, in theory at least, everything below it to the centre of the earth and everything above it. It is not enough just to check that the house has the right number of bedrooms and no rising damp.

The law treats land transactions differently from consumer transactions. Every contract to buy land has to be in writing and contain essential details: the price, who's buying and selling, and a description of the property. But even though a large amount of money is at stake you have in many ways much less legal protection than if you are buying a washing machine from a shop. There is no guarantee that a house is in good order, or even that the person who lives there has the right to sell it. That is why the legal side of house buying involves so much detective work. Your solicitor's job will be to find out if there are problems before you commit yourself to going ahead. Your best chance of making sure there are no nasty surprises is to work together with the person you appoint. Pass on any information which you think might be relevant and ask about things that seem odd or trouble you.

The two main stages

Up to exchange of contracts
Until contracts are exchanged either side is legally free to change his or her mind. It is the investigative period, when the buyer finds out as much as possible about the property; when the local and other pre-contract searches are carried out and preliminary enquiries are raised; when the documents are examined in great detail and if necessary the contract changed to suit your circumstances. Once you have exchanged contracts the buyer and seller are committed and cannot pull out.

From exchange of contracts to completion
This stage involves the more technical side of conveyancing – especially asking for requisitions and the preparation of the transfer and mortgage documentation.

The buyer's goal

This is to become the legal owner of the house, free from the claims of other people, and free from legal and other problems. Try to imagine the house and garden as your territory. You want to make sure that everything within that territory becomes yours and that no one else has any rights over it (or at least none that you do not know about – like shared driveways, drains etc.). Your territory must also have access to the outside world, which means that you must have the right for pipes, wires, drains etc. to be connected to the mains – and to be able legally to get to and from the property.

From the seller's point of view

Here the role is more passive. Questions are asked about the property, and what is included in the price. The seller must answer these truthfully, and not in a way that will lead to civil claims after completion. The seller (or his or her solicitor) has to ensure that all liabilities charged on the property (mortgages, hire purchase and the like) are cleared on completion and that the property is handed over, empty, and in accordance with the contract on completion day.

Calculating the cost

See **Chapter 2**, noting in particular the advice to obtain a written quotation from the solicitor or licensed conveyancer before giving instructions to start work.

Ask at an early stage how much the other fees will be, such as search fees and the Land Registry fee and stamp duty on the transfer. (These amounts depend on the price being paid for the property.)

Who will do the work?

As soon as you decide to sell or start hunting seriously for a new home, decide who you want to do the conveyancing work for you. The choice you have in England and Wales is to:

- appoint a solicitor
- appoint a licensed conveyancer
- do it yourself.

The advantage of d-i-y conveyancing is that you can save on solicitors' or conveyancers' fees (and VAT). Also, you are largely in control of events. It does away with the frustration of chasing up your solicitor/conveyancer to get him or her to chase up the seller's solicitor. To some extent you can dictate the pace and possibly eliminate delays. An outline of the procedures is given in **Chapter 11** but you will need to get to know not just what to do but how to do it before embarking on doing it yourself.

D-i-y conveyancing has become less popular in recent years partly because in real terms the fees charged by solicitors and licensed conveyancers have reduced dramatically and so, therefore, have the potential savings to be made.

Solicitors

Traditionally, solicitors have carried out the legal work on house buying and selling. Since the creation of licensed conveyancers they no longer have a monopoly on this work.

Solicitors (and licensed conveyancers, see below) are required by law to be on guard against money-laundering and other types of fraud. Do not take it amiss if you are asked to produce proof of your identity and your address, especially if you have not used the firm before or for some years.

Conveyancers

It is now unlawful for unqualified conveyancers (those who are not solicitors or licensed conveyancers) to draft conveyancing documents or contracts for a fee.

The Council for Licensed Conveyancers (CLC)* can give the name and address of any local licensed conveyancers in an area and, for a fee, can provide a list of all licensed conveyancers in England and Wales.

The Council deals with the licensing and supervision of non-solicitor conveyancers. It regulates the conduct of licence holders and has disciplinary machinery to deal with complaints against licensed conveyancers. It has set up a master policy to provide indemnity insurance and has established a compensation fund.

Making the choice

The choice is not so much between a solicitor and conveyancer (both of whom are qualified to do the work); rather, it is the choice of the best person to work with you. Price is not the only consideration: if you get a very low quotation, the solicitor/conveyancer may have had to take on a huge work load to make ends meet, and may have little time to give you personal attention. Worse than that, corners may be cut and the job could be done inadequately. On the other hand, the most expensive may not give the best service. House buying and selling is a stressful experience. It may be worth paying a little extra for a good service. The best indication of choice will come from someone who has used a particular licensed conveyancer or solicitor and still thinks that he or she is wonderful when it is all over.

If you have successfully used a firm of solicitors for any legal business in the past, you could start by asking to be put in touch with a member of the firm who specialises in conveyancing, or you could ask for a recommendation from a relative, friend, colleague at work, bank manager, building society manager, estate agent, or by consulting the Law Society's★ regional directory in your local reference library or Citizens Advice Bureau, or simply look for an advertisement in the local paper or *Yellow Pages*.

If you rely on personal recommendation, make sure that the professional you have chosen is recommended for skill in property transactions. Rumpole may be very good in court but he is unlikely to know the difference between a restrictive covenant and a puisne mortgage! (For that matter he is not even a solicitor!)

If you found the house you want to buy through a multi-firm solicitor's property centre, one of the other firms (not the one involved with the seller of your property) can be used. One solicitor can act for you in both transactions if you are buying and selling at the same time (and usually also deal with your mortgage). Except in very few cases, the same solicitor cannot act for both buyer and seller at the same time but two members of the same firm may act for the buyer and seller where both are already established clients of the firm, so long as there is no clash of interests between the buyer and seller. This is more likely to happen in a small rural town than in an urban area. However, where a newly built or converted house is being sold, a firm of solicitors can never act for both the builder/developer and the buyer, even if both are long-established clients.

It is not necessary for the solicitor to be local to the property being bought, although it can help, particularly if you are moving to another part of the country. Try to find someone you feel you will get on with, and who gives you confidence that matters are being well handled.

Do not expect a solicitor to be able to tell you precisely how long your transaction will take – but the reply may give you some impression of his or her tempo.

Delays that are not the making of your solicitor/conveyancer can include: the time it takes to obtain a mortgage offer; the time it takes to get the result of local searches – some local authorities take many weeks to deal with local searches. A good solicitor/conveyancer should advise a client about how long the procedure is likely to take, judging from experience of local conditions, and warn that there may be periods when nothing seems to be happening. In practice, however, it is difficult to estimate the exact time a transaction will take: a chain of buyers and sellers can proceed only at the pace of the slowest party in the chain.

When to appoint your solicitor or conveyancer

Consult your solicitor or conveyancer at as early a stage as possible, so that he or she can be ready when you decide to make an offer and advise you on any legal snags before you become too involved, such as:

- local restrictions (perhaps preventing or limiting extensions or alterations)
- the possibility of undesirable development in the neighbourhood.

Teamwork

The transaction is most likely to go smoothly if you work together with your solicitor/conveyancer. If you spend your time laying traps, and telephoning at three minutes past nine to say that there was a spelling mistake in the previous letter, you will only cause irritation. Work in tandem and the stress will be much less.

On the other hand, if you feel from the very start that you are just not going to get on, or that you do not have confidence in the person, consider changing to another straightaway. Your solicitor/conveyancer will probably not see the house: all he or she will have to work from will be the draft contract, the agent's particulars and information from the title deeds or the Land Registry. So, if you know of or can guess at any peculiarities about the property or if you have any proposals for using or changing the property in any particular way, pass on the details, in case they could create a legal problem.

The sort of items to be alert about include:

- the boundaries of a property (see below)
- any shared rights of access: for example, a drive shared with another property, and whether there is any obligation to contribute towards its upkeep
- a separate access to the back garden: you may need a right of way to it
- other 'easements', for example a short-cut through your property, or the way a neighbour's drains join yours
- any structural additions or alterations carried out by previous owners, such as an extension or a garage: these might have required planning permission or building regulation consent which may never have been obtained

- any remedial treatment for damp or woodworm or any re-roofing or double glazing for which guarantees still operate
- any reason for the sale which may give rise to problems over possession – e.g. matrimonial difficulties. If the seller's house is not jointly owned by husband and wife, it is important to get written consent for the house to be sold from the spouse who is not the owner in case of matrimonial dispute before completion; the solicitor/conveyancer can check whether that spouse has registered a claim
- any indication that the seller may be badly in debt. Your solicitor should know this at an early stage because he or she can then make preliminary searches and avoid trouble and delay later
- whether any part of the property is let or occupied.

Points like these will normally be dealt with in the contract, or cleared between the two parties before signing, but this can only be done if the points come to light. Do not assume that your solicitor/conveyancer is a clairvoyant or knows the property personally. Draw attention at an early stage to any features about the house, the neighbourhood or the sellers. Check the estate agent's particulars against what is in the house and what is stated in the contract. Tell the solicitor about anything which is shown up by the structural survey.

Some practical matters

The deposit

On exchange of contracts, a deposit has to be paid by the buyer to the seller. Traditionally, the deposit is 10 per cent of the purchase price but a lower figure (say 5 per cent) can usually be negotiated. This deposit (unlike any preliminary deposit paid to an estate agent) is non-refundable and is used as security for the performance of the contract. The amount will be deducted from the balance that has to be paid at completion.

Normally, the deposit is sent to the seller's solicitor/conveyancer as 'stakeholder', which means that he or she must hold it and not use it for the seller's purposes. Alternatively, a special condition of the contract may require the deposit to be paid to the solicitor/conveyancer as 'agent for the vendor', which means that it may be passed on to the seller. This is quite common in some areas of the UK. If the seller needs your deposit to pay the deposit on his or her new house, it is difficult for you to object to a request of this nature, especially if you are involved in a buying and selling chain and want to ask the same of the buyer of your house. But it does mean that you cannot be assured of regaining your deposit if someone in the chain defaults and does not honour the contract.

If you do not have the ready money for a deposit, you may have to arrange a bridging loan (see page 182), which will be paid off when you receive the mortgage loan or the money from the sale of the home. Alternatively, you can try the deposit guarantee scheme (see page 23), though this has never proved popular.

The chain situation

Unless you are a first-time buyer, you are likely to be selling your existing house as well as buying a new one, and will be trying to time the two operations to run as closely together as possible. The buyer of your present home might be in a similar situation. This is how a chain of buyer and seller, buyer and seller is created. Where there is a chain of transactions, each inter-dependent upon the other, the pace of the slowest can dictate the speed of the whole transaction. When a problem occurs along the chain, it affects all those in it. Obviously, the longer the chain, the greater the risk that one of the 'links' will collapse (see page 177 on chain breakers).

Buying a newly built house

Your solicitor or conveyancer must check:

- that the contract provides for the house to be properly built to specification with appropriate services laid on
- that the boundaries of the property are as shown on the plan

- that you are granted all necessary rights, such as rights of way and drainage
- that the builder has made an agreement with the appropriate local authority to construct the roads and that, when they are built, the authority will take them over and maintain them
- that the builder has a similar agreement to deal with drainage and sewerage
- what restrictions there may be: these are often connected with the appearance of the estate – for example, no parked caravans in front gardens, no cutting down of trees, no swimming-pools; there may be rules about keeping animals: e.g. forbidding the keeping of chickens or a pig. You may have to get the developer's approval before building an extension – even long after the estate has been finished
- whether the original planning permission for the estate contained conditions which restrict or remove the normal permitted development rights.

Registered or unregistered?

Where the property is 'registered', the owner has a Land Certificate (or Charge Certificate if the property is mortgaged) instead of the usual title deeds. The Certificate contains an exact copy of the information held in respect of the property at the Land Registry. The information is divided into three parts: the property register, the proprietorship register and the charges register. Every Land or Charge Certificate also has an official site plan of the property (known as 'the filed plan').

A buyer can get the information about ownership of the property (and matters such as other people's rights over it) from the Land Registry. This information is now publicly available. You do not need the seller's permission. Send the appropriate application to the relevant office of the Land Registry together with the fee (£10 from 1 March 1994 if you do not know the registered title, £5 if you do) and you will be sent details of everything that is registered against the property, along with (for a further £5 fee) a plan showing its location. This could well be useful if you want to find out more about the property before you make an offer.

Transferring registered property is easier than unregistered – some people do it themselves without a solicitor or licensed conveyancer. Not all the land in England and Wales is yet registered, but in all areas registration is now compulsory. This means that a property either has a registered title or, when the house is next sold, the title has to be registered by the new owner. (In Scotland, registration started during 1980.)

If the house you are buying does not yet have a registered title, ownership is proved by production of a copy of the title deeds. The seller's solicitor will prepare an epitome of title, consisting of a copy of all the relevant documentation going back at least 15 years. This will have to be checked by your solicitor/conveyancer who will deal with it as a purchase of unregistered property and, when you become the new owner, will register your ownership at the Land Registry. There is a two-month time limit for lodging the documents at the Land Registry after completion, but the Registry may take longer than you would wish – or expect – to record the change – often many months.

A fee is charged by the Land Registry for registration, based on the price paid for the house – see page 25. These Land Registry fees are always payable by the buyer.

Joint ownership

Where two or more people buy a house together – for example, husband and wife, or brother and sister – they should consult with their solicitor/conveyancer as early as possible as to which of the two kinds of joint ownership is more appropriate.

- **Joint tenancy** (the word 'tenancy' has nothing to do with rented property in this context) – under this arrangement, neither can sell without the other's agreement. When one dies, the survivor will automatically inherit the other's share. This may be a suitable arrangement for husband and wife, but may often not suit other kinds of shared ownership – e.g. two couples buying a house together.
- **Tenancy in common** – here, each joint owner is able to dispose of his or her share as he or she wishes, whether by

will or during his or her lifetime. This form of joint ownership is generally chosen by co-owners who are not married, who prefer to retain this independence. Joint tenants always hold the property in equal shares but tenants in common can have unequal shares in the property – for example, to reflect their different contributions to the price.

It is easy for a joint tenancy to be converted into a tenancy in common at any time – simply by one co-owner giving written notice to the other – but the reverse is more complicated and would need a lawyer.

The relevance of inheritance tax in the event of death of either or both of the co-owners is a factor in deciding whether a joint tenancy or a tenancy in common is preferable – see page 266.

In the event of a marriage breakdown, it is less complicated to preserve the rights of each spouse if the home is in joint names. A divorce court, however, has discretion to decide what is to happen to the home.

Buying extra items

Your solicitor/conveyancer needs to know the details of any items in the house which you have agreed to buy as an extra, as well as what fixtures and fittings you have agreed with the seller are to be included in the sale.

The standard form of enquiries contains a request for confirmation of items on the property which are included in the sale. The answer sometimes given by the seller's solicitor/conveyancer is: 'see agent's particulars', but an agent may not have been fully informed by the seller, or the seller may have changed his or her mind after the particulars were circulated. In order to avoid any misunderstanding or unpleasantness, the parties should reach a clear understanding with each other about what is and what is not included, and make a list in writing. Include this list with the other details you send to your solicitor/conveyancer, together with the agreed prices of those items you are buying separately. Insist that all of these are referred to in the contract, quoting relevant details such as brand names where appropriate.

If the TransAction Protocol procedures are being used you will be provided with a comprehensive fixtures, fittings and contents form.

This topic is covered in detail in **Chapter 4.**

Boundary walls and fences

It is most important to know where the boundaries lie before you commit yourself to buying a property. Boundary disputes are difficult to resolve and generate great animosity between neighbours.

Boundary hints

- A line of trees or a hedge at the side or far end of the garden does not necessarily indicate the limit of the property: it could be within or beyond that line.
- Ask to see the plan. Check (or ask your surveyor to investigate) exactly where the boundaries lie. If necessary, measure on the ground and compare the results with any dimensions given in the title documents or plan.
- The deeds are not always a help. Some deeds have no plan at all or are imprecise about where the boundaries actually are. Sometimes, the boundary is not where the deeds say it should be.
- Even established boundaries may not be accurate. Mistakes can be carried forward. Neighbours sometimes make their own adjustments without thinking to have the position regularised in their deeds.
- Traditionally, 'T' marks on a boundary line drawn on an original site plan indicate that that particular wall or fence belongs to the owner of the property inside which the 'T' mark appears.
- The deeds may say, or there may be other evidence, that a fence or wall on the boundary is on your land – in which case, you own it.
- If the house is registered at the Land Registry there will always be a plan but even this is not guaranteed to be accurate: it is still important to check for discrepancies.

Responsibility for boundaries
- Some deeds specify clearly what your obligations are as far as fencing is concerned (the type, or minimum or maximum height).
- If nothing is stated, you may not need to have a fence at all (unless one would be necessary to prevent damage or injury to others).
- Walls dividing semi-detached or terraced properties with supports on both sides are generally regarded as belonging to both, with repairs being a joint expense.
- Where there is a fence which you are not obliged to have, you generally cannot be made to repair it, but if it is likely to fall on your neighbour's land, it is up to you to make it safe or remove it.
- If you have to go on to a neighbour's land to repair a fence or wall, you will normally need permission unless the right is granted to you in your or his/her deeds.
- Sometimes you are not allowed to fence. Some new estates, for example, impose restrictions against front gardens being divided, and the original planning permission may have been granted on this basis. Corner properties may have special provisions about 'line(s) of sight' for traffic.
- Under general planning law, you may not erect a fence more than one metre high in front of a house, nor over two metres high at the rear.

  If there are doubts about the position of boundaries or the obligation to repair them it may be necessary to investigate further and obtain additional evidence, such as a sworn statement from someone familiar with the property. This should be dealt with before contracts are exchanged. It is the seller's responsibility. As the buyer, you should not be involved in the expense of sorting out these matters.

The Access to Neighbouring Land Act 1992
This Act came into force in January 1993 and gives the courts power to award access for certain necessary repairs and other works. An access order will only be made if it is impossible – or extremely difficult – to carry out the works without gaining access on to neighbouring land. The new legal provisions are

extremely complex and would undoubtedly be costly to invoke. It is therefore sensible to ensure that you buy a house which either already has rights of access over the neighbouring property to carry out repairs, or does not need them.

The conveyancing procedure – buying

The draft contract

It is the seller's solicitor/conveyancer who prepares a draft contract. He or she will produce this from the information to hand about the transaction (price, names of the parties and so on) and from the seller's title deeds. With the draft contract there will also be sent a 'package' consisting of a copy of the title deeds (or entries on the Land Register if the ownership is registered). If the solicitors are operating the TransAction Protocol (see page 257) the seller's solicitor will also send a copy of up-to-date searches, and a property information form.

The job of the buyer's solicitor/conveyancer is to make whatever enquiries may be necessary to ensure that there are no points which might affect your decision to buy, or your later enjoyment of the property. One of the main things that has to be done when you buy a house is to make sure that the seller really owns it and has the right to sell it.

With unregistered land, the solicitor/conveyancer has to check on all previous transactions which affect the title every time property changes hands – matters such as sales, mortgages, the granting of rights over the property, rights of way, drainage. This is done by investigating a summary (prepared by the seller or his or her solicitor/conveyancer) of the title deeds covering at least the previous 15 years (and often much longer). If the property is registered, it is a more simple matter of examining the registered details (office copy entries).

Ask your solicitor/conveyancer to send a copy of the draft contract if it has not been sent to you. If the seller has agreed to pay for remedial work, or to undertake any other obligations to you, make sure it gets put into the contract. Don't leave anything to chance: all material matters should be put into the contract. Human nature being what it is, people forget their promises once they achieve what they want! At this stage, the contract is only a draft because your solicitor/conveyancer has to be given the opportunity to check, change or add anything as a result of the enquiries and searches made, plus anything you may have told him or her.

Local searches

There are standard forms of questions; enquiries (called local searches) are sent off to the local authority, the answers to which may show, for example, whether there are any plans to build a trunk road nearby, or whether there are any serious defects which the local authority would require to be put right.

Note: these searches are mainly against the house itself. They do not show up information about nearby property (except matters like road proposals). If there is a derelict building or any vacant land nearby ask your solicitor/conveyancer to make a search on that too or go to the local authority and find out if anything is registered against it (such as planning permission for development or compulsory purchase).

Water and other searches

There is also now a separate set of standard questions which is sent to the water authority.

Your solicitor/conveyancer should consider carrying out other searches and enquiries if appropriate (there are many to choose from – see pages 25–6 – such as coal mining, commons searches etc.).

Preliminary enquiries

There is also a set of standard questions, known as 'preliminary enquiries' or 'enquiries before contract', concerning the property itself, boundaries, restrictions and so on. These are sent to the seller's solicitor/conveyancer with such additional questions as your solicitor/conveyancer thinks appropriate for the particular transaction, so as to get as much information about the property as possible before exchanging contracts.

Finalising the draft contract

It is essential that the contract contains everything that has been agreed between buyer and seller. Make sure you tell your solicitor/conveyancer about all agreements you have made with the seller.

Agreeing amendments to a draft contract can take time if the contract goes back and forth between the two professionals. Rather than sit at home fretting, do not be afraid to ask what is going on if there seem inexplicable delays or silences. But do not telephone daily – that would not help matters and you may find yourself paying for the time you take up.

THE LAW SOCIETY'S TRANSACTION PROTOCOL

This Law Society scheme is used by many solicitors. The seller's solicitor determines whether it is used. If it is used, the seller's solicitor provides a package containing the following:

- the draft contract
- copies of earlier title deeds (if unregistered) or official copies of the entries in the register (if registered)
- a special form of preliminary enquiries called the property information form
- the local authority search and any other appropriate searches (for example, land charges search, Index Map, coal mining or other searches). The cost of the searches is initially borne by the seller but if the sale goes ahead, the cost is reimbursed to the seller by the buyer on completion
- a fixtures, fittings and contents form, listing all the fixtures and fittings which are included in the price and those which will be removed by the seller. The idea behind the scheme is to get the paperwork under way quickly at the beginning of the transaction.

Exchange of contracts

Exchange of contracts means that the documents are physically swapped over. If you are buying, a contract with your signature goes to the seller's solicitor/conveyancer, who sends an identical contract signed by the seller to your solicitor/conveyancer.

Once contracts are exchanged, you (and the people selling to or buying from you) are locked into a legal agreement from which neither side can withdraw.

It is therefore a crucial point in the proceedings. A good solicitor/conveyancer will take time before you reach the stage of exchange of contracts to see you at the office and go through all the paperwork with you. Do not be afraid to ask questions on any points that are still unclear. It is important to make sure that everything is right *now*. It will be too late to change things after exchange of contracts.

Contracts should not be exchanged until:

- preliminary enquiries and local searches are completed
- any surveyor's report has been made and the facts accepted
- the source of funding is settled: a mortgage loan is offered in writing (and all conditions can be complied with)
- the deposit of 10 per cent of the purchase price (or less, by agreement) is available
- all terms are agreed between the parties. If there are matters which still have not been agreed it is not wise to leave matters to chance or goodwill. In a dispute, the contract will be relied on. If terms are missed out they cannot be put back once contracts are exchanged.
- the date for completion (i.e. the date to finalise the deal) has been agreed. (Completion day is often about two weeks from exchange of contracts, but this period can be longer or shorter, depending on the wishes of the people concerned.)

Buyer's exchange of contracts check list

- Survey report received and in order?
- Mortgage offer received and in order?
- Other finances calculated and in place?
- Deposit amount agreed and available?
- Removers lined up?
- Insurance (life and property) arranged and ready to be put in force?

- Completion date agreed with seller/own buyer/lender/all parties in chain?
- Terms of contract finalised and checked?

Contracts are then exchanged. There are two identical copies of the contract – one signed by the seller and one by the buyer. It is only when these documents have been exchanged that the two parties become legally bound to the transaction. Exchange of contracts now usually takes place between the seller's solicitor/ conveyancer and yours by telephone, using procedures laid down by the Law Society★.

After exchange of contracts, a buyer no longer needs to worry about gazumping or a seller whether the buyer really will go through with the deal. But it also means that you cannot change your mind. You have to buy (or sell) even if you lose your job or you discover some dreadful defect in the house you are buying.

Between exchange of contracts and completion

After exchange of contracts there is considerable activity between solicitors. It is the time when the transfer document is prepared. If the land is already registered this will be called a 'Transfer', but if the land is not yet registered your solicitor/ conveyancer may prepare a 'conveyance' or a special form of Transfer.

The Transfer must be signed by the seller and almost always by the buyer. This time will also be used to finalise the mortgage arrangements. Your solicitor/conveyancer (or that of the lender, if separate) will prepare the mortgage documents and arrange for the loan to be available on completion. If you are having an endowment mortgage, the life insurance policy must be in force by the completion date (it is best to put this on risk as soon as contracts are exchanged).

Final searches and enquiries will be carried out. Your solicitor/conveyancer will check whether anything is registered against the seller at the Land Registry (if the house is registered) or at the Land Charges Registry (if the house is not yet registered). The sort of things which might show up are undisclosed mortgages or disputes.

If you are buying from a company, your solicitor/conveyancer will make a company search if the property is not yet registered. He or she will also send 'Requisitions on Title' to the seller's solicitor/conveyancer to check on outstanding matters before completion.

The lead up to completion

Make sure you remain available to your solicitor/conveyancer in the weeks leading up to completion. There will be documents to sign and last-minute matters to arrange. You won't have to do any of the legal work but you will be needed to pay any sums due in sufficient time for cheques to clear before completion. This will include not only the balance of the money needed to buy, but also Land Registry fees and stamp duty. Some solicitors/conveyancers ask to be paid their own fee before completion.

It is most important to make sure *before* completion that outstanding obligations (e.g. remedial work) have been carried out in accordance with the contract. If not, you may have considerable difficulty in enforcing the contract once completion has taken place.

You should now be dealing with the logistics of moving. See **Chapter 9**.

Completion

This is the day when:

- the buyer pays the seller the balance of the price for the house (usually through solicitors or conveyancers)
- the seller's deeds are handed over to the buyer (through solicitors or conveyancers) and arrangements are made to pay off outstanding mortgages owed by the seller
- the seller *must* move out
- the keys are handed over to the buyer.

After completion

There is a lot of tidying up which has to be done by the buyer's solicitor/conveyancer after completion. Activities include:

- notifying the lender that completion has taken place
- giving other notifications (where appropriate) that completion has happened – such as to life insurance companies (where there is an endowment mortgage) or to the freeholder (where a leasehold has been transferred)
- producing the Transfer to the Inland Revenue and paying any stamp duty due
- registering the change of ownership at the Land Registry
- sending the deeds to the building society (or other lender) when the registration is complete
- sending you a 'completion statement', giving a complete financial summary of the transaction
- (and finally) sending you the bill!

The conveyancing procedure – selling

The same procedure takes place as under 'Buying' but from a different perspective.

Contract

The seller's solicitor/conveyancer will obtain the title deeds from the current lender (if the house is mortgaged) and from these prepare the draft contract. If the TransAction procedures are being used, together with the contract will be sent the answers to standard questions on the property and a detailed list of items to be included or excluded. Your solicitor/conveyancer will contact you and check that all information given is accurate. Make sure you give full and correct information. If in doubt, take advice at this stage. If difficulties appear only at a late stage (for instance because your solicitor/conveyancer did not know that there was a domestic dispute in your family), you could be liable for compensation if completion is delayed. If you have relevant documents (such as planning permissions, or treatment guarantees) these should be sent on to your solicitor/conveyancer.

Once the contract is sent out there may be further queries to be dealt with.

Negative equity

If there is any doubt that the price you sell at will cover the cost of repaying existing mortgages, ask your solicitor/conveyancer to obtain settlement figures (redemption statements) before contracts are exchanged.

Exchange

You may also be buying. It is essential that your transactions tie in. Make sure that the completion date is agreed all round. Make sure too that your finances are in order before you exchange contracts.

Completion

You must move all your possessions out of the house (except those which you have agreed to leave). It is a courtesy to clean the house before you go. Your solicitor/conveyancer will receive the purchase money, pay off existing mortgages and account to you for the balance after paying all expenses (or put the balance to your new house if you are buying another).

When things go wrong

Tens of thousands of house sales take place each year. Most of them go virtually without a hitch, but problems can occur very occasionally. These can range from minor irritations to major crises. The following are some of the things that go wrong and how they might be put right.

The seller fails to move out on completion day

If you get any warning that this might happen, instruct your solicitor/conveyancer immediately to hold up the transfer of the money. He or she will take steps to enforce the contract. A 'notice to complete' will be served. This will 'make time of the essence' and legally require the seller to complete the sale within a specified time. Your solicitor/conveyancer may also advise you on the question of issuing legal proceedings.

You can claim compensation if you are put to extra expense (e.g. hotel bills) if your move is delayed.

The buyer fails to pay the money due on completion

It goes without saying that you should not let the buyer move in. Once again, a notice to complete will be served, and other legal steps may be necessary to enforce the contract.

The money fails to get through

Much of the conveyancing process relies on high technology. It has been known for the computers operated by banks or building societies to fail, locking millions of pounds into the system while the problems are sorted out. There is very little that can be done in this situation, except to do the British thing and have a cup of tea while the problems are sorted out. Solicitors/conveyancers can often rely on local goodwill to get clients moved, and then pick up the financial pieces later.

The seller has taken away things which were included in the contract

Depending on what these are, a claim for the return of the original items (and the costs of re-installing them) can be made or the seller can be sued for compensation.

You find that you have not got what you bargained for

If the property is in worse condition than you expected, or there is a major defect in it, your remedy will depend on the circumstances:

- If it is something which should have been revealed in your survey, you could have a claim against your surveyor.
- If it is a new property with a Foundation 15 or NHBC guarantee, follow the claims procedures available under these schemes.
- If the problem is the result of false information, you may have a claim against the estate agent (under the Property Misdescriptions Act) or against the seller.

But, except in the cases of new houses, there is generally no guarantee about the state and condition of a house. This underlines the need to have proper checks carried out before you exchange contracts.

You find that there are legal problems

It must be stressed that the conveyancing procedure cannot be certain to unearth all problems, but it should protect you against most.

If you have received poor service but have not suffered financially you may have a right of complaint either to the Office for the Supervision of Solicitors (OSS)★ (complaints against solicitors) or to the Council for Licensed Conveyancers (CLC)★ (complaints against licensed conveyancers). Both have disciplinary powers. The OSS can order a refund of fees and/or compensation (up to £1,000). If you are not satisfied with the way in which the OSS has handled your complaint you may complain further to the Legal Services Ombudsman★.

If your solicitor or licensed conveyancer has not delivered the required level of service, and you have suffered financially as a result, you will have a compensation claim. This could happen, for instance, if steps are not taken to ensure that the seller's mortgage is repaid on completion, or if the solicitor/conveyancer fails to find out about (or tell you about) a restriction which prevents you using the house as a home.

Solicitors and licensed conveyancers are required by law to be covered by negligence insurance. Neither the OSS nor the CLC will handle negligence claims. Here seek advice from an independent solicitor. The Law Society★ has a 'negligence panel' of solicitors prepared to take on cases against other solicitors. They will offer a free preliminary consultation. Contact them through the OSS.

Total disaster: the solicitor/conveyancer defaults and keeps your money

This is fortunately very rare. If it happens, take immediate steps to contact an independent solicitor. The Law Society administers a fund (paid for by solicitors) to compensate clients who have lost out in these circumstances. The CLC operates a similar scheme.

Other legal matters

A will

If you have become a property owner for the first time, it is important to make a will or amend an existing one, making clear what you wish to be done with your estate after your death. It is not too difficult for the average person to draw up a will but it is essential that this is done correctly. The Consumers' Association publication *Wills and Probate* explains how to draw up your own will.

If you think your case is at all complicated, it would be worth consulting a solicitor (also if you have moved to or from Scotland). Some solicitors will make a deal with you over fees if you make a will at the same time as you move if the firm is handling the conveyancing.

Keep your will in a safe place – and tell your executors where this is.

Tax

Capital gains tax

Normally, you do not have to worry about capital gains tax (CGT) when you are selling your home. So long as you have lived in the house throughout your ownership and have lived in (or owned) no other house as your principal residence, no tax will be payable. But tax might be payable if, for instance, you have spent time abroad and let the home to tenants, or if you have not actually occupied the home (even if you owned no other). You might also have to pay tax if part of the house was used for business purposes or the land sold with it was more than an acre.

Capital gains tax is payable only on the net profit on the sale (after knocking off the costs of buying and selling and improvements – other than things such as redecoration). The first £6,300 is exempt (1996–7 tax year) and tax is payable at your income tax rate on the rest. The profit is based either on the value of the property in 1982 or, if acquired after 31 March 1982, on the price you paid when you bought it.

There are specific exemptions to having to pay CGT. For instance, you can overlap two houses if you buy your new home before selling your old one but for no more than two years. The 'dependent relative exemption', which enables a second house to be sold free of CGT if it has been occupied throughout your ownership rent-free by certain relatives, applies only to property which was acquired for this purpose before 6 April 1988.

Inheritance tax

House buying is often accompanied by additional life insurance arrangements, which may result in the value of your estate on death being considerably increased. This could give rise to inheritance tax (formerly estate duty or capital gains tax) considerations. The threshold for inheritance tax is £200,000 in the 1996-7 tax year (value of estate at death but taking into account gifts made during the previous seven years). Tax at the rate of 40 per cent is payable on the excess over £200,000. There are various exemptions. Notably, gifts at any time between husband and wife (but *not* people simply living together as man and wife) are always exempt.

Various steps can be taken to minimise inheritance tax, such as equalising assets between husband and wife, so that full advantage can be taken of the exemptions on the death of both. It often helps in these circumstances for a house to be owned as tenants in common (see page 251–2). If your assets are approaching the inheritance tax limit, it would be worthwhile taking advice on tax planning from your solicitor.

Credit blacklisting

In the past, home buyers have found that they are unable to obtain credit because of debts run up by previous owners or occupiers of the property. When a potential lender checked with a credit reference agency, details of everyone who had lived in the property in recent years and their bad debts would show up. Since 1 August 1993 this has no longer been the case because only information about the person applying for credit and people in the house closely associated with him or her can be given. However, this will not protect new owners from being harassed by debt collectors trying to obtain payment of bills left unpaid by previous owners or occupiers.

Normally, a credit reference agency will not give you information about an individual or an address, unless you live at the address. If you are worried that there may be a problem with the seller, tell your solicitor. You have no right to be given credit, but if you are refused a loan you are entitled to know which credit reference agency has been used by your lender, as long as you request the information within 28 days of the decision. Once you have the details of the credit reference agency you can (on payment of a fee of £1) request details of the information it holds on you. If any of it is incorrect, you have a right to have it corrected.

Another source of information about credit is the Registry of County Court Judgments*. For a small fee you can check against any name and address.

DOING IT YOURSELF

YOU WOULD be unwise to attempt to do-it-yourself where the property you are buying or selling is:

- not freehold
- not registered
- not in England or Wales
- not a house
- part of a property. There are special considerations where part of a garden or house is sold, or where part of the property is let to tenants. This should always be dealt with by a solicitor
- sold at auction
- not wholly occupied by the seller
- being sold to you as new by a builder or developer
- a 'hybrid transaction' – housing associations and other bodies have developed schemes to help first-time buyers get a foot on the house-owning ladder. These usually involve complex documentation which is part freehold and part leasehold
- being sold by a divorcing or separating couple. Buying or selling a house in these circumstances requires specialist skill and knowledge
- not through a solicitor or licensed conveyancer. You should be very careful if you are dealing with either an unlicensed conveyancer or a private individual acting for him/herself. There is nothing wrong with two unqualified people handling their own transactions, but the scope for problems does increase greatly.

If you are getting a mortgage, the saving may not be great: you will still have to pay the lender's solicitor's charge.

Usually, your own solicitor will do the building society work as well and charge an all-in fee. If you do your own conveyancing, you will be charged at a higher rate for the building society's solicitor's work.

Getting started

To have a chance of doing it yourself successfully you must know as much as you can about what you are doing. You will need to have knowledge of the law and the procedures and will have to be able to devote time to the exercise. You will need to be on hand during the working day and will probably have to travel around quite a bit. The protocols which are available to solicitors and licensed conveyancers (such as exchange of contracts by telephone, completion through the post) will not be available to you.

You should have access to a daytime telephone and preferably also a fax machine – virtually all solicitors and licensed conveyancers are now on fax. You should also adopt basic office techniques – have your letters typed (and keep copies), keep a file, and so on.

This book contains much background information about house transactions. Read it and become familiar with it.

You will need to get hold of some forms, but this will not always be easy. Some law stationers feel protective about the legal profession and may not be prepared to sell you what you need. That is a little short-sighted: if someone is going to go it alone, it is far better that he or she has the right forms. In each section of this chapter you will be told the forms that you will need.

The steps to take

The stages have been outlined earlier in the book. In practice this converts into the following action. This is not a detailed guide to doing it yourself and you should not use it as such. It is simply a check list of the steps that are taken in a normal, straightforward transaction, where the land is already registered.

Buying

The forms you will need are:

- Con 29 (local search) (2)
- LLC1 (1)
- Water search. Some water companies have their own search forms. Enquire of the company covering the area where the house is
- Preliminary enquiries (2)
- Land Registry search form 94A
- Land Registry application to register A4
- Requisitions on title (2)
- Transfer (3)
- Inland Revenue form L(A)451
- Inland Revenue Stamps form 61.

Step 1
Once terms have been agreed, the legal side of house buying begins in earnest. Your first step is to write to the seller's solicitor asking to be sent a draft contract.

Step 2
Make the mortgage application. Tell the lender that you will be doing it yourself and ask what the requirements will be.

Step 3
Arrange survey.

Step 4
The seller's solicitors will send you:

- copies of the draft contract
- office copies (i.e. certified copies) of Land Registry entries.

As part of the TransAction procedure you may also receive the following:

- a recent local search result (for which reimbursement of the fee might be needed)
- answers to standard preliminary enquiries
- copies of relevant documents like NHBC (National House Building Council★) guarantee, planning permissions etc.
- fixtures, fittings and contents form.

Step 5
Acknowledge them. Send in your local and other searches (2 × form Con 29 + 1 × LLC1 + fee) as soon as possible, unless (in the case of a local search) you have already been sent a search by the seller's solicitor. Even then you may have to send off your own search. These searches are valid for only two months. If it is already several weeks old, make your own search.

You should already have been told either by the estate agents or the solicitors for the sellers which is the relevant local authority. In London, it will be one of the London boroughs. Outside London it will be a council of District Council status.

Step 6
Carry out water search.

Step 7
Decide if you want to make other searches (see pages 25–6) or enquiries; if so, get them under way.

Step 8
Check all the documents. Go through every detail of and approve (or make changes to) the contract and send one copy back to the seller's solicitor. At the same time make preliminary enquiries (or extra preliminary enquiries if you have already received the standard answers).

Step 9
Check the plan with the contract or office copy entries against the property itself.

Step 10
Check very thoroughly each of the following as they come in:

the result of your local searches, the answers to preliminary enquiries and all other searches and enquiries you make. Query and resolve any problems that arise.

Step 11
Deal with the requirements of your lender's solicitors.

Step 12
Discuss and agree a completion date with your seller.

Step 13
Agree the amount of deposit you will pay on exchange of contracts.

Step 14
Check survey result and, if appropriate, have the contract amended to deal with any problems.

Step 15
Make sure that: your survey is satisfactory; your mortgage offer is received and has no conditions which would cause problems (including insurance conditions if you are having an endowment mortgage: you will need to have received acceptance terms for any new endowment policies required for the mortgage); your searches disclose no problems; your answers to preliminary enquiries are full, detailed and accurate; the amount of deposit you can pay is acceptable.

Step 16
Make sure that the terms of the contract are agreed, with all detail completed. Both parts of the contract must be identically worded.

Step 17
All buyers sign the contract and send it to the seller's solicitor with the agreed deposit. Stipulate that contracts are to be exchanged within x days and that completion is to be the date you have agreed.

Step 18
Put property insurance (and life insurance if applicable) on cover.

Step 19
After exchange of contracts you will receive the contract signed by the seller. If the TransAction scheme is being used you will also receive the completion particulars form (instead of requisitions on title).

Step 20
Confirm your removal arrangements.

Step 21
Notify the lender's solicitor of exchange of contracts and remind him or her of the completion date. Deal with all requirements as soon as possible.

Step 22
Prepare the transfer and send two copies to the seller's solicitor for approval. At the same time send two copies of requisitions on title if completion particulars form not received.

Step 23
Carry out final searches at Land Registry using form 94A (fee £5).

Step 24
Receive back transfer from the seller's solicitor approved/amended. If you agree to the amendments, prepare fair copy (engrossment – see Glossary). All buyers to sign and have their signatures witnessed.

Step 25
Send signed transfer back to the seller's solicitor and ask the seller to sign in readiness for completion.

Step 26
Check the result of final searches and ask the seller's solicitors to clear off any entries revealed (not previously disclosed).

Step 27
A few days before completion date, make final arrangements for the finances. If you are having a mortgage, the lender's solicitor will attend on completion and will need to be assured that you will pay the necessary balance plus all expenses (such as stamp duty and Land Registry fees).

If you are not having a mortgage, arrange for a bank draft to be issued (a personal cheque will not be acceptable). Check that even a bank draft will be accepted by the seller's solicitor. A bank draft represents guaranteed funds but these still take several days to reach the solicitor's bank account. The solicitor will need to have 'cleared funds' in his or her account so that he or she can account to the client for the money – or pay it on for a connected transaction. In order to achieve this, you may be asked to arrange for your bank to transfer the money to the solicitor's bank account by the computerised system (known as CHAPS) for transferring funds. It will cost you approximately £20 + VAT. You would have to obtain from the solicitor an undertaking not to account to his or her client for the money until completion had taken place. If you do use a bank draft, keep it safe. It is virtually impossible to 'stop' a bank draft.

Step 28
The day before completion make an appointment with the seller's solicitor to complete the purchase. Note that most contracts require completion to take place before the end of the morning.

Step 29
On completion day (if not having a mortgage), attend in good time for the appointment. **Receive**: the title deeds (i.e. Land or Charge Certificate) and other documents (e.g. the originals of all guarantees, certificates, planning permissions, building control consents etc.) in accordance with details previously supplied to you; the transfer (check that it is signed by the sellers)` which should be dated the day of completion; an undertaking from the solicitor to pay off all outstanding mortgages (or form 53 discharges in respect of them all); the keys. **Hand over**: a bank draft for the balance of the money (if

not transferring under the CHAPS system – see Step 27).

If having a mortgage you may still need to attend to provide the balance of the money, collect the keys etc.

Step 30

Move in!

Step 31

If stamp duty is payable, send the transfer with the necessary stamp duty to the Controller of Stamps★ at the Inland Revenue with form L(A)451 and form 61. (This must be done within 30 days.) The transfer will be returned to you with the duty marked on it. If below stamp duty threshold, send L(A)451 to the Land Registry with an application to register. (See below.)

Step 32

Before the expiry date of the priority period shown in your Land Registry search (and allowing for delays in the post), complete A4 application to register and send off with the appropriate documents (the land or charge certificate, form 53, if applicable, the result of your Land Registry search, the transfer and correct fee) to the Land Registry office which covers the property.

Step 33

Deal with any queries raised by the Land Registry within the time limit set.

Step 34

Receive back from the Land Registry the Land Certificate, showing you to be the registered proprietor – check it very carefully. Keep it in a safe place, preferably not at your house.

Selling

The forms you will need are:

- Contract (2)
- Application for Land Registry office copy entries form 109
- Form 53 discharge if you have a mortgage.

Step 1

Send off for office copy entries (form 109 + fee of £10) to the relevant Land Registry. If you do not have your deeds (because you have a mortgage) you will need to find out from your lender the title number of your house.

Step 2

If you have a mortgage, find out from your lender what procedure will be required for releasing the deeds on completion.

Step 3

On receipt of office copy entries, prepare contract and send two copies to buyer's solicitors, along with office copy entries.

Step 4

Answer the preliminary enquiries raised by the buyer's solicitors and send copies of accompanying documentation.

Step 5

Deal with the amendments to the contract suggested by the seller's solicitors and agree its terms. All sellers must sign the contract.

Step 6

Agree method of holding the deposit. The buyer's solicitor will not agree for you to hold it. There are three possibilities: open an account in the joint names of yourself and the buyer's solicitor; or allow the buyer's solicitor to hold it as a stake holder; if you are buying a house simultaneously, the buyer's solicitor may agree to pay the deposit direct to the solicitor acting for your seller.

Step 7

Agree a completion date (which may need to tie in with your purchase).

Step 8

If you have a mortgage, find out from your lenders what their requirements will be for the repayment of the mortgage and release of the deeds to your buyer. Communicate these to the buyer's solicitor.

Step 9
Exchange contracts.

Step 10
The buyer's solicitor will send you a draft transfer and requisitions on title in duplicate.

Step 11
Approve (or amend) and return to the buyer's solicitor the draft transfer, along with answers to requisitions on title asked by the buyer's solicitor or licensed conveyancer. Provide a statement showing the amount you require to be paid on completion.

Step 12
When the engrossment copy of the transfer is sent to you, all sellers must sign it in the presence of an independent witness in readiness for completion. Do not date it yet.

Step 13
Make arrangements for completion. **Hand over** to the buyer's solicitor or licensed conveyancer the Land Certificate, the transfer, all other relevant deeds and documents and, of course, the keys. If you have a mortgage, the Charge Certificate will have to be handed over instead of the Land Certificate, along with a form 53 discharge. The charge certificate will not be released to you, and completion will either have to take place at the lender's office or will have to be attended by the lender's solicitor. **Receive** from the buyer's solicitor the balance of the purchase money.

Step 14
Move out.

CHAPTER 12

AUCTIONS

Buying a house at auction

AN ESTATE agent may advertise or give you details of a house which is going to be sold by auction. The method of sale in this case differs fundamentally from a sale 'by private treaty' in that when the house is 'knocked down' to a bidder, he or she exchanges contracts there and then with the auctioneer and cannot back out of the purchase later. The buyer is legally bound to it, even if he or she were to flee from the sale room without signing anything.

Before the day of the auction, the would-be buyer should therefore have taken all the steps which are normally taken before exchange of contracts: made the preliminary enquiries and local searches, checked the title documents, had a survey carried out, and completed the organisation of his or her finances.

Because an auction is likely to attract a number of interested house buyers all needing the answers to a number of questions about the property, a set of particulars more detailed than usual is prepared by the agent. This normally takes the form of a brochure, sometimes with photographs, containing full details of the house itself, with additional facts about the tenure, possession, fixtures and fittings, Council Tax band, and Special Conditions of Sale. These, along with the Memorandum of Agreement (contained in the brochure) are the equivalent of a contract for sale by private treaty. The problem is that there is no scope for negotiating its terms.

The price

Check if one of the conditions of sale is that the seller is selling 'subject to reserve price' – how much this is is usually not disclosed, although the agent may be able to give you a guideline figure. The auctioneer may, during the bidding, use a phrase like 'I'm going to sell this property', as an indication that the reserve price has been reached. If the bidding does not reach the reserve, the auctioneer withdraws the property. If you were among the last bidders for a property that is withdrawn, tell the agent afterwards at what figure you are prepared to buy – the seller may accept your offer.

The publicity for the auction may contain the proviso 'unless previously sold'. In this case, the seller's agent is open to offers and is prepared to negotiate a sale by private treaty before, and instead of, the auction. The seller will still, however, expect to sell on the auction contract so you may have only a few days (or hours) in which to make enquiries and raise funds.

Check straightaway whether the intention really is to go to auction; it may be more of an incentive for offers than an intention to go to auction and you may lose your chance by waiting for auction day.

Some properties have to go to auction for legal reasons connected with proving that a proper price has been obtained when it is sold by executors or creditors. If the property is one of these, you will see a phrase such as 'sold by order of executors or trustees'. Do not make a prior offer as this may colour the reserve price.

Steps to take

- Study the agent's brochure extremely carefully, reading all the small print. There may be conditions or disclaimers which would make the property unsuitable. Look for mention of any planning restrictions or refusals, in case you would want to make any alterations or improvements.
- View the house in the normal way and be sure that it is what you want. Remember that you cannot back out after the auction.

- As early as possible, send to your solicitor or conveyancer the brochure with all the details, and arrange for him or her to carry out the usual enquiries and searches and check the title before the day of the auction. Sometimes the seller's solicitor will carry out the searches and send a copy to yours. Arrange to have a survey and a valuation done and to get the results before the auction.
- Fix your price limit, and complete arrangements for the necessary finance for the purchase before the day of the auction. A building society or other lender will have to inspect and value the property in the usual way before making an offer of a mortgage.

Resolve not to get carried away during the bidding and so exceed your price limit. If you have doubts about this, appoint someone else to bid for you – such as your solicitor (who will charge for his or her time).

If you are outbid, you lose not only the house but the expenses of a survey and solicitor, just as you do if you fail to buy by private treaty.

If you are successful, you will have to pay 10 per cent of your bid to the auctioneer straightaway. The Memorandum of Agreement is countersigned by the seller's agent as confirmation of the sale and acknowledgement of receipt of the 10 per cent deposit. The rest of the transaction then follows in the same way as with a sale by private treaty arrangement. Completion usually takes place 28 days after the auction, and the balance of the purchase money has to be paid then.

If you cannot complete, the seller can sue you for the difference between your agreed bid and what he or she realises on a subsequent sale if this is less, and for any expenses incurred.

Sale by tender

An alternative to an auction is a tender, which invites buyers to put their offer, together with a 10 per cent deposit, in a sealed envelope and return it to the agent by a specified date. A 'Form of Tender' is included in the sale particulars. Check whether the terms of the tender include a contract, in which case you may be bound to the purchase. In other cases, you may still be able to back out after your tender has been accepted.

This method is not normally used for sales of private houses, although a simplified version of it may be, in cases where two or three offers have been made near to or at the asking price.

Selling a house by auction

Having assessed your property in the light of prevailing market conditions, the estate agent may recommend that you should not sell by private treaty (the most usual method) but by auction. Holding an auction creates a situation where the price may be forced upwards by a number of keen bidders.

An agent may find a house difficult to put a price on because of its unusual nature – a converted mill, chapel or barn, for instance – and if it is the only one of its kind in the district, he or she may have no precedent for an accurate valuation. The agent may, therefore, suggest that an auction would be the best way of ensuring that the seller gets a good price for it. Most firms of estate agents are also property auctioneers.

The seller has to pay the auctioneer a percentage of the price reached (2½ per cent is usual). You should agree beforehand what this will be and whether it will be the same if the property is sold before the auction.

Before the auction

A brochure, sometimes with a photograph, describing the house in detail and containing the particulars, is prepared and printed.

The estate agent arranges for extensive advertising (for which the seller pays) in order to get the widest possible coverage for the auction. Posters and advertisements in specialist magazines add to the cost.

Discuss what the expenses may amount to (not forgetting photographs for the brochure: a professional photographer may be expensive) and try to agree on limits. You can either agree to pay all the publicity expenses incurred, or fix a set sum for them. Some agents require a lump sum in advance for advertising purposes.

The brochure will include the Special Conditions of Sale (which should be drawn up by your solicitor). It should also include the auction contract with blank spaces for the buyer's name and the purchase price to be inserted.

Some auctions are advertised for three or four weeks, others for two or three months, depending on the kind of property involved. Top-of-the-market houses or investment properties usually attract cash buyers rather than buyers needing a mortgage (which takes time to arrange), so the period leading up to the auction can be shorter.

A good auctioneer/estate agent will consult the client halfway to the auction date on whether further expenditure on advertising is justified in view of the response to date.

If, during the period before the auction, a number of would-be buyers emerge, they will want to have surveys and valuations carried out, and you must be prepared to accommodate these. You will probably also have a larger proportion of 'just curious' viewers as well as genuine potential buyers.

The auctioneer's terms may be that you give his or her firm sole selling rights up to the date of auction and for some specified period afterwards. This means that you would have to pay the commission even if you found a private buyer yourself.

Ask the agent to include in the brochure and advertisement that the auction will take place 'unless previously sold'. This gives you the option of accepting an offer from a private buyer. There are many people who would make satisfactory buyers who will not come to buy at an auction. The idea of bidding at an auction is a daunting prospect, and a keen purchaser may be induced to make an attractive offer beforehand. Whether or not you decide to let the property 'go to the room' a buyer will, in any case, have to sign the auction contract. A great advantage of this is that it avoids the pre-contract stress of a sale by private treaty.

But consider carefully before agreeing to accept an offer: the auction may still be the best conclusion.

The agent should help you decide what the reserve price should be. This is usually not revealed to bidders: the sale particulars just state 'subject to reserve price'. If the figure is not reached, the auctioneer withdraws the house. A fee may be payable to the auctioneer in place of commission: this should be part of the agreement made between seller and auctioneer.

At the auction

Public auctions are held on a specified day in a particular auction room, hotel or rented hall. A number of properties may be being sold at the same time.

Bidding takes place along similar lines to the auctioning of goods such as antiques or second-hand furniture. The prospective buyers will be people prepared to go through the preliminaries (including the expenses) without any guarantee of getting the house, or people who have enough cash and confidence to risk bidding without prior investigation.

The reserve price not being revealed, it cannot be leaked beforehand. Also, if you think signs are propitious (lots of enquiries and a rising market), you can lift it a bit. If, on the contrary, signs are bad, you can pare it down a shade.

When the bidding has reached the reserve, it is usual for the auctioneer to let the audience know, particularly if it seems that competition is flagging. This tends to sharpen things up a bit. On the other hand, if it is rolling along in a lively style, he or she will not let on that the reserve has been passed, so that it does not take the steam out of things.

At the fall of the hammer, the successful bidder is committed to buy. He or she has to sign the auction contract and pay 10 per cent of the price there and then to the auctioneer. This should be held by the auctioneer as stakeholder.

The advantage of selling by auction is that there is an immediate binding contract without the uncertainty of the 'subject to contract, subject to survey' stage. The buyer cannot be gazumped and the seller cannot be let down. Completion is usually within four weeks of the auction.

Drawbacks when selling by auction are:

- the cost to the seller is more, sometimes considerably more, than a sale by private treaty – although this may be offset by a better sale price

- the house may be sold before auction so that some of the extra cost will have been unnecessary
- the seller has no choice over who is to be the next owner
- the house could fail to sell if the reserve price is not reached
- you must be prepared to get out of the house and give vacant possession 28 days after the auction.

CHAPTER 13

BUYING AND SELLING IN SCOTLAND

THERE are major differences between Scottish and English law, particularly in the law relating to the purchase and sale of houses and flats. If you are moving from England to Scotland, while the practical aspects of the move are much the same as they would be in England, you will find that the legal aspects are very different.

You are strongly advised not to do your own conveyancing or missives. You will have to employ a solicitor as there are no licensed conveyancers in Scotland.

Prices of houses outside the main cities and suburbs in Scotland are generally rather below the United Kingdom average. Properties in outlying rural areas are relatively inexpensive, less so when they are within easy commuting distance of a major city. But properties in the most sought-after residential areas command high prices.

The inner areas of the major Scottish cities have many good residential areas, where there are many purpose-built old stone tenements (or blocks of flats) and terraced houses.

Virtually all this chapter applies to flats in the same way that it applies to detached, semi-detached or terraced houses. However, in considering whether to buy a flat you would need to look at the condition of the whole tenement, as well as the flat itself, and make sure that the cost of repairing the structure and common parts of the tenement is shared on some equitable basis amongst the proprietors. The word 'house' is used to include a flat unless the text states otherwise.

Tenure

The term freehold is not used in Scotland. Most houses and flats, and indeed most other kinds of property, are owned on 'feudal tenure'. For practical purposes, this means that they are owned absolutely and can be disposed of freely in the same way as freehold land and property in England. The property offered for sale is sometimes referred to in Scotland as 'the feu'.

The main distinguishing feature of feudal tenure is that the original developer of the land or estate owner, who is known as the superior, can impose conditions on its future use – for instance, by prohibiting commercial use, extensions or alterations without his or her consent. It is also usual for the superior to require the maintenance of the property in good condition and reinstatement following damage or destruction.

Once feuing conditions have been imposed, they remain in force in perpetuity unless the superior agrees to waive or modify them. Any purchaser will be bound by the feuing conditions, but it may be possible, once he or she has bought the property, to negotiate with the superior for a waiver. Normally, the superior charges a capital payment for agreeing to waive feuing conditions. If a superior refuses to vary unreasonable conditions, or if the existence of a condition impedes some reasonable use of land, the owner (or 'feuar') can apply to the Lands Tribunal for Scotland* for an order to vary them. A leaflet on land obligations and how they may be varied or discharged, and the fees payable, is obtainable from the Lands Tribunal for Scotland. If you think that you may be justified in seeking such an order, consult your solicitor in the first instance.

In the past, the feuar paid an annual cash sum or 'feuduty' to the superior. Since 1974, the creation of new feuduties has been prohibited, and the feuar is obliged to redeem the feuduty when he or she sells the property. This means that the majority of feuduties have ceased to exist. The feuing conditions, however, still apply even if the feuduty has been redeemed.

Flats

Flats are owned absolutely on feudal tenure, in the same way as houses, rather than on long leases as is the practice in England;

long leases of residential property in Scotland are rare. In the case of flats, the *solum* (the ground on which the block of flats is built), the roof, stairs and common services are normally owned by the proprietors in the block equally or on some other equitable basis. The external walls bounding each flat are owned by the proprietor of it but all the proprietors have an interest to see that they are properly maintained. The title deeds normally set out the basis on which the costs of repairs and maintenance are shared between the various owners.

Solicitors, their role and charges

You will need a solicitor; there are no licensed conveyancers in Scotland. Although in theory you could do all the legal work yourself it is not usually considered practicable to do so.

If you do not know a solicitor, the best recommendation may be that of a friend or colleague who has used one for this type of work and who can give you a personal introduction. English solicitors are not permitted to practise in Scotland, but if you are moving from England, your English solicitor may have a Scottish solicitor with whom he or she deals regularly. A *Directory of General Services* issued by the Law Society of Scotland★ giving the names, addresses and telephone numbers of solicitors is available at Citizens Advice Bureaux and libraries; it also publishes leaflets explaining the role of solicitors in buying and selling houses. You will find a full list of solicitors in the *Yellow Pages*.

You should ask your solicitor, at the outset, to give you an estimate of the fees involved and the outlays (disbursements) he or she will have to make. There are no set fees, so you can shop around for competitive estimates. The outlays are substantial and should be budgeted for.

Pricing

The general practice in Scotland is that houses are offered for sale at 'offers over' a stated figure, sometimes referred to as the 'upset price'. The quoted figure may be the minimum which the seller will consider accepting, but it may have been set low in order to attract purchasers and encourage competitive bidding. Purchasers will generally have to pay more than the upset but much depends on the demand, the condition of the property and market conditions. Houses in modern estates or blocks of flats where there are many similar properties tend to sell for close to the upset. On the other hand, older and more individual properties in sought-after residential areas tend to go for considerably more than the upset.

Sometimes houses are offered for sale at a fixed price. This may be because a quick sale is sought or because earlier attempts to sell it at an 'offers over' price have been unsuccessful. If you want to buy a house which is offered for sale at a fixed price, you should be ready to proceed very quickly, since the first acceptable offer at the stated price will secure the house. Builders and developers invariably sell at fixed prices.

Buying a house

The main steps involved are:

- finding a suitable house
- arranging a loan and having the house surveyed
- making an offer
- obtaining a legal title to the house.

It is advisable to see your solicitor as early on in the procedure as possible. Things can move very fast and if you have not made contact you may miss your chance to make an offer for the house you have decided on. Solicitors can also give useful general advice about buying and assist you in obtaining a loan.

Finding a suitable house

There are three main sources of information about houses for sale in Scotland:

- newspapers
- solicitors' property centres and solicitors' offices
- estate agents.

If you are thinking about a new house, you could contact the sales departments of building firms in the area or go to see the various developments.

A quarterly list of buildings of historic or architectural interest for sale in Scotland is available from the Scottish Civic Trust*.

Newspapers

The English national daily and Sunday newspapers tend to advertise only a limited selection of Scottish houses and do not reflect the range of properties on the market. However, many more are advertised in the principal Scottish 'quality' daily newspapers and each has its main property day – *The Scotsman* (Edinburgh and the Lothians) on Thursdays; *The Herald* (Glasgow and Strathclyde) on Wednesdays; the *Press and Journal* (Aberdeen and Grampian) on Tuesdays, *Courier and Advertiser* (Dundee, Perth and Tayside) on Thursdays. A good range of properties for sale is also advertised in the smaller local newspapers circulating in various districts.

Solicitors' property centres and solicitors' offices

More properties in Scotland are sold by solicitors than by estate agents. This is particularly so in the Edinburgh, Aberdeen and Dundee areas and in many large towns, where the vast majority of houses are sold by solicitors and where solicitors' property centres (sometimes called Solicitors' Estate Agencies Ltd, or SEAL) have become established. These are run by solicitors on a co-operative basis and are situated in shopping areas. They provide details of all properties being sold by solicitors in the area. There is a solicitors' property centre in Berwick-upon-Tweed, unique in that it deals with properties for sale on both sides of the border – England and Scotland.

Most solicitors' property centres operate only as information centres and not as selling agents – the solicitors themselves retain the selling role. The staff at a centre are conversant with house purchase and sale procedures and will give general advice and information but will direct a customer who is interested in a property to the solicitor actually selling it. All properties are displayed (most with photographs) and full estate agency-type particulars are available for each property, including the name of the solicitor handling the sale. The biggest centres, in Aberdeen and Edinburgh, each have several thousand properties on display at any one time. The service is free to people looking for property to buy.

Some solicitors' property centres publish regular property lists, most of them weekly, with full listings of all properties registered at the centre in question. Copies can be mailed to prospective purchasers if requested and are available from the particular centre and from all the solicitors practising in the area.

A list of solicitors' property centres with addresses and telephone numbers is available from the Law Society of Scotland*.

Solicitors are allowed to call themselves 'Solicitors and Estate Agents' and often do so. Some firms of solicitors have their own property department where details of available properties are displayed and from whom you can obtain particulars of properties for sale. Many firms of solicitors employ specialist sales staff who deal with the non-legal aspects of buying and selling property.

Estate agents

There are many estate agents in Scotland. Many are part of chains owned by UK insurance companies or building societies, others are local firms.

The larger estate agencies issue regular property lists and most estate agents maintain mailing lists. Estate agents in Edinburgh have grouped together to publish a fortnightly property list *Real Homes* which is available through offices of its member firms.

Generally, estate agents in Scotland operate in the same way as those in England and Wales, and the points to bear in mind when dealing with an estate agent in Scotland are the same.

When you have found a house

When you have found a house that you would like to buy, tell your solicitor immediately. You can discuss with the seller the date of entry and what contents, such as carpets, curtains, light fittings etc., are included, although these should be in the particulars of sale. You can try to negotiate a price, but many sellers will simply ask you to put in a formal offer via your solicitor. An oral agreement for the sale of land or a house cannot create a binding contract and can be repudiated by either party without any consequences. But you should never write letters or sign any documents relating to a sale or purchase without consulting your solicitor. Developers usually have their own documents for intending purchasers to sign and it is very difficult to negotiate different terms. Even so, you should show the document to your solicitor before signing it so that he or she can explain the terms and effect of the document to you.

When you tell your solicitor that you are interested in buying a particular property, the first thing he or she will do is to telephone the seller's solicitor or estate agent to notify him or her of your interest. The seller's solicitor or estate agent will give you a chance to offer, once your interest has been notified, although he or she is not legally obliged to do so.

Mortgage loan

If you have not already made your loan arrangements, the next thing to do is to arrange with a building society, bank or other source of finance to lend you the money you need to borrow. If you have difficulty in finding a loan, your solicitor will probably be able to help you.

It is wise to make sure at an early stage that the necessary loan finance will be available when it is needed. Most of the leading English building societies and banks, and all the Scottish banks and building societies, will lend on the security of Scottish properties.

Even before you have a specific house in mind, you should establish that the amount you require will be available on the type of property which you are seeking and that it will be available when you want it – subject always to a satisfactory survey report on the chosen house. See also **Chapter 6**.

Survey

Building societies and banks require the property to be surveyed before committing themselves to making you a loan. Even if you are paying for the house without a loan you are strongly advised to have the property surveyed before making an offer. In Scotland it is customary to have a survey carried out before you make an offer for a property. An offer made 'subject to survey' is almost certain to be rejected by the seller unless the property requires expensive specialist surveys or market conditions are unusual.

The survey is usually instructed by your solicitor once he or she is informed that you are interested and wish to go ahead. If your offer is unsuccessful you will have wasted the survey fee and your solicitor will expect you to pay for it there and then.

The range of types of survey is similar to that in England. The briefest and cheapest is the building society survey, which is little more than a mortgage valuation; the home buyers' report gives a wider range of fairly standard information; a full structural survey normally costs much more and is rarely instructed in Scotland.

A building society valuation is undertaken merely for the purpose of satisfying the building society that the house or flat will provide suitable security for its loan to you. The survey is commissioned by the building society which is making the loan, although it is you who pays the surveyor's fee. The surveyor or building society will tell your solicitor whether the property in question is suitable for the loan which you require, the valuation placed on it, and the main points about the condition of the property. Many building societies now make a practice of giving the borrower a brief written survey report or a copy of the surveyor's report.

Making an offer

If the survey report is favourable, the next thing to do is to make an offer to buy the property. An offer is a formal document, usually a letter running to several pages, or sometimes a shorter letter with a schedule of conditions attached. It specifies all the conditions on which you are willing to buy the property. You are strongly advised not to make an offer yourself. Your solicitor will prepare it and send it to the seller's solicitor or estate agent.

In making the offer, you will have to decide, with guidance from your solicitor, how much to pay. You should also be clear when you want to move in and what extras you want to buy. If you are the only person interested in the property, your solicitor may be able to find this out from the seller's solicitor or estate agent and may be able to negotiate an acceptable price.

If more than one person is interested in buying the same property, the seller's solicitor or estate agent will normally fix a closing date, intimating to each person interested that offers must be submitted by a stated time on a stated date. You will have to offer 'blind', without knowing how much other people will offer. There may be quite a large gap between the highest and the next highest offers. It is not possible to get round this by making a bid of '£100 more than the highest offer you receive'.

Your solicitor will normally help you decide how much over the upset price you should offer (he or she probably has access to information about prices achieved for similar properties to guide you in making your decision; the solicitor's knowledge of the market locally is important and usually helpful to you). But the final decision is yours.

Date of entry

Stating the date on which you want to move in is part of your formal offer. Whether this is acceptable is largely governed by when the seller wants to move out. The date of entry is a matter for negotiation between you and the seller. If there are no compelling reasons on either side for a very early or very far-off date of entry, the period between making the offer and moving in is typically between one and two months. This gives you a reasonable period in which to sell your house and have all the legal work completed.

Extras

What extras, such as carpets, curtains, kitchen equipment, etc., you wish to purchase may be relevant if there is competition for the house and one prospective purchaser is offering a better price than another for the contents. Sale particulars normally specify what is, and what is not, included in the price and your offer will normally be drawn up accordingly.

If the extra items included in your price are valuable, you may want to allocate part of the price on them – for example, house £75,000, moveable property £3,000 – as this will give you a small saving in stamp duty. For stamp duty to be saved, the items must be moveable. Heritable fittings and fixtures (fitted kitchens, built-in bedroom furniture etc.) are transferred by the disposition. This will therefore contain a statement of the value of the building + heritable fittings and fixtures.

The remaining conditions of the offer are taken up with technical legal matters such as ensuring that you will receive a good marketable title, that the property is not adversely affected by planning proposals, that structural alterations/extensions have received local authority approval and that you can withdraw from the contract if the house and contents included in the sale are not in substantially the same condition when you move in as when you offered for them.

If there is some special use to which you want to put the property, such as using part of it as an office or as a guest house, or if you plan to make major alterations, you must tell your solicitor so that he or she can include conditions in the offer to make sure that there are no relevant prohibitions in the title. If you are planning alterations or a change of use, you may have to make the offer conditional upon obtaining planning and/or building control permission. Sellers are not very keen on such offers but sometimes they are unavoidable.

Concluding the contract

If a closing date has been fixed and there is more than one offer, the seller and the solicitor or estate agent will consider all the offers made and decide which one, if any, to accept. Although the highest offer is normally the one accepted, the seller can, and sometimes does, take other factors into consideration, such as the date of entry proposed and the extras to be included in the sale.

Your solicitor will usually be informed by the seller's solicitor or estate agent, by telephone, within an hour or so after the closing time, whether your offer has been successful.

Your offer will stipulate that the property is not subject to any local authority proposals, notices or orders which might adversely affect it and oblige the seller to obtain and exhibit local authority certificates to this effect. Should the certificates disclose any adverse matter, you are permitted to withdraw from the purchase or you could renegotiate the price. You should ask your solicitor to explain the legal and practical effects of any matters disclosed, such as the building being listed as being of architectural or historic interest.

An oral acceptance is not legally binding; usually the selling solicitor will deliver an acceptance modifying or adjusting some of the terms of your offer, such as the date of entry, or making provision for payment of interest on the price of the house if settlement of the price on the date of entry is delayed through no fault of the seller, and to what extent (if any) the contract to be concluded will form a continuing contract after the date of entry. This is called a qualified acceptance and is often delivered within a day or so of receipt of the offer. If the modifications are acceptable to you (your solicitor will advise you on this), your solicitor sends a letter to the selling solicitor confirming that a binding contract is concluded. This is usually done within a day or so of receipt of the qualified acceptance. Thus, the contract can be concluded within a few days of making the offer.

The written offer and subsequent letters between the buyer's and seller's solicitors relating to it are known as 'the missives'. Missives constitute a binding legal contract and neither the buyer nor the seller can withdraw without liability to pay damages. Missives are concluded by the solicitors; there is nothing for the buyer or seller to sign.

Insurance

At common law in Scotland the purchaser becomes responsible for insurance of the property from the date when missives are concluded. However, it is now usual for the missives to provide that the seller will remain liable for any damage to the property until the date of entry, and for its insurance until that date, and that the purchaser can withdraw from the purchase without penalty if the house and any extras included in the sale are seriously damaged or destroyed before the date of entry.

Completing the purchase

Once missives have been concluded, your solicitor will put in hand examination of the title and the conveyancing procedures to ensure that the disposition (the legal document transferring the house to you) in your favour is ready for delivery by the date of entry in exchange for payment of the price.

If you are buying the house together with your husband or wife or some other person, you will need to think about how the title is to be taken. The terms of the title will regulate the ownership, the respective shares of the co-owners and what happens to their shares on their death. You should discuss these matters with your co-owners and your solicitor before the disposition is prepared.

A title simply in the names of two people gives each of them a separate and distinct equal share in the property. If you and your co-owner are to have unequal shares (say one-third to you and two-thirds to your brother) the title must state this. During life, each co-owner can dispose of his or her share (by sale or gift) or can demand that the whole property be sold and his or her share of the proceeds paid over. It is possible for co-owners to agree not to demand a sale. Where the co-owners are a married couple the Matrimonial Homes (Family Protection) (Scotland) Act 1981 requires both spouses (or the court) to agree to any sale of the whole property or any disposal by one spouse of his or her separate share.

Two co-owners, particularly spouses, often take the title in name of each of them and the survivor. Then the survivor automatically becomes entitled to the whole property. Such a survivorship title cannot usually be altered without the agreement of both co-owners and it will in general prevail over any will made by either of the co-owners.

Mortgage

As soon as the missives have been concluded, complete your loan application papers if you have not already done so.

If you are borrowing from a building society, bank or other lender, your solicitor normally acts for the lender as well as for you. He or she will report to the lender on the title and prepare the necessary mortgage document, called a 'standard security'. Sometimes there is additional security by way of assignation of a life policy or pension plan. He or she will also arrange for the loan money to be available in time for the date of entry, and will ask you to sign the standard security and other documents by that date.

If you are in any doubt about the terms of the mortgage documents, ask your solicitor to explain them to you before you sign them. Almost all such documents prohibit letting of the property without the lender's consent. They also set out detailed conditions about maintenance, insurance, and so on, and give the lender a wide range of remedies, including the right to sell the house if you fail to maintain your payments or otherwise fail to observe the loan conditions.

The building society's or other lender's cheque will be sent to your solicitor before the date of entry and he or she will ask you to pay the difference between the price and your mortgage loan. If you are selling another house, whether in Scotland or England, and you are relying on the money from the sale, you should make bridging loan arrangements at an early stage and tell your solicitor.

Documents

On the date of settlement, your solicitor will arrange with the seller's solicitor to hand over a cheque for the full price in return for the title deeds, including the disposition in your favour. This may be done by sending someone along or by post. The keys are usually handed over at settlement unless other arrangements have been agreed.

Your solicitor will register the disposition and the standard security in the General Register of Sasines or, if your property is in an area where registration of title has been introduced, in the Land Register of Scotland. In a couple of months the documents will be returned to your solicitor. If you had a loan, the solicitor will send the documents to the building society or other lender. If there is no loan, your solicitor will hand the title deeds over to you once the registration process has been completed. He or she may offer to hold them in safe custody for you, for which there is generally no charge.

Solicitors' charges

After completing the purchase (or sometimes before doing so) your solicitor will send you the account for his or her fees and outlays (disbursements). Solicitors in Scotland do not charge according to fixed scales.

In addition to the solicitors' fees for the preliminary work leading up to and concluding missives, the conveyancing and the mortgage (on all of which you will have to pay VAT), there will be stamp duty of 1 per cent of the price if it is over £60,000, and registration dues for recording the documents in the Register of Sasines or Land Register.

Outlays must be paid by the date of entry; the solicitor may agree to accept payments of fees a month later or to have payment by instalments, but is not obliged to do so.

Succession

If you buy a house in Scotland intending it as your residence or principal residence, you will acquire a Scottish domicile. This may affect, amongst other things, the way your property is inherited on your death.

If you die without a will, Scottish law will regulate the distribution of your heritable property (that is, land and buildings) in Scotland and moveable property (all property other than 'heritable') in Scotland and elsewhere.

If you die leaving a will, it regulates the distribution of your estate, but the provisions of your will are subject to Scottish rules of succession which differ in a number of important respects from English law. The most important difference is that a spouse and children cannot be cut out of the succession to the moveable estate, no matter what the will may say. They are always entitled to their 'legal rights' which, depending on the circumstances, may be either one-third or one-half of the net moveable estate.

With heritable property (land and buildings), regardless of the domicile of the owner, succession is governed by the law of the country in which the property is. So, even if only a holiday home is bought in Scotland, so that there is no question of the buyer thereby acquiring Scottish domicile, the succession to heritable property in Scotland is governed by Scottish law.

In Scotland, a will is not automatically revoked if the person making it subsequently marries, nor are provisions in favour of a spouse automatically revoked on divorce.

Selling your house

If you are selling in Scotland, you are likely to have been a purchaser already and thus familiar with the Scottish system. Many matters dealt with in the previous section *Buying a house* will be of interest to you as a seller.

The main steps involved in selling a house in Scotland are:

- advertising and showing your house
- dealing with offers
- transferring title to the seller and repaying any loan.

You should alert your solicitor, before putting it on the market, to the fact that you are about to sell your house. This is because a binding contract for the sale will usually be concluded within a few days of a purchaser making a formal offer and this cannot normally be done quickly unless your solicitor has had an opportunity to:

- look over your title deeds to ensure they are in order and that you have good title to the property. (He or she will borrow them from your building society or other lender if you have an outstanding loan over the property)
- order local authority searches to make sure that the property is not affected by any outstanding local authority notices, orders or proposals.

Someone who has been used to the English method of sale, where the solicitor becomes involved at only a relatively late stage, should be aware of the need to bring a solicitor into the picture early in Scotland.

Consent to sale

Where a house is owned by two or more people, all of them must consent to its sale, although a sale can be forced by the court. Try to get agreement because legal proceedings are expensive.

The Matrimonial Homes (Family Protection) (Scotland) Act 1981 makes it imperative for a married seller whose spouse is not a co-owner to obtain the spouse's consent to a sale at the earliest opportunity and certainly before missives are concluded. Failure to do so may mean that the seller finds he or she cannot give the purchaser possession of the property as provided for in the missives. This is especially important where the couple are separated or estranged.

Advertising and showing your house

The three most common ways of marketing your house are to:

- employ a solicitor
- employ an estate agent
- do it yourself.

Even if you employ a solicitor or an estate agent you will probably be showing prospective purchasers round the house yourself. As the owner, you will show the property to its best advantage and know the answers to all the questions people are likely to ask. Moreover, solicitors and estate agents will generally charge extra for showing prospective purchasers round property.

Selling through a solicitor

The majority of houses in Scotland are sold by solicitors rather than by estate agents. If you ask your solicitor to sell your house, you should expect him or her to provide a full estate agency service.

He or she will normally also register your property in the local solicitors' property centre, for which a charge of approximately £150 plus VAT (more in some centres) is made. This covers display of the house in the solicitors' property centre for six months, and insertion in the property centre's regular property listing or mailing where there is one.

Although solicitors are entitled to charge a sales commission of 1½ per cent, many charge 1 per cent or slightly less. Legal fees for conveyancing are in addition to the commission. It is quite common for a solicitor to charge a single percentage fee (usually 1½ per cent) to cover both the selling and the conveyancing. VAT is due on commission and fees. Ask your solicitor for an estimate of charges before instructing him or her to act for you, and if you are not satisfied with the estimate, discuss it with him or her, or seek an alternative estimate from another solicitor.

If you decide to handle the sale yourself and only need your solicitor to attend to certain specific items, make sure that the basis of the charge is agreed in advance.

Selling through an estate agent

Generally speaking, estate agents' terms of business are similar in Scotland to those in England. Commissions are generally 1½ per cent of the achieved selling price, although lower charges may be negotiated, and higher charges normally apply in the case of large country houses or other specialised properties. Ask the estate agent for an estimate and make sure you understand what is included in the charge, whether VAT is included and whether advertising costs are extra; you may be charged for the insertion of the property in the estate agent's house magazine.

Even if you instruct an estate agent to sell your house for you, he or she will normally pass to your solicitor any formal offers which are made. It is important to realise that as well as the estate agent's commission, you will have to pay the solicitor's fee for concluding missives and the conveyancing fees.

Selling it yourself

This entails advertising the property, showing people round it, letting surveyors inspect it, answering questions about room sizes, the price and what items are and are not included in the sale. You should prepare written particulars similar to those issued by solicitors and estate agents, but stress to people viewing the house that these are provided only as a guide and are not to form part of any contract.

If you decide to sell your house yourself, the only costs which you need incur are those for advertising. Although it is probably not sensible to 'go it alone' the first time you sell, if you have been through the process of buying and selling before, and if you have a readily saleable house in which a large number of people are likely to be interested, you may feel that the saving in sales commission is justified. ·

If you decide to sell your house yourself, you will still need a solicitor to do the conveyancing and should tell him or her in advance, and tell prospective buyers that formal written offers are to be submitted to him or her.

The advertisement

If you are selling through a solicitor or an estate agent, he or she will prepare the advertisement for you and agree its terms with you, and will also advise you on the upset price and the price you should expect to achieve.

Arrangements for viewing are normally stated in the advertisement. There may be fixed viewing times or viewing by telephone appointment, or a mixture of both. Remember that the easier you make it for people to view a house, the more people are likely to do so and the quicker you may find a buyer. Evenings and weekend afternoons are popular viewing times.

The advertisement also normally states an upset price and invites offers over that price. The upset is generally fixed below the actual price that a seller hopes to obtain in order to attract purchasers and encourage competition. You should be able to judge what upset to put on your house by looking at advertisements for comparable houses in the neighbourhood. A surveyor will carry out a quick pre-sale valuation for £80–£100 + VAT. (See also **Chapter 7**.)

After the advertisement

You may gain an impression of whether people are seriously interested or not when they come to view, particularly if they return a second time. However, this is not always so and the first sign that you may be going to receive an offer is usually when a solicitor telephones your solicitor or estate agent to say that he or she has a client interested in your property. You should then not sell to anyone without giving everyone who has notified an interest to you or your solicitor or estate agent an opportunity of offering.

Noting interest is usually followed by a visit from a surveyor. If the survey is favourable, it is likely to be followed by an offer.

If you are doing the selling of your house yourself, ask purchasers to lodge formal offers with your solicitor. Never sign a written acceptance of an offer or exchange letters with a prospective purchaser without consulting your solicitor.

Receiving offers

If several people have expressed an interest in your house, it is usual to fix a closing date for offers – that is, a date and time at which you will consider all offers which have been lodged. All those people whose interest has been noted will be asked to submit formal written offers through their solicitor by the date and time fixed. Your solicitor or estate agent will advise you whether to fix a closing date or not, and will suggest when it should be. Often estate agents will advise clients to negotiate with the first person who registers serious interest in the house, whereas solicitors encourage sellers to generate interest from several people before fixing a closing date. Where there is competition, a higher price may be achieved if you do not rush the sale, but this may be nerve-racking for the seller.

On the closing date, you and your solicitor or estate agent will have to decide which offer to accept. You are not under an obligation to accept the highest offer or any offer. If offers are close, you may take into account other factors such as the proposed date of entry, what extras are included in the price, or even whether or not you liked the highest offeror. If the price is acceptable but other conditions of the offer are not, your solicitor or estate agent can negotiate these other conditions with the offeror or his or her solicitor. If the top offer is too low, you may have to re-advertise. It is unethical to try to get the top offeror to pay more without giving the other offerors a chance to re-offer.

Concluding the missives

If you are selling through an estate agent, he or she will normally pass the offers, or at least the offer which is to be accepted, to your solicitor. Once you have received an offer which you want to accept, or identified which of competing offers is to be accepted, your solicitor will adjust points of details with the solicitor acting for the successful offeror. When these adjustments have been made, they are confirmed in writing: this exchange of letters is referred to as the 'missives'. This process normally takes a few days. As with buying a house, the conclusion of missives constitutes a binding contract from which neither party can withdraw. The solicitor will accept the offer and conduct the bargain on your behalf. Make sure therefore that you understand exactly what you are agreeing to.

In theory, it would be possible for 'gazumping' to take place between the date when an acceptable offer is received and the date when missives are concluded, but it would be unethical for a solicitor acting for a seller to negotiate with a third party during this period. If in such circumstances you decided to withdraw from negotiations with the successful offerors and to negotiate with someone else, your solicitor would have to stop acting for you and you would have to appoint another solicitor. The absence of gazumping, and the short time between offers being made and becoming binding, are advantages of the Scottish system.

Completing the sale

Once the missives have been concluded, your solicitor will send the title deeds of the property to the purchaser's solicitor so that he or she can examine them and prepare the disposition (the document transferring title to the purchaser) in favour of the purchaser. He or she will also inform your building society, bank or other lender that missives have been concluded and obtain a redemption statement to show the amount of loan to be repaid on completion of the sale. He or she will prepare the discharge document and have it signed by the lender before the date of entry.

Your solicitor will instruct searches in the Registers to demonstrate to the purchaser that there are no adverse entries in respect of the property or against you as seller. He or she answers any questions raised by the purchaser's solicitor, adjusting the terms of the disposition with him or her. You have to sign it before the date of entry. Date of entry is the date on which the purchaser obtains physical possession of the property. The purchaser may or may not move in then. The date of settlement is when the disposition is handed over in exchange for the price.

Immediately prior to the date of entry, your solicitor will agree with you what arrangements are to be made about handing over the keys (often it is best to deliver these to your solicitor on the date of entry).

The disposition in favour of the purchaser is handed over in return for the purchaser's solicitor's cheque for the full purchase price. Out of that amount, he or she repays your outstanding mortgage loan, and any bridging loan, in accordance with instructions received from you or your bank and will then let you have a cheque for the balance of the price payable to you, after deducting fees and outlays. He or she should provide you with a detailed statement showing all the financial details; if not, make sure you ask for one. You should normally expect your solicitor to send you the balance of the price and his or her statement on the day on which the sale is completed, or at the latest on the following day.

EPILOGUE

And, finally...

If moving has turned out to be particularly complicated or strenuous in spite of trying to foresee all the hazards, try to get away, even if only for a couple of days. A break at this point from the physical and mental effort can make all the difference. You should find that you return eagerly to your new home, ready to enjoy it in a new period of your life.

Glossary

Here are some terms you may come across in connection with conveyancing, insurance, or arranging a mortgage.

Advance The mortgage loan (also capital sum, principal sum).

All risks insurance Insurance that covers all happenings that are not specifically excluded in the policy (as opposed to a policy of specified perils, which covers only the happenings that are listed).

APR Annual percentage rates of the total charge for credit: standard way (laid down by the Consumer Credit Act 1974) of working out the true interest rate; by law, the APR has to be shown by banks and building societies alongside their quoted rates for each mortgage term, to enable potential borrowers to compare equally what is being offered.

Assignment The transfer of ownership to another person of some kinds of property, such as an insurance policy in the case of an endowment mortgage, or a lease.

Balance outstanding The amount of loan owed at any one time.

Bonus Additional amounts paid on with-profits policies – periodically (reversionary) or at the end of the policy term.

Bridging loan A loan, usually from a bank, to tide a person over between the time when he or she has to pay the purchase price of one house and the time when the proceeds of sale of another and/or mortgage funds become available.

Capital The mortgage loan (also advance, principal).

Capital reducing mortgage Repayment mortgage.

Cash-in value see *surrender value*

Charge Any right or interest, subject to which freehold or leasehold property may be held, especially a mortgage; also used to denote a debit, or a claim for payment.

Charges Register One of the three registers maintained by the Land Registry for a property. It records interests adverse to the owner.

Completion date The finalisation of a transaction. The day when the money is paid, the deeds are handed over, the keys are released and you can move into the house.

Conditions of sale The detailed standard terms which govern the rights and duties of the buyer and the seller of a house, as laid down in the contract which they sign; these may be the National Standard, or the Law Society's conditions of sale.

Contract The agreement to sell the property. Not binding until exchange of contracts.

Conveyance A written document transferring unregistered land from the seller to the buyer.

Conveyancing The legal and administrative process involved in transferring the ownership of land or any buildings on it from one owner to another.

Covenant A promise in a deed to undertake (if covenant is positive) or to abstain from doing (if restrictive covenant) specified things.

Creditor Someone owed money; the lender.

Deeds see *title deeds*

Differentials When a lender operates a 'banding system' under which extra interest is charged on larger loans; the 'bands' are known as differentials.

Early redemption Paying off a loan before the end of the mortgage term.

Early redemption charge The sum charged by a lender to cover administration costs in the event of a loan being repaid before the end of the mortgage term (usually in the first three to five years).

Easement The legal right of a property owner to use the facilities of another's land – for example, a right of way.

Endowment insurance Life insurance which will pay out a specified sum, or more, on a specified date (or on death, if sooner).

Endowment mortgage A loan on which only interest is paid throughout the term; it is paid off in one lump sum at the end with the proceeds of an endowment insurance policy.

Engrossment Effectively, the top or final copy of a legal document.

Exchange of contracts The process of making an agreement to buy and sell a house legally binding.

Freehold Property held absolutely (that is, until the end of time). Also known as 'fee simple'.

Indemnity covenant A clause in the transfer in which the buyer undertakes to indemnify the seller in respect of breaches in any of the restrictions in the title deeds which affect the property.

Index Map Search A search to find out if ownership of a property is registered at the Land Registry.

Joint tenants Two or more people holding property as co-owners; when one dies, his or her share of the property automatically passes to the survivor(s).

Land Certificate The certificate, akin to a log book, from the Land Registry to say that you own a house.

Land Registry A government department (head office in London and district registries in various other places in England and Wales) responsible for opening, maintaining and amending the registers of all properties in England and Wales which have registered titles.

Leasehold Ownership of property for a fixed number of years granted by a lease which sets out the obligations of the lessee (or tenant), for example, regarding payment of rent to the landlord, repairs and insurance; as opposed to freehold property, where ownership is absolute.

Legal Charge To all intents and purposes the same as a mortgage.

Lessee A person who takes a lease (i.e. the tenant).

Lessor A person who grants a lease (i.e. the landlord).

Local Search Certificate An application made to the local authority for a certificate providing certain information about a property and the surrounding area.

Low-cost endowment mortgage A mortgage secured by a mixture of endowment with-profits and decreasing convertible term insurance, so that the guaranteed sum insured payable on death is equal to the loan; the bonuses added to the endowment policy normally ensure (but do not guarantee) that the loan can be repaid at the end of the term.

Low start mortgage Premiums start low and increase by a certain percentage each year until the full level premium is reached.

Making time of the essence If either party is late for completion, the contract can be enforced only by serving a notice to complete setting a time limit to finalise the transaction. This step has serious legal consequences.

MIRAS Mortgage Interest Relief At Source; mortgage payments are paid net of basic rate tax (rather than paying the gross amount with adjustment to the tax code).

Mortgage A loan (usually for house purchase) for which a house is the security or collateral. It gives to the lender (usually a building society or bank) certain rights in the property, including the power to sell if the mortgage payments are not made. These rights are cancelled when the money advanced is repaid with interest, in accordance with the agreed terms.

Mortgage deed The document enshrining the conditions of a loan secured on a property (also called a Legal Charge).

Mortgagee The lender.

Mortgage indemnity policy Compulsory insurance required by building society for a loan which is above the percentage of the valuation of the property at which the society will normally lend (also called mortgage guarantee policy or high-lending fee).

Mortgage protection policy Life insurance taken out by borrower which would pay off the outstanding mortgage loan in case of borrower's death, usually taken out with a repayment mortgage.

Mortgagor The borrower (whose property is security for the loan).

Office Copy (Entries) A copy (officially prepared by the Land Registry) of the entries on a Land Register. The term also applies to other official copies – such as probates or letters of administration.

Preliminary enquiries The questions asked about a property before exchange of contracts.

Premium Payment (one-off or periodical) for an insurance policy, the amount depending on the sum insured and the type and degree of risk to the insurer.

Principal The amount of money that has been borrowed and on which interest is calculated.

Property Register One of the three parts of a Land or Charge Certificate. It describes the property and rights that go with it.

Proprietorship Register Another of the parts of a Land or Charge Certificate. It records the names of the owners and any restrictions on their right to sell.

Purchaser The buyer.

Redemption Paying off a loan; the final payment of principal, interest and costs of the mortgage; if all or part of the loan is repaid early, an additional charge may be payable.

Registered land Land (including buildings, houses on it), the title to which is registered at the Land Registry, with the result that ownership is guaranteed fully or to some degree by the state; in all parts of England and Wales, registration of title is compulsory.

Repayment mortgage Loan on which part of the capital as well as interest is paid back throughout the period of the loan.

Requisitions on title The questions asked about the seller's title to land, and the matters raised before completion.

Retention The withholding of part of a mortgage loan, should structural defects need to be repaired on the property in question; the amount is normally the sum required to carry out the repairs, and it will be withheld until the work has been completed satisfactorily.

Right(s) This is an interest protected by law (as opposed to mere permission or licence, which can always be terminated). In house buying it often amounts to a right for the benefit of one property over another (this is an easement). There are many types of rights, such as rights of light, air, way and drainage. Rights for the benefit of the property appear in the property register and rights adverse to the property show in the charges register.

Stakeholder One who holds a deposit as an intermediary between the buyer and seller, so that the deposit may only be passed on to the seller with the permission of the buyer, or returned to the buyer with the permission of the seller.

'Subject to contract' The words you should put in every letter to the seller, his or her solicitor or agent before contracts are exchanged. It is an accepted formula to stop a contract being created in correspondence. (Since September 1989 this procedure has not been strictly necessary. However, it does no harm and might still provide you with protection in rare cases.)

Sum insured The amount that will be paid out when a term insurance policy matures or the event insured for happens (such as, for life insurance, the death of the policyholder; for household insurance, loss of or damage to property).

Surrender value The amount of money a policyholder receives if a life insurance policy is terminated before the expiry date (other than on death), for instance, when the endowment mortgage is paid off early.

Tenants in common Two (or more) people who together hold property in such a way that, when one dies, his or her share does not pass automatically to the survivor but forms part of his or her own property and passes under his or her will or intestacy (this is in contrast with what happens in the case of joint tenants).

Term insurance A life insurance contract which pays out only on death within a specified period (also known as temporary insurance); is used to cover the period of a mortgage.

Term of mortgage The number of years at the end of which the loan is to be repaid; the shorter the term, the higher the monthly repayments (and the APR).

Title The right to ownership of property.

Title deeds The documents conferring and evidencing ownership of land. In registered land transactions the 'Title deeds' will be the Land Certificate or the Charge Certificate.

Title number The unique number allocated to each property by the Land Registry. Make a note of yours. You will need to refer to it in any correspondence with the Land Registry.

Top-up mortgage Additional mortgage from another lender when the first lender does not provide enough finance to purchase a house.

Transfer The Land Registry document transferring the ownership of the property from the seller to the buyer.

Vendor The seller.

With-profits policy A life insurance policy where bonuses (varying according to the company's profits) are added regularly to the original sum assured paid when the policy matures; the type of policy often used for an endowment mortgage.

ADDRESSES

The Advisory Centre for Education
1B Aberdeen Studios
22 Highbury Grove
London N5 2EA
Tel 0171–354 8321 (2-5 p.m.)

The Architects and Surveyors
Institute (ASI)
St Mary House
15 St Mary Street
Chippenham
Wiltshire SN15 3WD
Tel (01249) 444505

The Architectural Association
34-36 Bedford Square
London WC1B 3ES
Tel 0171–636 0974

The Association of British Insurers
(ABI)
51 Gresham Street
London EC2V 7HQ
Tel 0171–600 3333

The Association of Building
Engineers (ABE)
Jubilee House
Billing Brook Road
Weston Favell
Northamptonshire NN3 8NW
Tel (01604) 404121

The Association of Relocation
Agents
PO Box 108
Edinburgh EH7 5JQ
Tel 031–558 3060

The British Association of
Removers (BAR)
3 Churchill Court
58 Station Road
North Harrow
Middlesex HA2 7SA
Tel 0181–861 3331

The British Insurance and
Investment Brokers Association
(BIIBA)
BIIBA House
14 Bevis Marks
London EC3A 7NT
Tel 071–623 9043

British Rail Property Board
1 Eversholt Street
London NW1 2DD
Tel 0171–214 9898

The British Wood Preserving and
Damp-proofing Association
6 The Office Village
4 Romford Road
London E15 4EA
Tel 0181–519 2588

The Building Employers
Confederation (BEC)
82 New Cavendish Street
London W1M 8AD
Tel 0171–580 5588

The Building Societies Association/
Council of Mortgage Lenders
(BSA/CML)
3 Savile Row
London W1X 1AF
Tel 0171–437 0655

The Controller of Stamps
Stamp Offices
South West Wing
Bush House
Strand
London WC2B 4QN
Tel 0171–438 7452
(counter service only; phone for address of local offices)

The Corporation of Insurance and
Financial Advisers (CIFA)
174 High Street
Guildford
Surrey GU1 3HW
Tel (01483) 39121

Council for Licensed Conveyancers
(CLC)
16 Glebe Road
Chelmsford
Essex CM1 1QG
Tel (01245) 349599

Department of the Environment
(Public Enquiry Point)
Eland House
Bressington Place
London SW1E 5PV
Tel 0171–890 3000

The Electrical Contractors'
Association (ECA)
ESCA House
34 Palace Court
London W2 4HY
Tel 0171–229 1266

The Electrical Contractors'
Association of Scotland (ECA
Scotland)
Bush House
Bush Estate
Midlothian EH26 0SB
Tel 0131–445 5577

English Heritage
23 Savile Row
London W1X 1AB
Tel 0171–973 3000

The Federation of Master Builders
(FMB)
14/15 Great James Street
London WC1N 3DP
Tel 0171–242 7583

The Forestry Commission
231 Corstorphine Road
Edinburgh EH1 7AT
Tel 0131–334 0303

The Guarantee Protection Trust
27 London Road
High Wycombe
Buckinghamshire HP11 1BW
Tel (01494) 447049

The Heating and Ventilating
Contractors Association (HVCA)
34 Palace Court
London W2 4JG
Tel 0171–229 2488

HMSO Books
Publications Centre
PO Box 276
London SW8 5DT
Tel 0171–873 0011 (*enquiries*)
or 0171–873 9090 (*orders*)

The Housing Corporation
149 Tottenham Court Road
London W1P 0BN
Tel 0171–393 2000

The Incorporated Society of
Valuers and Auctioneers (ISVA)
3 Cadogan Gate
London SW1X 0AS
Tel 0171–235 2282

The Independent Schools
Information Service (ISIS)
56 Buckingham Gate
London SW1E 6AG
Tel 0171–630 8793

ISIS (Scotland)
21 Melville Street
Edinburgh EH3 7PE
Tel 0131–220 2106

The Institute of Plumbing
64 Station Lane
Hornchurch
Essex RM12 6NB
Tel (01708) 472791

The Lands Tribunal for Scotland
1 Grosvenor Crescent
Edinburgh EH12 5ER
Tel 0131–225 7996

The Law Commission
Conquest House
37–38 John Street
Theobalds Road
London WC1N 2BQ
Tel 0171–453 1220

The Law Society
113 Chancery Lane
London WC2A 1PL
Tel 0171–242 1222

The Law Society of Scotland
26 Drumsheugh Gardens
Edinburgh EH3 7YR
Tel 0131–226 7411

Legal Services Ombudsman
22 Oxford Court
Oxford Street
Manchester M2 3WQ
Tel 0161–236 9532

The National Association of Estate
Agents (NAEA)
Arbon House
21 Jury Street
Warwick
Warwickshire CV34 4EH
Tel (01926) 496800
or call the Homelink Hotline direct on:
(01926) 410785

The National Association of
Plumbing, Heating and Mechanical
Services Contractors (NAPHMSC)
14/15 Ensign House
Ensign Business Centre
Westwood Way
Coventry CV4 8JA
Tel (01203) 470626

The National House Building
Council (NHBC)
Buildmark House
Chiltern Avenue
Amersham
Buckinghamshire HP6 5AP
Tel (01494) 434477

The National Inspection Council
for Electrical Installation
Contracting (NICEIC)
Vintage House
37 Albert Embankment
London SE1 7UJ
Tel 0171–582 7746

National Approval Council for
Security Systems (NACOSS)
Queensgate House
14 Cookham Road
Maidenhead
Berkshire SL6 8AJ
Tel (01628) 37512

The New Homes Marketing Board
(NHMB)
82 New Cavendish Street
London W1M 8AD
Tel 0171–580 5588

Office for the Supervision of
Solicitors (OSS)
Victoria Court
8 Dormer Place
Leamington Spa
Warwickshire CV32 5AE
Tel (01926) 820082

The Pre-school Learning
Alliance
(PLA)
69 King's Cross Road
London WC1X 9LL
Tel 0171–833 0991

Registry of County Court
Judgments
173–175 Cleveland Street
London W1P 5PE
Tel 0171–380 0133

The Royal Incorporation of
Architects in Scotland (RIA
Scotland)
15 Rutland Square
Edinburgh EH1 2BE
Tel 0131–229 7205

The Royal Institute of British
Architects (RIBA)
Client's Advisory Service
66 Portland Place
London W1N 4AD
Tel 0171–580 5533

The Royal Institute of Chartered
Surveyors (RICS)
12 Great George Street
London SWIP 3AD
Tel 0171–222 7000

The Royal Institution of Chartered
Surveyors in Scotland (RICS
Scotland)
9 Manor Place
Edinburgh EH3 7DN
Tel 0131–225 7078

The Royal Society of Architects
in Wales
75a Llandennis Road
Rhydypennau
Cardiff CF2 6EE
Tel (01222) 762215

The Royal Society of Ulster
Architects (RSUA)
2 Mount Charles
Belfast BT7 1NZ
Tel (01232) 323760

The Royal Town Planning Institute
26 Portland Place
London WIN 4BE
Tel 0171–636 9107

The School Government
Publishing Company
Darby House
Bletchingley Road
Merstham
Redhill
Surrey RH1 3DN
Tel (01737) 642223

The Scottish Building Employers
Federation (SBEF)
13 Woodside Crescent
Glasgow G3 7UP
Tel 0141–332 7144

The Scottish Civic Trust
24 George Square
Glasgow G2 1EF
Tel 0141–221 1466

The Scottish Education
Department
Victoria Quay
Edinburgh EH6 6QQ
Tel 0131–556 8400

The Society for the Protection of
Ancient Buildings (SPAB)
37 Spital Square
London E1 6DY
Tel 0171–377 1644

Solicitors Property Group
30 Station Road
Cuffley
Hertfordshire EN6 4HE
Tel (01707) 873126

The Telecommunications Industry
Association
Douglas House
32–34 Simpson Road
Fenny Stratford
Milton Keynes
Buckinghamshire MK1 1BA
Tel (01908) 645000 (1-4 p.m.)

The Timber & Brick Homes
Information Council (TBHIC)
Gable House
40 High Street
Rickmansworth
Hertfordshire WD1 3ES
Tel (01923) 778136

Zurich Municipal
Hermes House
Southwood Crescent
Farnborough
Hampshire GU14 0NJ
Tel (01252) 522000

INDEX